DICTIONARY

THEME–BASED

British English Collection

ENGLISH-
KOREAN

The most useful words
To expand your lexicon and sharpen
your language skills

9000 words

Theme-based dictionary British English-Korean - 9000 words

By Andrey Taranov

T&P Books vocabularies are intended for helping you learn, memorize and review foreign words. The dictionary is divided into themes, covering all major spheres of everyday activities, business, science, culture, etc.

The process of learning words using T&P Books' theme-based dictionaries gives you the following advantages:

- Correctly grouped source information predetermines success at subsequent stages of word memorization
- Availability of words derived from the same root allowing memorization of word units (rather than separate words)
- Small units of words facilitate the process of establishing associative links needed for consolidation of vocabulary
- Level of language knowledge can be estimated by the number of learned words

T&P Books Publishing
www.tpbooks.com

This book is also available in E-book formats.
Please visit www.tpbooks.com or the major online bookstores.

KOREAN THEME-BASED DICTIONARY
British English collection

T&P Books vocabularies are intended to help you learn, memorize, and review foreign words. The vocabulary contains over 9000 commonly used words arranged thematically.

- Vocabulary contains the most commonly used words
- Recommended as an addition to any language course
- Meets the needs of beginners and advanced learners of foreign languages
- Convenient for daily use, revision sessions, and self-testing activities
- Allows you to assess your vocabulary

Special features of the vocabulary

- Words are organized according to their meaning, not alphabetically
- Words are presented in three columns to facilitate the reviewing and self-testing processes
- Words in groups are divided into small blocks to facilitate the learning process
- The vocabulary offers a convenient and simple transcription of each foreign word

The vocabulary has 256 topics including:

Basic Concepts, Numbers, Colors, Months, Seasons, Units of Measurement, Clothing & Accessories, Food & Nutrition, Restaurant, Family Members, Relatives, Character, Feelings, Emotions, Diseases, City, Town, Sightseeing, Shopping, Money, House, Home, Office, Working in the Office, Import & Export, Marketing, Job Search, Sports, Education, Computer, Internet, Tools, Nature, Countries, Nationalities and more ...

TABLE OF CONTENTS

PRONUNCIATION GUIDE

Letter	Korean example	T&P phonetic alphabet	English example

Consonants

Letter	Korean example	T&P phonetic alphabet	English example
ㄱ [1]	개	[k]	clock, kiss
ㄱ [2]	아기	[g]	game, gold
ㄲ	껌	[k]	tense [k]
ㄴ	눈	[n]	name, normal
ㄷ [3]	달	[t]	tourist, trip
ㄷ [4]	사다리	[d]	day, doctor
ㄸ	딸	[t]	tense [t]
ㄹ [5]	라디오	[r]	rice, radio
ㄹ [6]	십팔	[l]	lace, people
ㅁ	문	[m]	magic, milk
ㅂ [7]	봄	[p]	pencil, private
ㅂ [8]	아버지	[b]	baby, book
ㅃ	빵	[p]	tense [p]
ㅅ [9]	실	[s]	city, boss
ㅅ [10]	옷	[t]	tourist, trip
ㅆ	쌀	[ja:]	royal
ㅇ [11]	강	[ŋg]	language, single
ㅈ [12]	집	[tɕ]	cheer
ㅈ [13]	아주	[dʑ]	jeans, gene
ㅉ	짬	[tɕ]	tense [tch]
ㅊ	차	[tɕh]	hitchhiker
ㅌ	택시	[th]	don't have
ㅋ	칼	[kh]	work hard
ㅍ	포도	[ph]	top hat
ㅎ	한국	[h]	home, have

Vowels and combinations with vowels

Letter	Korean example	T&P phonetic alphabet	English example
ㅏ	사	[a]	shorter than in 'ask'
ㅑ	향	[ja]	Kenya, piano
ㅓ	머리	[ʌ]	lucky, sun

Letter	Korean example	T&P phonetic alphabet	English example
ㅕ	병	[jɑ]	young, yard
ㅗ	몸	[o]	pod, John
ㅛ	표	[jɔ]	New York
ㅜ	물	[u]	book
ㅠ	슈퍼	[ju]	youth, usually
ㅡ	음악	[ɪ]	big, America
ㅣ	길	[i], [iː]	feet, Peter
ㅐ	뱀	[ɛ], [ɛː]	habit, bad
ㅒ	애기	[je]	yesterday, yen
ㅔ	펜	[e]	elm, medal
ㅖ	계산	[je]	yesterday, yen
ㅘ	왕	[wa]	watt, white
ㅙ	왜	[ʊə]	pure, fuel
ㅚ	회의	[ø], [we]	first, web
ㅝ	권	[uɔ]	to order, to open
ㅞ	웬	[ʊə]	pure, fuel
ㅟ	쥐	[wi]	whiskey
ㅢ	거의	[ɯi]	combination [ɪi]

Comments

[1] at the beginning of words
[2] between voiced sounds
[3] at the beginning of words
[4] between voiced sounds
[5] at the beginning of a syllable
[6] at the end of a syllable
[7] at the beginning of words
[8] between voiced sounds
[9] at the beginning of a syllable
[10] at the end of a syllable
[11] at the end of a syllable
[12] at the beginning of words
[13] between voiced sounds

ABBREVIATIONS
used in the dictionary

English abbreviations

ab.	-	about
adj	-	adjective
adv	-	adverb
anim.	-	animate
as adj	-	attributive noun used as adjective
e.g.	-	for example
etc.	-	et cetera
fam.	-	familiar
fem.	-	feminine
form.	-	formal
inanim.	-	inanimate
masc.	-	masculine
math	-	mathematics
mil.	-	military
n	-	noun
pl	-	plural
pron.	-	pronoun
sb	-	somebody
sing.	-	singular
sth	-	something
v aux	-	auxiliary verb
vi	-	intransitive verb
vi, vt	-	intransitive, transitive verb
vt	-	transitive verb

BASIC CONCEPTS

Basic concepts. Part 1

1. Pronouns

I, me	나, 저	na
you	너	neo
he	그, 그분	geu, geu-bun
she	그녀	geu-nyeo
it	그것	geu-geot
we	우리	u-ri
you (to a group)	너희	neo-hui
you (polite, sing.)	당신	dang-sin
they	그들	geu-deul

2. Greetings. Salutations. Farewells

Hello! (fam.)	안녕!	an-nyeong!
Hello! (form.)	안녕하세요!	an-nyeong-ha-se-yo!
Good morning!	안녕하세요!	an-nyeong-ha-se-yo!
Good afternoon!	안녕하세요!	an-nyeong-ha-se-yo!
Good evening!	안녕하세요!	an-nyeong-ha-se-yo!
to say hello	인사하다	in-sa-ha-da
Hi! (hello)	안녕!	an-nyeong!
greeting (n)	인사	in-sa
to greet (vt)	인사하다	in-sa-ha-da
How are you?	잘 지내세요?	jal ji-nae-se-yo?
What's new?	어떻게 지내?	eo-tteo-ke ji-nae?
Bye-Bye! Goodbye!	안녕히 가세요!	an-nyeong-hi ga-se-yo!
See you soon!	또 만나요!	tto man-na-yo!
Farewell! (to a friend)	잘 있어!	jal ri-seo!
Farewell! (form.)	안녕히 계세요!	an-nyeong-hi gye-se-yo!
to say goodbye	작별인사를 하다	jak-byeo-rin-sa-reul ha-da
Cheers!	안녕!	an-nyeong!
Thank you! Cheers!	감사합니다!	gam-sa-ham-ni-da!
Thank you very much!	대단히 감사합니다!	dae-dan-hi gam-sa-ham-ni-da!
My pleasure!	천만이에요	cheon-man-i-e-yo
Don't mention it!	천만의 말씀입니다	cheon-man-ui mal-sseum-im-ni-da
It was nothing	천만에	cheon-man-e

Excuse me! (fam.)	실례!	sil-lye!
Excuse me! (form.)	실례합니다!	sil-lye-ham-ni-da!
to excuse (forgive)	용서하다	yong-seo-ha-da

to apologize (vi)	사과하다	sa-gwa-ha-da
My apologies	사과드립니다	sa-gwa-deu-rim-ni-da
I'm sorry!	죄송합니다!	joe-song-ham-ni-da!
to forgive (vt)	용서하다	yong-seo-ha-da
please (adv)	부탁합니다	bu-tak-am-ni-da

Don't forget!	잊지 마십시오!	it-ji ma-sip-si-o!
Certainly!	물론이에요!	mul-lon-i-e-yo!
Of course not!	물론 아니에요!	mul-lon a-ni-e-yo!
Okay! (I agree)	그래요!	geu-rae-yo!
That's enough!	그만!	geu-man!

3. How to address

mister, sir	선생	seon-saeng
madam	여사님	yeo-sa-nim
miss	아가씨	a-ga-ssi
young man	젊은 분	jeol-meun bun
young man (little boy)	꼬마	kko-ma
miss (little girl)	꼬마	kko-ma

4. Cardinal numbers. Part 1

0 zero	영	yeong
1 one	일	il
2 two	이	i
3 three	삼	sam
4 four	사	sa

5 five	오	o
6 six	육	yuk
7 seven	칠	chil
8 eight	팔	pal
9 nine	구	gu

10 ten	십	sip
11 eleven	십일	si-bil
12 twelve	십이	si-bi
13 thirteen	십삼	sip-sam
14 fourteen	십사	sip-sa

15 fifteen	십오	si-bo
16 sixteen	십육	si-byuk
17 seventeen	십칠	sip-chil
18 eighteen	십팔	sip-pal
19 nineteen	십구	sip-gu
20 twenty	이십	i-sip
21 twenty-one	이십일	i-si-bil

22 twenty-two	이십이	i-si-bi
23 twenty-three	이십삼	i-sip-sam

30 thirty	삼십	sam-sip
31 thirty-one	삼십일	sam-si-bil
32 thirty-two	삼십이	sam-si-bi
33 thirty-three	삼십삼	sam-sip-sam

40 forty	사십	sa-sip
41 forty-one	사십일	sa-si-bil
42 forty-two	사십이	sa-si-bi
43 forty-three	사십삼	sa-sip-sam

50 fifty	오십	o-sip
51 fifty-one	오십일	o-si-bil
52 fifty-two	오십이	o-si-bi
53 fifty-three	오십삼	o-sip-sam

60 sixty	육십	yuk-sip
61 sixty-one	육십일	yuk-si-bil
62 sixty-two	육십이	yuk-si-bi
63 sixty-three	육십삼	yuk-sip-sam

70 seventy	칠십	chil-sip
71 seventy-one	칠십일	chil-si-bil
72 seventy-two	칠십이	chil-si-bi
73 seventy-three	칠십삼	chil-sip-sam

80 eighty	팔십	pal-sip
81 eighty-one	팔십일	pal-si-bil
82 eighty-two	팔십이	pal-si-bi
83 eighty-three	팔십삼	pal-sip-sam

90 ninety	구십	gu-sip
91 ninety-one	구십일	gu-si-bil
92 ninety-two	구십이	gu-si-bi
93 ninety-three	구십삼	gu-sip-sam

5. Cardinal numbers. Part 2

100 one hundred	백	baek
200 two hundred	이백	i-baek
300 three hundred	삼백	sam-baek
400 four hundred	사백	sa-baek
500 five hundred	오백	o-baek

600 six hundred	육백	yuk-baek
700 seven hundred	칠백	chil-baek
800 eight hundred	팔백	pal-baek
900 nine hundred	구백	gu-baek

1000 one thousand	천	cheon
2000 two thousand	이천	i-cheon
3000 three thousand	삼천	sam-cheon

10000 ten thousand	만	man
one hundred thousand	십만	sim-man
million	백만	baeng-man
billion	십억	si-beok

6. Ordinal numbers

first (adj)	첫 번째의	cheot beon-jjae-ui
second (adj)	두 번째의	du beon-jjae-ui
third (adj)	세 번째의	se beon-jjae-ui
fourth (adj)	네 번째의	ne beon-jjae-ui
fifth (adj)	다섯 번째의	da-seot beon-jjae-ui
sixth (adj)	여섯 번째의	yeo-seot beon-jjae-ui
seventh (adj)	일곱 번째의	il-gop beon-jjae-ui
eighth (adj)	여덟 번째의	yeo-deol beon-jjae-ui
ninth (adj)	아홉 번째의	a-hop beon-jjae-ui
tenth (adj)	열 번째의	yeol beon-jjae-ui

7. Numbers. Fractions

fraction	분수	bun-su
one half	이분의 일	i-bun-ui il
one third	삼분의 일	sam-bun-ui il
one quarter	사분의 일	sa-bun-ui il
one eighth	팔분의 일	pal-bun-ui il
one tenth	십분의 일	sip-bun-ui il
two thirds	삼분의 이	sam-bun-ui i
three quarters	사분의 삼	sa-bun-ui sam

8. Numbers. Basic operations

subtraction	빼기	ppae-gi
to subtract (vi, vt)	빼다	ppae-da
division	나누기	na-nu-gi
to divide (vt)	나누다	na-nu-da
addition	더하기	deo-ha-gi
to add up (vt)	합하다	ha-pa-da
to add (vi)	더하다	deo-ha-da
multiplication	곱하기	go-pa-gi
to multiply (vt)	곱하다	go-pa-da

9. Numbers. Miscellaneous

| digit, figure | 숫자 | sut-ja |
| number | 숫자 | sut-ja |

numeral	수사	su-sa
minus sign	마이너스	ma-i-neo-seu
plus sign	플러스	peul-leo-seu
formula	공식	gong-sik

calculation	계산	gye-san
to count (vi, vt)	세다	se-da
to count up	헤아리다	he-a-ri-da
to compare (vt)	비교하다	bi-gyo-ha-da

How much?	얼마?	eol-ma?
How many?	얼마나?	eo-di-ro?
sum, total	총합	chong-hap
result	결과	gyeol-gwa
remainder	나머지	na-meo-ji

a few (e.g., ~ years ago)	몇	myeot
little (I had ~ time)	조금	jo-geum
the rest	나머지	na-meo-ji
one and a half	일과 이분의 일	il-gwa i-bun-ui il
dozen	다스	da-seu

in half (adv)	반으로	ba-neu-ro
equally (evenly)	균등하게	gyun-deung-ha-ge
half	절반	jeol-ban
time (three ~s)	번	beon

10. The most important verbs. Part 1

to advise (vt)	조언하다	jo-eon-ha-da
to agree (say yes)	동의하다	dong-ui-ha-da
to answer (vi, vt)	대답하다	dae-da-pa-da
to apologize (vi)	사과하다	sa-gwa-ha-da
to arrive (vi)	도착하다	do-chak-a-da

| to ask (~ oneself) | 묻다 | mut-da |
| to ask (~ sb to do sth) | 부탁하다 | bu-tak-a-da |

to be afraid	무서워하다	mu-seo-wo-ha-da
to be hungry	배가 고프다	bae-ga go-peu-da
to be interested in ...	··· 에 관심을 가지다	... e gwan-si-meul ga-ji-da
to be needed	필요하다	pi-ryo-ha-da
to be surprised	놀라다	nol-la-da

to be thirsty	목마르다	mong-ma-reu-da
to begin (vt)	시작하다	si-jak-a-da
to belong to ...	··· 에 속하다	... e sok-a-da
to boast (vi)	자랑하다	ja-rang-ha-da
to break (split into pieces)	깨뜨리다	kkae-tteu-ri-da
to call (~ for help)	부르다, 요청하다	bu-reu-da, yo-cheong-ha-da

can (v aux)	할 수 있다	hal su it-da
to catch (vt)	잡다	jap-da
to change (vt)	바꾸다	ba-kku-da

| to choose (select) | 선택하다 | seon-taek-a-da |
| to come down (the stairs) | 내려오다 | nae-ryeo-o-da |

to compare (vt)	비교하다	bi-gyo-ha-da
to complain (vi, vt)	불평하다	bul-pyeong-ha-da
to confuse (mix up)	혼동하다	hon-dong-ha-da
to continue (vt)	계속하다	gye-sok-a-da
to control (vt)	제어하다	je-eo-ha-da
to cook (dinner)	요리하다	yo-ri-ha-da

to cost (vt)	값이 … 이다	gap-si … i-da
to count (add up)	세다	se-da
to count on …	… 에 의지하다	… e ui-ji-ha-da
to create (vt)	창조하다	chang-jo-ha-da
to cry (weep)	울다	ul-da

11. The most important verbs. Part 2

to deceive (vi, vt)	속이다	so-gi-da
to decorate (tree, street)	장식하다	jang-sik-a-da
to defend (a country, etc.)	방어하다	bang-eo-ha-da
to demand (request firmly)	요구하다	yo-gu-ha-da
to dig (vt)	파다	pa-da

to discuss (vt)	의논하다	ui-non-ha-da
to do (vt)	하다	ha-da
to doubt (have doubts)	의심하다	ui-sim-ha-da
to drop (let fall)	떨어뜨리다	tteo-reo-tteu-ri-da
to enter (room, house, etc.)	들어가다	deu-reo-ga-da

to exist (vi)	존재하다	jon-jae-ha-da
to expect (foresee)	예상하다	ye-sang-ha-da
to explain (vt)	설명하다	seol-myeong-ha-da
to fall (vi)	떨어지다	tteo-reo-ji-da

to fancy (vt)	좋아하다	jo-a-ha-da
to find (vt)	찾다	chat-da
to finish (vt)	끝내다	kkeun-nae-da
to fly (vi)	날다	nal-da
to follow … (come after)	… 를 따라가다	… reul tta-ra-ga-da

to forget (vi, vt)	잊다	it-da
to forgive (vt)	용서하다	yong-seo-ha-da
to give (vt)	주다	ju-da
to give a hint	힌트를 주다	hin-teu-reul ju-da
to go (on foot)	가다	ga-da

to go for a swim	수영하다	su-yeong-ha-da
to go out (for dinner, etc.)	나가다	na-ga-da
to guess (the answer)	추측하다	chu-cheuk-a-da

to have (vt)	가지다	ga-ji-da
to have breakfast	아침을 먹다	a-chi-meul meok-da
to have dinner	저녁을 먹다	jeo-nyeo-geul meok-da

| to have lunch | 점심을 먹다 | jeom-si-meul meok-da |
| to hear (vt) | 듣다 | deut-da |

to help (vt)	도와주다	do-wa-ju-da
to hide (vt)	숨기다	sum-gi-da
to hope (vi, vt)	희망하다	hui-mang-ha-da
to hunt (vi, vt)	사냥하다	sa-nyang-ha-da
to hurry (vi)	서두르다	seo-du-reu-da

12. The most important verbs. Part 3

to inform (vt)	알리다	al-li-da
to insist (vi, vt)	주장하다	ju-jang-ha-da
to insult (vt)	모욕하다	mo-yok-a-da
to invite (vt)	초대하다	cho-dae-ha-da
to joke (vi)	농담하다	nong-dam-ha-da

to keep (vt)	보관하다	bo-gwan-ha-da
to keep silent, to hush	침묵을 지키다	chim-mu-geul ji-ki-da
to kill (vt)	죽이다	ju-gi-da
to know (sb)	알다	al-da
to know (sth)	알다	al-da
to laugh (vi)	웃다	ut-da

to liberate (city, etc.)	해방하다	hae-bang-ha-da
to look for ... (search)	··· 를 찾다	... reul chat-da
to love (sb)	사랑하다	sa-rang-ha-da
to make a mistake	실수하다	sil-su-ha-da
to manage, to run	운영하다	u-nyeong-ha-da

to mean (signify)	의미하다	ui-mi-ha-da
to mention (talk about)	언급하다	eon-geu-pa-da
to miss (school, etc.)	결석하다	gyeol-seok-a-da
to notice (see)	알아차리다	a-ra-cha-ri-da
to object (vi, vt)	반대하다	ban-dae-ha-da

to observe (see)	지켜보다	ji-kyeo-bo-da
to open (vt)	열다	yeol-da
to order (meal, etc.)	주문하다	ju-mun-ha-da
to order (mil.)	명령하다	myeong-nyeong-ha-da
to own (possess)	소유하다	so-yu-ha-da

to participate (vi)	참가하다	cham-ga-ha-da
to pay (vi, vt)	지불하다	ji-bul-ha-da
to permit (vt)	허가하다	heo-ga-ha-da
to plan (vt)	계획하다	gye-hoek-a-da
to play (children)	놀다	nol-da

to pray (vi, vt)	기도하다	gi-do-ha-da
to prefer (vt)	선호하다	seon-ho-ha-da
to promise (vt)	약속하다	yak-sok-a-da
to pronounce (vt)	발음하다	ba-reum-ha-da
to propose (vt)	제안하다	je-an-ha-da
to punish (vt)	처벌하다	cheo-beol-ha-da

13. The most important verbs. Part 4

to read (vi, vt)	읽다	ik-da
to recommend (vt)	추천하다	chu-cheon-ha-da
to refuse (vi, vt)	거절하다	geo-jeol-ha-da
to regret (be sorry)	후회하다	hu-hoe-ha-da
to rent (sth from sb)	임대하다	im-dae-ha-da
to repeat (say again)	반복하다	ban-bok-a-da
to reserve, to book	예약하다	ye-yak-a-da
to run (vi)	달리다	dal-li-da
to save (rescue)	구조하다	gu-jo-ha-da
to say (~ thank you)	말하다	mal-ha-da
to scold (vt)	꾸짖다	kku-jit-da
to see (vt)	보다	bo-da
to sell (vt)	팔다	pal-da
to send (vt)	보내다	bo-nae-da
to shoot (vi)	쏘다	sso-da
to shout (vi)	소리치다	so-ri-chi-da
to show (vt)	보여주다	bo-yeo-ju-da
to sign (document)	서명하다	seo-myeong-ha-da
to sit down (vi)	앉다	an-da
to smile (vi)	미소를 짓다	mi-so-reul jit-da
to speak (vi, vt)	말하다	mal-ha-da
to steal (money, etc.)	훔치다	hum-chi-da
to stop (for pause, etc.)	정지하다	jeong-ji-ha-da
to stop (please ~ calling me)	그만두다	geu-man-du-da
to study (vt)	공부하다	gong-bu-ha-da
to swim (vi)	수영하다	su-yeong-ha-da
to take (vt)	잡다	jap-da
to think (vi, vt)	생각하다	saeng-gak-a-da
to threaten (vt)	협박하다	hyeop-bak-a-da
to touch (with hands)	닿다	da-ta
to translate (vt)	번역하다	beo-nyeok-a-da
to trust (vt)	신뢰하다	sil-loe-ha-da
to try (attempt)	해보다	hae-bo-da
to turn (e.g., ~ left)	돌다	dol-da
to underestimate (vt)	과소평가하다	gwa-so-pyeong-ga-ha-da
to understand (vt)	이해하다	i-hae-ha-da
to unite (vt)	연합하다	yeon-ha-pa-da
to wait (vt)	기다리다	gi-da-ri-da
to want (wish, desire)	원하다	won-ha-da
to warn (vt)	경고하다	gyeong-go-ha-da
to work (vi)	일하다	il-ha-da
to write (vt)	쓰다	sseu-da
to write down	적다	jeok-da

14. Colours

colour	색	sae
shade (tint)	색조	saek-jo
hue	색상	saek-sang
rainbow	무지개	mu-ji-gae

white (adj)	흰	huin
black (adj)	검은	geo-meun
grey (adj)	회색의	hoe-sae-gui

green (adj)	초록색의	cho-rok-sae-gui
yellow (adj)	노란	no-ran
red (adj)	빨간	ppal-gan

blue (adj)	파란	pa-ran
light blue (adj)	하늘색의	ha-neul-sae-gui
pink (adj)	분홍색의	bun-hong-sae-gui
orange (adj)	주황색의	ju-hwang-sae-gui
violet (adj)	보라색의	bo-ra-sae-gui
brown (adj)	갈색의	gal-sae-gui

| golden (adj) | 금색의 | geum-sae-gui |
| silvery (adj) | 은색의 | eun-sae-gui |

beige (adj)	베이지색의	be-i-ji-sae-gui
cream (adj)	크림색의	keu-rim-sae-gui
turquoise (adj)	청록색의	cheong-nok-sae-gui
cherry red (adj)	암적색의	am-jeok-sae-gui
lilac (adj)	연보라색의	yeon-bo-ra-sae-gui
crimson (adj)	진홍색의	jin-hong-sae-gui

light (adj)	밝은	bal-geun
dark (adj)	짙은	ji-teun
bright, vivid (adj)	선명한	seon-myeong-han

coloured (pencils)	색의	sae-gui
colour (e.g. ~ film)	컬러의	keol-leo-ui
black-and-white (adj)	흑백의	heuk-bae-gui
plain (one-coloured)	단색의	dan-sae-gui
multicoloured (adj)	다색의	da-sae-gui

15. Questions

Who?	누구?	nu-gu?
What?	무엇?	mu-eot?
Where? (at, in)	어디?	eo-di?
Where (to)?	어디로?	eo-di-ro?
From where?	어디로부터?	eo-di-ro-bu-teo?
When?	언제?	eon-je?
Why? (What for?)	왜?	wae?
Why? (~ are you crying?)	왜?	wae?
What for?	무엇을 위해서?	mu-eos-eul rwi-hae-seo?

How? (in what way)	어떻게?	eo-tteo-ke?
What? (What kind of ...?)	어떤?	eo-tteon?
Which?	어느?	eo-neu?

To whom?	누구에게?	nu-gu-e-ge?
About whom?	누구에 대하여?	nu-gu-e dae-ha-yeo?
About what?	무엇에 대하여?	mu-eos-e dae-ha-yeo?
With whom?	누구하고?	nu-gu-ha-go?

| How many? How much? | 얼마? | eol-ma? |
| Whose? | 누구의? | nu-gu-ui? |

16. Prepositions

with (accompanied by)	··· 하고	... ha-go
without	없이	eop-si
to (indicating direction)	··· 에	... e
about (talking ~ ...)	··· 에 대하여	... e dae-ha-yeo
before (in time)	전에	jeon-e
in front of ...	··· 앞에	... a-pe

under (beneath, below)	밑에	mi-te
above (over)	위에	wi-e
on (atop)	위에	wi-e
from (off, out of)	··· 에서	... e-seo
of (made from)	··· 로	... ro

| in (e.g. ~ ten minutes) | ··· 안에 | ... a-ne |
| over (across the top of) | 너머 | dwi-e |

17. Function words. Adverbs. Part 1

Where? (at, in)	어디?	eo-di?
here (adv)	여기	yeo-gi
there (adv)	거기	geo-gi

| somewhere (to be) | 어딘가 | eo-din-ga |
| nowhere (not in any place) | 어디도 | eo-di-do |

| by (near, beside) | 옆에 | yeo-pe |
| by the window | 창문 옆에 | chang-mun nyeo-pe |

Where (to)?	어디로?	eo-di-ro?
here (e.g. come ~!)	여기로	yeo-gi-ro
there (e.g. to go ~)	거기로	geo-gi-ro
from here (adv)	여기서	yeo-gi-seo
from there (adv)	거기서	geo-gi-seo

close (adv)	가까이	ga-kka-i
far (adv)	멀리	meol-li
near (e.g. ~ Paris)	근처에	geun-cheo-e
nearby (adv)	인근에	in-geu-ne

not far (adv)	멀지 않게	meol-ji an-ke
left (adj)	왼쪽의	oen-jjo-gui
on the left	왼쪽에	oen-jjo-ge
to the left	왼쪽으로	oen-jjo-geu-ro
right (adj)	오른쪽의	o-reun-jjo-gui
on the right	오른쪽에	o-reun-jjo-ge
to the right	오른쪽으로	o-reun-jjo-geu-ro
in front (adv)	앞쪽에	ap-jjo-ge
front (as adj)	앞의	a-pui
ahead (the kids ran ~)	앞으로	a-peu-ro
behind (adv)	뒤에	dwi-e
from behind	뒤에서	dwi-e-seo
back (towards the rear)	뒤로	dwi-ro
middle	가운데	ga-un-de
in the middle	가운데에	ga-un-de-e
at the side	옆에	yeo-pe
everywhere (adv)	모든 곳에	mo-deun gos-e
around (in all directions)	주위에	ju-wi-e
from inside	내면에서	nae-myeon-e-seo
somewhere (to go)	어딘가에	eo-din-ga-e
straight (directly)	똑바로	ttok-ba-ro
back (e.g. come ~)	뒤로	dwi-ro
from anywhere	어디에서든지	eo-di-e-seo-deun-ji
from somewhere	어디로부터인지	eo-di-ro-bu-teo-in-ji
firstly (adv)	첫째로	cheot-jjae-ro
secondly (adv)	둘째로	dul-jjae-ro
thirdly (adv)	셋째로	set-jjae-ro
suddenly (adv)	갑자기	gap-ja-gi
at first (in the beginning)	처음에	cheo-eum-e
for the first time	처음으로	cheo-eu-meu-ro
long before ...	··· 오래 전에	... o-rae jeon-e
anew (over again)	다시	da-si
for good (adv)	영원히	yeong-won-hi
never (adv)	절대로	jeol-dae-ro
again (adv)	다시	da-si
now (at present)	이제	i-je
often (adv)	자주	ja-ju
then (adv)	그때	geu-ttae
urgently (quickly)	급히	geu-pi
usually (adv)	보통으로	bo-tong-eu-ro
by the way, ...	그건 그렇고, ···	geu-geon geu-reo-ko, ...
possibly	가능한	ga-neung-han
probably (adv)	아마	a-ma
maybe (adv)	어쩌면	eo-jjeo-myeon
besides ...	게다가 ···	ge-da-ga ...

that's why ...	그래서 …	geu-rae-seo ...
in spite of ...	… 에도 불구하고	… e-do bul-gu-ha-go
thanks to ...	… 덕분에	… deok-bun-e

something	무엇인가	mu-eon-nin-ga
anything (something)	무엇이든지	mu-eon-ni-deun-ji
nothing	아무것도	a-mu-geot-do

| someone | 누구 | nu-gu |
| somebody | 누군가 | nu-gun-ga |

nobody	아무도	a-mu-do
nowhere (a voyage to ~)	아무데도	a-mu-de-do
nobody's	누구의 것도 아닌	nu-gu-ui geot-do a-nin
somebody's	누군가의	nu-gun-ga-ui

so (I'm ~ glad)	그래서	geu-rae-seo
also (as well)	역시	yeok-si
too (as well)	또한	tto-han

18. Function words. Adverbs. Part 2

Why?	왜?	wae?
for some reason	어떤 이유로	eo-tteon ni-yu-ro
because ...	왜냐하면 …	wae-nya-ha-myeon ...
for some purpose	어떤 목적으로	eo-tteon mok-jeo-geu-ro

and	그리고	geu-ri-go
or	또는	tto-neun
but	그러나	geu-reo-na
for (e.g. ~ me)	위해서	wi-hae-seo

too (excessively)	너무	neo-mu
only (exclusively)	… 만	… man
exactly (adv)	정확하게	jeong-hwak-a-ge
about (more or less)	약	yak

approximately (adv)	대략	dae-ryak
approximate (adj)	대략적인	dae-ryak-jeo-gin
almost (adv)	거의	geo-ui
the rest	나머지	na-meo-ji

each (adj)	각각의	gak-ga-gui
any (no matter which)	아무	a-mu
many, much (a lot of)	많이	ma-ni
many people	많은 사람들	ma-neun sa-ram-deul
all (everyone)	모두	mo-du

in return for ...	… 의 교환으로	… ui gyo-hwa-neu-ro
in exchange (adv)	교환으로	gyo-hwa-neu-ro
by hand (made)	수공으로	su-gong-eu-ro
hardly (negative opinion)	거의	geo-ui
probably (adv)	아마	a-ma
on purpose (intentionally)	일부러	il-bu-reo

by accident (adv)	우연히	u-yeon-hi
very (adv)	아주	a-ju
for example (adv)	예를 들면	ye-reul deul-myeon
between	사이에	sa-i-e
among	중에	jung-e
so much (such a lot)	이만큼	i-man-keum
especially (adv)	특히	teuk-i

Basic concepts. Part 2

19. Opposites

rich (adj)	부유한	bu-yu-han
poor (adj)	가난한	ga-nan-han
ill, sick (adj)	아픈	a-peun
well (not sick)	건강한	geon-gang-han
big (adj)	큰	keun
small (adj)	작은	ja-geun
quickly (adv)	빨리	ppal-li
slowly (adv)	천천히	cheon-cheon-hi
fast (adj)	빠른	ppa-reun
slow (adj)	느린	neu-rin
glad (adj)	기쁜	gi-ppeun
sad (adj)	슬픈	seul-peun
together (adv)	같이	ga-chi
separately (adv)	따로	tta-ro
aloud (to read)	큰소리로	keun-so-ri-ro
silently (to oneself)	묵독	muk-dok
tall (adj)	높은	no-peun
low (adj)	낮은	na-jeun
deep (adj)	깊은	gi-peun
shallow (adj)	얕은	ya-teun
yes	네	ne
no	아니오	a-ni-o
distant (in space)	먼	meon
nearby (adj)	인근의	in-geu-nui
far (adv)	멀리	meol-li
nearby (adv)	인근에	in-geu-ne
long (adj)	긴	gin
short (adj)	짧은	jjal-beun
good (kindhearted)	착한	cha-kan
evil (adj)	사악한	sa-a-kan

| married (adj) | 결혼한 | gyeol-hon-han |
| single (adj) | 미혼의 | mi-hon-ui |

| to forbid (vt) | 금지하다 | geum-ji-ha-da |
| to permit (vt) | 허가하다 | heo-ga-ha-da |

| end | 끝 | kkeut |
| beginning | 시작 | si-jak |

| left (adj) | 왼쪽의 | oen-jjo-gui |
| right (adj) | 오른쪽의 | o-reun-jjo-gui |

| first (adj) | 첫 번째의 | cheot beon-jjae-ui |
| last (adj) | 마지막의 | ma-ji-ma-gui |

| crime | 범죄 | beom-joe |
| punishment | 벌 | beol |

| to order (vt) | 명령하다 | myeong-nyeong-ha-da |
| to obey (vi, vt) | 복종하다 | bok-jong-ha-da |

| straight (adj) | 곧은 | go-deun |
| curved (adj) | 굽은 | gu-beun |

| paradise | 천국 | cheon-guk |
| hell | 지옥 | ji-ok |

| to be born | 태어나다 | tae-eo-na-da |
| to die (vi) | 죽다 | juk-da |

| strong (adj) | 강한 | gang-han |
| weak (adj) | 약한 | yak-an |

| old (adj) | 늙은 | neul-geun |
| young (adj) | 젊은 | jeol-meun |

| old (adj) | 낡은 | nal-geun |
| new (adj) | 새로운 | sae-ro-un |

| hard (adj) | 단단한 | dan-dan-han |
| soft (adj) | 부드러운 | bu-deu-reo-un |

| warm (tepid) | 따뜻한 | tta-tteu-tan |
| cold (adj) | 추운 | chu-un |

| fat (adj) | 뚱뚱한 | ttung-ttung-han |
| thin (adj) | 마른 | ma-reun |

| narrow (adj) | 좁은 | jo-beun |
| wide (adj) | 넓은 | neol-beun |

| good (adj) | 좋은 | jo-eun |
| bad (adj) | 나쁜 | na-ppeun |

| brave (adj) | 용감한 | yong-gam-han |
| cowardly (adj) | 비겁한 | bi-geo-pan |

20. Weekdays

Monday	월요일	wo-ryo-il
Tuesday	화요일	hwa-yo-il
Wednesday	수요일	su-yo-il
Thursday	목요일	mo-gyo-il
Friday	금요일	geu-myo-il
Saturday	토요일	to-yo-il
Sunday	일요일	i-ryo-il

today (adv)	오늘	o-neul
tomorrow (adv)	내일	nae-il
the day after tomorrow	모레	mo-re
yesterday (adv)	어제	eo-je
the day before yesterday	그저께	geu-jeo-kke

day	낮	nat
working day	근무일	geun-mu-il
public holiday	공휴일	gong-hyu-il
day off	휴일	hyu-il
weekend	주말	ju-mal

all day long	하루종일	ha-ru-jong-il
the next day (adv)	다음날	da-eum-nal
two days ago	이틀 전	i-teul jeon
the day before	전날	jeon-nal
daily (adj)	일간의	il-ga-nui
every day (adv)	매일	mae-il

week	주	ju
last week (adv)	지난 주에	ji-nan ju-e
next week (adv)	다음 주에	da-eum ju-e
weekly (adj)	주간의	ju-ga-nui
every week (adv)	매주	mae-ju
twice a week	일주일에 두번	il-ju-i-re du-beon
every Tuesday	매주 화요일	mae-ju hwa-yo-il

21. Hours. Day and night

morning	아침	a-chim
in the morning	아침에	a-chim-e
noon, midday	정오	jeong-o
in the afternoon	오후에	o-hu-e

evening	저녁	jeo-nyeok
in the evening	저녁에	jeo-nyeo-ge
night	밤	bam
at night	밤에	bam-e
midnight	자정	ja-jeong

second	초	cho
minute	분	bun
hour	시	si

half an hour	반시간	ban-si-gan
a quarter-hour	십오분	si-bo-bun
fifteen minutes	십오분	si-bo-bun
24 hours	이십사시간	i-sip-sa-si-gan
sunrise	일출	il-chul
dawn	새벽	sae-byeok
early morning	이른 아침	i-reun a-chim
sunset	저녁 노을	jeo-nyeok no-eul
early in the morning	이른 아침에	i-reun a-chim-e
this morning	오늘 아침에	o-neul ra-chim-e
tomorrow morning	내일 아침에	nae-il ra-chim-e
this afternoon	오늘 오후에	o-neul ro-hu-e
in the afternoon	오후에	o-hu-e
tomorrow afternoon	내일 오후에	nae-il ro-hu-e
tonight (this evening)	오늘 저녁에	o-neul jeo-nyeo-ge
tomorrow night	내일 밤에	nae-il bam-e
at 3 o'clock sharp	3시 정각에	se-si jeong-ga-ge
about 4 o'clock	4시쯤에	ne-si-jjeu-me
by 12 o'clock	12시까지	yeoldu si-kka-ji
in 20 minutes	20분 안에	sib-bun na-ne
in an hour	한 시간 안에	han si-gan na-ne
on time (adv)	제시간에	je-si-gan-e
a quarter to ...	··· 십오 분	... si-bo bun
within an hour	한 시간 내에	han si-gan nae-e
every 15 minutes	15분 마다	sibo-bun ma-da
round the clock	하루종일	ha-ru-jong-il

22. Months. Seasons

January	일월	i-rwol
February	이월	i-wol
March	삼월	sam-wol
April	사월	sa-wol
May	오월	o-wol
June	유월	yu-wol
July	칠월	chi-rwol
August	팔월	pa-rwol
September	구월	gu-wol
October	시월	si-wol
November	십일월	si-bi-rwol
December	십이월	si-bi-wol
spring	봄	bom
in spring	봄에	bom-e
spring (as adj)	봄의	bom-ui
summer	여름	yeo-reum

in summer	여름에	yeo-reum-e
summer (as adj)	여름의	yeo-reu-mui
autumn	가을	ga-eul
in autumn	가을에	ga-eu-re
autumn (as adj)	가을의	ga-eu-rui
winter	겨울	gyeo-ul
in winter	겨울에	gyeo-u-re
winter (as adj)	겨울의	gyeo-ul
month	월, 달	wol, dal
this month	이번 달에	i-beon da-re
next month	다음 달에	da-eum da-re
last month	지난 달에	ji-nan da-re
a month ago	한달 전에	han-dal jeon-e
in a month (a month later)	한 달 안에	han dal ra-ne
in 2 months (2 months later)	두 달 안에	du dal ra-ne
the whole month	한 달 내내	han dal lae-nae
all month long	한달간 내내	han-dal-gan nae-nae
monthly (~ magazine)	월간의	wol-ga-nui
monthly (adv)	매월, 매달	mae-wol, mae-dal
every month	매달	mae-dal
twice a month	한 달에 두 번	han da-re du beon
year	년	nyeon
this year	올해	ol-hae
next year	내년	nae-nyeon
last year	작년	jang-nyeon
a year ago	일년 전	il-lyeon jeon
in a year	일 년 안에	il lyeon na-ne
in two years	이 년 안에	i nyeon na-ne
the whole year	한 해 전체	han hae jeon-che
all year long	일년 내내	il-lyeon nae-nae
every year	매년	mae-nyeon
annual (adj)	연간의	yeon-ga-nui
annually (adv)	매년	mae-nyeon
4 times a year	일년에 네 번	il-lyeon-e ne beon
date (e.g. today's ~)	날짜	nal-jja
date (e.g. ~ of birth)	월일	wo-ril
calendar	달력	dal-lyeok
half a year	반년	ban-nyeon
six months	육개월	yuk-gae-wol
season (summer, etc.)	계절	gye-jeol
century	세기	se-gi

23. Time. Miscellaneous

time	시간	si-gan
moment	순간	sun-gan

instant (n)	찰나	chal-la
instant (adj)	찰나의	chal-la-ui
lapse (of time)	기간	gi-gan
life	일생	il-saeng
eternity	영원	yeong-won
epoch	시대	si-dae
era	시대	si-dae
cycle	주기	ju-gi
period	기간	gi-gan
term (short-~)	기간	gi-gan
the future	미래	mi-rae
future (as adj)	미래의	mi-rae-ui
next time	다음번	da-eum-beon
the past	과거	gwa-geo
past (recent)	지나간	ji-na-gan
last time	지난 번에	ji-nan beon-e
later (adv)	나중에	na-jung-e
after (prep.)	··· 후에	... hu-e
nowadays (adv)	요즘	yo-jeum
now (at this moment)	이제	i-je
immediately (adv)	즉시	jeuk-si
soon (adv)	곧	got
in advance (beforehand)	미리	mi-ri
a long time ago	오래 전	o-rae jeon
recently (adv)	최근	choe-geun
destiny	운명	un-myeong
recollections	회상, 추억	hoe-sang, chu-eok
archives	기록	gi-rok
during ...	··· 동안	... dong-an
long, a long time (adv)	오래	o-rae
not long (adv)	길지 않은	gil-ji a-neun
early (in the morning)	일찍	il-jjik
late (not early)	늦게	neut-ge
forever (for good)	영원히	yeong-won-hi
to start (begin)	시작하다	si-jak-a-da
to postpone (vt)	연기하다	yeon-gi-ha-da
at the same time	동시에	dong-si-e
permanently (adv)	영구히	yeong-gu-hi
constant (noise, pain)	끊임없는	kkeu-nim-eom-neun
temporary (adj)	일시적인	il-si-jeo-gin
sometimes (adv)	가끔	ga-kkeum
rarely (adv)	드물게	deu-mul-ge
often (adv)	자주	ja-ju

24. Lines and shapes

square	정사각형	jeong-sa-gak-yeong
square (as adj)	사각의	sa-ga-gui

circle	원	won
round (adj)	원형의	won-hyeong-ui
triangle	삼각형	sam-gak-yeong
triangular (adj)	삼각형의	sam-gak-yeong-ui
oval	타원	ta-won
oval (as adj)	타원의	ta-won-ui
rectangle	직사각형	jik-sa-gak-yeong
rectangular (adj)	직사각형의	jik-sa-gak-yeong-ui
pyramid	피라미드	pi-ra-mi-deu
rhombus	마름모	ma-reum-mo
trapezium	사다리꼴	sa-da-ri-kkol
cube	정육면체	jeong-yung-myeon-che
prism	각기둥	gak-gi-dung
circumference	원주	won-ju
sphere	구	gu
ball (solid sphere)	구체	gu-che
diameter	지름	ji-reum
radius	반경	ban-gyeong
perimeter (circle's ~)	둘레	dul-le
centre	중심	jung-sim
horizontal (adj)	가로의	ga-ro-ui
vertical (adj)	세로의	se-ro-ui
parallel (n)	평행	pyeong-haeng
parallel (as adj)	평행한	pyeong-haeng-han
line	선, 줄	seon, jul
stroke	획	hoek
straight line	직선	jik-seon
curve (curved line)	곡선	gok-seon
thin (line, etc.)	얇은	yal-beun
contour (outline)	외곽선	oe-gwak-seon
intersection	교점	gyo-jeom
right angle	직각	jik-gak
segment	활꼴	hwal-kkol
sector (circular ~)	부채꼴	bu-chae-kkol
side (of a triangle)	변	byeon
angle	각	gak

25. Units of measurement

weight	무게	mu-ge
length	길이	gi-ri
width	폭, 너비	pok, neo-bi
height	높이	no-pi
depth	깊이	gi-pi
volume	부피	bu-pi
area	면적	myeon-jeok
gram	그램	geu-raem
milligram	밀리그램	mil-li-geu-raem

kilogram	킬로그램	kil-lo-geu-raem
ton	톤	ton
pound	파운드	pa-un-deu
ounce	온스	on-seu
metre	미터	mi-teo
millimetre	밀리미터	mil-li-mi-teo
centimetre	센티미터	sen-ti-mi-teo
kilometre	킬로미터	kil-lo-mi-teo
mile	마일	ma-il
inch	인치	in-chi
foot	피트	pi-teu
yard	야드	ya-deu
square metre	제곱미터	je-gom-mi-teo
hectare	헥타르	hek-ta-reu
litre	리터	ri-teo
degree	도	do
volt	볼트	bol-teu
ampere	암페어	am-pe-eo
horsepower	마력	ma-ryeok
quantity	수량, 양	su-ryang, yang
a little bit of ...	... 조금	... jo-geum
half	절반	jeol-ban
dozen	다스	da-seu
piece (item)	조각	jo-gak
size	크기	keu-gi
scale (map ~)	축척	chuk-cheok
minimal (adj)	최소의	choe-so-ui
the smallest (adj)	가장 작은	ga-jang ja-geun
medium (adj)	중간의	jung-gan-ui
maximal (adj)	최대의	choe-dae-ui
the largest (adj)	가장 큰	ga-jang keun

26. Containers

canning jar (glass ~)	유리병	yu-ri-byeong
tin, can	캔, 깡통	kaen, kkang-tong
bucket	양동이	yang-dong-i
barrel	통	tong
wash basin (e.g., plastic ~)	대야	dae-ya
tank (100L water ~)	탱크	taeng-keu
hip flask	휴대용 술병	hyu-dae-yong sul-byeong
jerrycan	통	tong
tank (e.g., tank car)	탱크	taeng-keu
mug	머그컵	meo-geu-keop
cup (of coffee, etc.)	컵	keop

saucer	받침 접시	bat-chim jeop-si
glass (tumbler)	유리잔	yu-ri-jan
wine glass	와인글라스	wa-in-geul-la-seu
stock pot (soup pot)	냄비	naem-bi
bottle (~ of wine)	병	byeong
neck (of the bottle, etc.)	병목	byeong-mok
carafe (decanter)	디캔터	di-kaen-teo
pitcher	물병	mul-byeong
vessel (container)	용기	yong-gi
pot (crock, stoneware ~)	항아리	hang-a-ri
vase	화병	hwa-byeong
flacon, bottle (perfume ~)	향수병	hyang-su-byeong
vial, small bottle	약병	yak-byeong
tube (of toothpaste)	튜브	tyu-beu
sack (bag)	자루	ja-ru
bag (paper ~, plastic ~)	봉투	bong-tu
packet (of cigarettes, etc.)	갑	gap
box (e.g. shoebox)	박스	bak-seu
crate	상자	sang-ja
basket	바구니	ba-gu-ni

27. Materials

material	재료	jae-ryo
wood (n)	목재	mok-jae
wood-, wooden (adj)	목재의	mok-jae-ui
glass (n)	유리	yu-ri
glass (as adj)	유리의	yu-ri-ui
stone (n)	돌	dol
stone (as adj)	돌의	do-rui
plastic (n)	플라스틱	peul-la-seu-tik
plastic (as adj)	플라스틱의	peul-la-seu-ti-gui
rubber (n)	고무	go-mu
rubber (as adj)	고무의	go-mu-ui
cloth, fabric (n)	직물	jing-mul
fabric (as adj)	직물의	jing-mu-rui
paper (n)	종이	jong-i
paper (as adj)	종이의	jong-i-ui
cardboard (n)	판지	pan-ji
cardboard (as adj)	판지의	pan-ji-ui
polyethylene	폴리에틸렌	pol-li-e-til-len
cellophane	셀로판	sel-lo-pan

plywood	합판	hap-pan
porcelain (n)	도자기	do-ja-gi
porcelain (as adj)	도자기의	do-ja-gi-ui
clay (n)	점토	jeom-to
clay (as adj)	점토의	jeom-to-ui
ceramic (n)	세라믹	se-ra-mik
ceramic (as adj)	세라믹의	se-ra-mi-gui

28. Metals

metal (n)	금속	geum-sok
metal (as adj)	금속제의	geum-sok-je-ui
alloy (n)	합금	hap-geum

gold (n)	금	geum
gold, golden (adj)	금의	geum-ui
silver (n)	은	eun
silver (as adj)	은의	eun-ui

iron (n)	철	cheol
iron-, made of iron (adj)	철제의	cheol-je-ui
steel (n)	강철	gang-cheol
steel (as adj)	강철의	gang-cheo-rui
copper (n)	구리	gu-ri
copper (as adj)	구리의	gu-ri-ui

aluminium (n)	알루미늄	al-lu-mi-nyum
aluminium (as adj)	알루미늄의	al-lu-mi-nyum-ui
bronze (n)	청동	cheong-dong
bronze (as adj)	청동의	cheong-dong-ui

brass	황동	hwang-dong
nickel	니켈	ni-kel
platinum	백금	baek-geum
mercury	수은	su-eun
tin	주석	ju-seok
lead	납	nap
zinc	아연	a-yeon

HUMAN BEING

Human being. The body

29. Humans. Basic concepts

human being	사람	sa-ram
man (adult male)	남자	nam-ja
woman	여자	yeo-ja
child	아이, 아동	a-i, a-dong
girl	소녀	so-nyeo
boy	소년	so-nyeon
teenager	청소년	cheong-so-nyeon
old man	노인	no-in
old woman	노인	no-in

30. Human anatomy

organism (body)	생체	saeng-che
heart	심장	sim-jang
blood	피	pi
artery	동맥	dong-maek
vein	정맥	jeong-maek
brain	두뇌	du-noe
nerve	신경	sin-gyeong
nerves	신경	sin-gyeong
vertebra	척추	cheok-chu
spine (backbone)	등뼈	deung-ppyeo
stomach (organ)	위	wi
intestines, bowels	창자	chang-ja
intestine (e.g. large ~)	장	jang
liver	간	gan
kidney	신장	sin-jang
bone	뼈	ppyeo
skeleton	뼈대	ppyeo-dae
rib	늑골	neuk-gol
skull	두개골	du-gae-gol
muscle	근육	geu-nyuk
biceps	이두근	i-du-geun
tendon	힘줄, 건	him-jul, geon
joint	관절	gwan-jeol

lungs	폐	pye
genitals	생식기	saeng-sik-gi
skin	피부	pi-bu

31. Head

head	머리	meo-ri
face	얼굴	eol-gul
nose	코	ko
mouth	입	ip

eye	눈	nun
eyes	눈	nun
pupil	눈동자	nun-dong-ja
eyebrow	눈썹	nun-sseop
eyelash	속눈썹	song-nun-sseop
eyelid	눈꺼풀	nun-kkeo-pul

tongue	혀	hyeo
tooth	이	i
lips	입술	ip-sul
cheekbones	광대뼈	gwang-dae-ppyeo
gum	잇몸	in-mom
palate	입천장	ip-cheon-jang

nostrils	콧구멍	kot-gu-meong
chin	턱	teok
jaw	턱	teok
cheek	뺨, 볼	ppyam, bol

forehead	이마	i-ma
temple	관자놀이	gwan-ja-no-ri
ear	귀	gwi
back of the head	뒤통수	dwi-tong-su
neck	목	mok
throat	목구멍	mok-gu-meong

hair	머리털, 헤어	meo-ri-teol, he-eo
hairstyle	머리 스타일	meo-ri seu-ta-il
haircut	헤어컷	he-eo-keot
wig	가발	ga-bal

moustache	콧수염	kot-su-yeom
beard	턱수염	teok-su-yeom
to have (a beard, etc.)	기르다	gi-reu-da
plait	땋은 머리	tta-eun meo-ri
sideboards	구레나룻	gu-re-na-rut

red-haired (adj)	빨강머리의	ppal-gang-meo-ri-ui
grey (hair)	흰머리의	huin-meo-ri-ui
bald (adj)	대머리인	dae-meo-ri-in
bald patch	땜통	ttaem-tong
ponytail	말총머리	mal-chong-meo-ri
fringe	앞머리	am-meo-ri

32. Human body

hand	손	son
arm	팔	pal
finger	손가락	son-ga-rak
thumb	엄지손가락	eom-ji-son-ga-rak
little finger	새끼손가락	sae-kki-son-ga-rak
nail	손톱	son-top
fist	주먹	ju-meok
palm	손바닥	son-ba-dak
wrist	손목	son-mok
forearm	전박	jeon-bak
elbow	팔꿈치	pal-kkum-chi
shoulder	어깨	eo-kkae
leg	다리	da-ri
foot	발	bal
knee	무릎	mu-reup
calf	종아리	jong-a-ri
hip	엉덩이	eong-deong-i
heel	발뒤꿈치	bal-dwi-kkum-chi
body	몸	mom
stomach	배	bae
chest	가슴	ga-seum
breast	가슴	ga-seum
flank	옆구리	yeop-gu-ri
back	등	deung
lower back	허리	heo-ri
waist	허리	heo-ri
navel (belly button)	배꼽	bae-kkop
buttocks	엉덩이	eong-deong-i
bottom	엉덩이	eong-deong-i
beauty spot	점	jeom
birthmark (café au lait spot)	모반	mo-ban
tattoo	문신	mun-sin
scar	흉터	hyung-teo

Clothing & Accessories

33. Outerwear. Coats

clothes	옷	ot
outerwear	겉옷	geo-tot
winter clothing	겨울옷	gyeo=u=rot
coat (overcoat)	코트	ko-teu
fur coat	모피 외투	mo-pi oe-tu
fur jacket	짧은 모피 외투	jjal-beun mo-pi oe-tu
down coat	패딩점퍼	pae-ding-jeom-peo
jacket (e.g. leather ~)	재킷	jae-kit
raincoat (trenchcoat, etc.)	트렌치코트	teu-ren-chi-ko-teu
waterproof (adj)	방수의	bang-su-ui

34. Men's & women's clothing

shirt (button shirt)	셔츠	syeo-cheu
trousers	바지	ba-ji
jeans	청바지	cheong-ba-ji
suit jacket	재킷	jae-kit
suit	양복	yang-bok
dress (frock)	드레스	deu-re-seu
skirt	치마	chi-ma
blouse	블라우스	beul-la-u-seu
knitted jacket (cardigan, etc.)	니트 재킷	ni-teu jae-kit
jacket (of a woman's suit)	재킷	jae-kit
T-shirt	티셔츠	ti-syeo-cheu
shorts (short trousers)	반바지	ban-ba-ji
tracksuit	운동복	un-dong-bok
bathrobe	목욕가운	mo-gyok-ga-un
pyjamas	파자마	pa-ja-ma
jumper (sweater)	스웨터	seu-we-teo
pullover	폴오버	pu-ro-beo
waistcoat	조끼	jo-kki
tailcoat	연미복	yeon-mi-bok
dinner suit	턱시도	teok-si-do
uniform	제복	je-bok
workwear	작업복	ja-geop-bok
boiler suit	작업바지	ja-geop-ba-ji
coat (e.g. doctor's smock)	가운	ga-un

35. Clothing. Underwear

underwear	속옷	so-got
vest (singlet)	러닝 셔츠	reo-ning syeo-cheu
socks	양말	yang-mal
nightdress	잠옷	jam-ot
bra	브라	beu-ra
knee highs (knee-high socks)	무릎길이 스타킹	mu-reup-gi-ri seu-ta-king
tights	팬티 스타킹	paen-ti seu-ta-king
stockings (hold ups)	밴드 스타킹	baen-deu seu-ta-king
swimsuit, bikini	수영복	su-yeong-bok

36. Headwear

hat	모자	mo-ja
trilby hat	중절모	jung-jeol-mo
baseball cap	야구 모자	ya-gu mo-ja
flatcap	플랫캡	peul-laet-kaep
beret	베레모	be-re-mo
hood	후드	hu-deu
panama hat	파나마 모자	pa-na-ma mo-ja
knit cap (knitted hat)	니트 모자	ni-teu mo-ja
headscarf	스카프	seu-ka-peu
women's hat	여성용 모자	yeo-seong-yong mo-ja
hard hat	안전모	an-jeon-mo
forage cap	개리슨 캡	gae-ri-seun kaep
helmet	헬멧	hel-met

37. Footwear

footwear	신발	sin-bal
shoes (men's shoes)	구두	gu-du
shoes (women's shoes)	구두	gu-du
boots (e.g., cowboy ~)	부츠	bu-cheu
carpet slippers	슬리퍼	seul-li-peo
trainers	운동화	un-dong-hwa
trainers	스니커즈	seu-ni-keo-jeu
sandals	샌들	saen-deul
cobbler (shoe repairer)	구둣방	gu-dut-bang
heel	굽	gup
pair (of shoes)	켤레	kyeol-le
lace (shoelace)	끈	kkeun
to lace up (vt)	끈을 매다	kkeu-neul mae-da
shoehorn	구둣주걱	gu-dut-ju-geok
shoe polish	구두약	gu-du-yak

38. Textile. Fabrics

cotton (n)	면	myeon
cotton (as adj)	면의	myeo-nui
flax (n)	리넨	ri-nen
flax (as adj)	린넨의	rin-ne-nui
silk (n)	실크	sil-keu
silk (as adj)	실크의	sil-keu-ui
wool (n)	모직, 울	mo-jik, ul
wool (as adj)	모직의	mo-ji-gui
velvet	벨벳	bel-bet
suede	스웨이드	seu-we-i-deu
corduroy	코듀로이	ko-dyu-ro-i
nylon (n)	나일론	na-il-lon
nylon (as adj)	나일론의	na-il-lo-nui
polyester (n)	폴리에스테르	pol-li-e-seu-te-reu
polyester (as adj)	폴리에스테르의	pol-li-e-seu-te-reu-ui
leather (n)	가죽	ga-juk
leather (as adj)	가죽의	ga-ju-gui
fur (n)	모피	mo-pi
fur (e.g. ~ coat)	모피의	mo-pi-ui

39. Personal accessories

gloves	장갑	jang-gap
mittens	벙어리장갑	beong-eo-ri-jang-gap
scarf (muffler)	목도리	mok-do-ri
glasses	안경	an-gyeong
frame (eyeglass ~)	안경테	an-gyeong-te
umbrella	우산	u-san
walking stick	지팡이	ji-pang-i
hairbrush	빗, 솔빗	bit, sol-bit
fan	부채	bu-chae
tie (necktie)	넥타이	nek-ta-i
bow tie	나비넥타이	na-bi-nek-ta-i
braces	멜빵	mel-ppang
handkerchief	손수건	son-su-geon
comb	빗	bit
hair slide	머리핀	meo-ri-pin
hairpin	머리핀	meo-ri-pin
buckle	버클	beo-keul
belt	벨트	bel-teu
shoulder strap	어깨끈	eo-kkae-kkeun
bag (handbag)	가방	ga-bang
handbag	핸드백	haen-deu-baek
rucksack	배낭	bae-nang

40. Clothing. Miscellaneous

fashion	패션	pae-syeon
in vogue (adj)	유행하는	yu-haeng-ha-neun
fashion designer	패션 디자이너	pae-syeon di-ja-i-neo

collar	옷깃	ot-git
pocket	주머니, 포켓	ju-meo-ni, po-ket
pocket (as adj)	주머니의	ju-meo-ni-ui
sleeve	소매	so-mae
hanging loop	거는 끈	geo-neun kkeun
flies (on trousers)	바지 지퍼	ba-ji ji-peo

zip (fastener)	지퍼	ji-peo
fastener	조임쇠	jo-im-soe
button	단추	dan-chu
buttonhole	단춧 구멍	dan-chut gu-meong
to come off (ab. button)	떨어지다	tteo-reo-ji-da

to sew (vi, vt)	바느질하다	ba-neu-jil-ha-da
to embroider (vi, vt)	수놓다	su-no-ta
embroidery	자수	ja-su
sewing needle	바늘	ba-neul
thread	실	sil
seam	솔기	sol-gi

to get dirty (vi)	더러워지다	deo-reo-wo-ji-da
stain (mark, spot)	얼룩	eol-luk
to crease, to crumple	구겨지다	gu-gyeo-ji-da
to tear, to rip (vt)	찢다	jjit-da
clothes moth	좀	jom

41. Personal care. Cosmetics

toothpaste	치약	chi-yak
toothbrush	칫솔	chit-sol
to clean one's teeth	이를 닦다	i-reul dak-da

razor	면도기	myeon-do-gi
shaving cream	면도용 크림	myeon-do-yong keu-rim
to shave (vi)	깎다	kkak-da

| soap | 비누 | bi-nu |
| shampoo | 샴푸 | syam-pu |

scissors	가위	ga-wi
nail file	손톱줄	son-top-jul
nail clippers	손톱깎이	son-top-kka-kki
tweezers	족집게	jok-jip-ge

cosmetics	화장품	hwa-jang-pum
face mask	얼굴 마스크	eol-gul ma-seu-keu
manicure	매니큐어	mae-ni-kyu-eo

to have a manicure	매니큐어를 칠하다	mae-ni-kyu-eo-reul chil-ha-da
pedicure	페디큐어	pe-di-kyu-eo

make-up bag	화장품 가방	hwa-jang-pum ga-bang
face powder	분	bun
powder compact	콤팩트	kom-paek-teu
blusher	블러셔	beul-leo-syeo

perfume (bottled)	향수	hyang-su
toilet water (lotion)	화장수	hwa-jang-su
lotion	로션	ro-syeon
cologne	오드콜로뉴	o-deu-kol-lo-nyu

eyeshadow	아이섀도	a-i-syae-do
eyeliner	아이라이너	a-i-ra-i-neo
mascara	마스카라	ma-seu-ka-ra

lipstick	립스틱	rip-seu-tik
nail polish	매니큐어	mae-ni-kyu-eo
hair spray	헤어 스프레이	he-eo seu-peu-re-i
deodorant	데오도란트	de-o-do-ran-teu

cream	크림	keu-rim
face cream	얼굴 크림	eol-gul keu-rim
hand cream	핸드 크림	haen-deu keu-rim
anti-wrinkle cream	주름제거 크림	ju-reum-je-geo keu-rim
day (as adj)	낮의	na-jui
night (as adj)	밤의	ba-mui

tampon	탐폰	tam-pon
toilet paper (toilet roll)	화장지	hwa-jang-ji
hair dryer	헤어 드라이어	he-eo deu-ra-i-eo

42. Jewellery

jewellery, jewels	보석	bo-seok
precious (e.g. ~ stone)	귀중한	gwi-jung-han
hallmark stamp	품질 보증 마크	pum-jil bo-jeung ma-keu

ring	반지	ban-ji
wedding ring	결혼반지	gyeol-hon-ban-ji
bracelet	팔찌	pal-jji

earrings	귀걸이	gwi-geo-ri
necklace (~ of pearls)	목걸이	mok-geo-ri
crown	왕관	wang-gwan
bead necklace	구슬 목걸이	gu-seul mok-geo-ri

diamond	다이아몬드	da-i-a-mon-deu
emerald	에메랄드	e-me-ral-deu
ruby	루비	ru-bi
sapphire	사파이어	sa-pa-i-eo
pearl	진주	jin-ju
amber	호박	ho-bak

43. Watches. Clocks

watch (wristwatch)	손목 시계	son-mok si-gye
dial	문자반	mun-ja-ban
hand (clock, watch)	바늘	ba-neul
metal bracelet	금속제 시계줄	geum-sok-je si-gye-jul
watch strap	시계줄	si-gye-jul
battery	건전지	geon-jeon-ji
to be flat (battery)	나가다	na-ga-da
to change a battery	배터리를 갈다	bae-teo-ri-reul gal-da
to run fast	빨리 가다	ppal-li ga-da
to run slow	늦게 가다	neut-ge ga-da
wall clock	벽시계	byeok-si-gye
hourglass	모래시계	mo-rae-si-gye
sundial	해시계	hae-si-gye
alarm clock	알람 시계	al-lam si-gye
watchmaker	시계 기술자	si-gye gi-sul-ja
to repair (vt)	수리하다	su-ri-ha-da

Food. Nutricion

44. Food

meat	고기	go-gi
chicken	닭고기	dak-go-gi
poussin	영계	yeong-gye
duck	오리고기	o-ri-go-gi
goose	거위고기	geo-wi-go-gi
game	사냥감	sa-nyang-gam
turkey	칠면조고기	chil-myeon-jo-go-gi
pork	돼지고기	dwae-ji-go-gi
veal	송아지 고기	song-a-ji go-gi
lamb	양고기	yang-go-gi
beef	소고기	so-go-gi
rabbit	토끼고기	to-kki-go-gi
sausage (bologna, etc.)	소시지	so-si-ji
vienna sausage (frankfurter)	비엔나 소시지	bi-en-na so-si-ji
bacon	베이컨	be-i-keon
ham	햄	haem
gammon	개먼	gae-meon
pâté	파테	pa-te
liver	간	gan
mince (minced meat)	다진 고기	da-jin go-gi
tongue	혀	hyeo
egg	계란	gye-ran
eggs	계란	gye-ran
egg white	흰자	huin-ja
egg yolk	노른자	no-reun-ja
fish	생선	saeng-seon
seafood	해물	hae-mul
caviar	캐비어	kae-bi-eo
crab	게	ge
prawn	새우	sae-u
oyster	굴	gul
spiny lobster	대하	dae-ha
octopus	문어	mun-eo
squid	오징어	o-jing-eo
sturgeon	철갑상어	cheol-gap-sang-eo
salmon	연어	yeon-eo
halibut	넙치	neop-chi
cod	대구	dae-gu
mackerel	고등어	go-deung-eo

| tuna | 참치 | cham-chi |
| eel | 뱀장어 | baem-jang-eo |

trout	송어	song-eo
sardine	정어리	jeong-eo-ri
pike	강꼬치고기	gang-kko-chi-go-gi
herring	청어	cheong-eo

bread	빵	ppang
cheese	치즈	chi-jeu
sugar	설탕	seol-tang
salt	소금	so-geum

rice	쌀	ssal
pasta (macaroni)	파스타	pa-seu-ta
noodles	면	myeon

butter	버터	beo-teo
vegetable oil	식물유	sing-mu-ryu
sunflower oil	해바라기유	hae-ba-ra-gi-yu
margarine	마가린	ma-ga-rin

| olives | 올리브 | ol-li-beu |
| olive oil | 올리브유 | ol-li-beu-yu |

milk	우유	u-yu
condensed milk	연유	yeo-nyu
yogurt	요구르트	yo-gu-reu-teu
soured cream	사워크림	sa-wo-keu-rim
cream (of milk)	크림	keu-rim

| mayonnaise | 마요네즈 | ma-yo-ne-jeu |
| buttercream | 버터크림 | beo-teo-keu-rim |

groats (barley ~, etc.)	곡물	gong-mul
flour	밀가루	mil-ga-ru
tinned food	통조림	tong-jo-rim

cornflakes	콘플레이크	kon-peul-le-i-keu
honey	꿀	kkul
jam	잼	jaem
chewing gum	껌	kkeom

45. Drinks

water	물	mul
drinking water	음료수	eum-nyo-su
mineral water	미네랄 워터	mi-ne-ral rwo-teo

still (adj)	탄산 없는	tan-san neom-neun
carbonated (adj)	탄산의	tan-sa-nui
sparkling (adj)	탄산이 든	tan-san-i deun
ice	얼음	eo-reum
with ice	얼음을 넣은	eo-reu-meul leo-eun

non-alcoholic (adj)	무알코올의	mu-al-ko-o-rui
soft drink	청량음료	cheong-nyang-eum-nyo
refreshing drink	청량 음료	cheong-nyang eum-nyo
lemonade	레모네이드	re-mo-ne-i-deu
spirits	술	sul
wine	와인	wa-in
white wine	백 포도주	baek po-do-ju
red wine	레드 와인	re-deu wa-in
liqueur	리큐르	ri-kyu-reu
champagne	샴페인	syam-pe-in
vermouth	베르무트	be-reu-mu-teu
whisky	위스키	wi-seu-ki
vodka	보드카	bo-deu-ka
gin	진	jin
cognac	코냑	ko-nyak
rum	럼	reom
coffee	커피	keo-pi
black coffee	블랙 커피	beul-laek keo-pi
white coffee	밀크 커피	mil-keu keo-pi
cappuccino	카푸치노	ka-pu-chi-no
instant coffee	인스턴트 커피	in-seu-teon-teu keo-pi
milk	우유	u-yu
cocktail	칵테일	kak-te-il
milkshake	밀크 셰이크	mil-keu sye-i-keu
juice	주스	ju-seu
tomato juice	토마토 주스	to-ma-to ju-seu
orange juice	오렌지 주스	o-ren-ji ju-seu
freshly squeezed juice	생과일주스	saeng-gwa-il-ju-seu
beer	맥주	maek-ju
lager	라거	ra-geo
bitter	흑맥주	heung-maek-ju
tea	차	cha
black tea	홍차	hong-cha
green tea	녹차	nok-cha

46. Vegetables

vegetables	채소	chae-so
greens	녹황색 채소	nok-wang-saek chae-so
tomato	토마토	to-ma-to
cucumber	오이	o-i
carrot	당근	dang-geun
potato	감자	gam-ja
onion	양파	yang-pa
garlic	마늘	ma-neul

cabbage	양배추	yang-bae-chu
cauliflower	컬리플라워	keol-li-peul-la-wo
Brussels sprouts	방울다다기 양배추	bang-ul-da-da-gi yang-bae-chu
broccoli	브로콜리	beu-ro-kol-li

beetroot	비트	bi-teu
aubergine	가지	ga-ji
courgette	애호박	ae-ho-bak
pumpkin	호박	ho-bak
turnip	순무	sun-mu

parsley	파슬리	pa-seul-li
dill	딜	dil
lettuce	양상추	yang-sang-chu
celery	쎌러리	sel-leo-ri
asparagus	아스파라거스	a-seu-pa-ra-geo-seu
spinach	시금치	si-geum-chi

pea	완두	wan-du
beans	콩	kong
maize	옥수수	ok-su-su
kidney bean	강낭콩	gang-nang-kong

sweet paper	피망	pi-mang
radish	무	mu
artichoke	아티초크	a-ti-cho-keu

47. Fruits. Nuts

fruit	파일	gwa-il
apple	사과	sa-gwa
pear	배	bae
lemon	레몬	re-mon
orange	오렌지	o-ren-ji
strawberry (garden ~)	딸기	ttal-gi

tangerine	귤	gyul
plum	자두	ja-du
peach	복숭아	bok-sung-a
apricot	살구	sal-gu
raspberry	라즈베리	ra-jeu-be-ri
pineapple	파인애플	pa-in-ae-peul

banana	바나나	ba-na-na
watermelon	수박	su-bak
grape	포도	po-do
sour cherry	신양	si-nyang
sweet cherry	양벚나무	yang-beon-na-mu
melon	멜론	mel-lon

grapefruit	자몽	ja-mong
avocado	아보카도	a-bo-ka-do
papaya	파파야	pa-pa-ya

mango	망고	mang-go
pomegranate	석류	seong-nyu
redcurrant	레드커런트	re-deu-keo-ren-teu
blackcurrant	블랙커런트	beul-laek-keo-ren-teu
gooseberry	구스베리	gu-seu-be-ri
bilberry	빌베리	bil-be-ri
blackberry	블랙베리	beul-laek-be-ri
raisin	건포도	geon-po-do
fig	무화과	mu-hwa-gwa
date	대추야자	dae-chu-ya-ja
peanut	땅콩	ttang-kong
almond	아몬드	a-mon-deu
walnut	호두	ho-du
hazelnut	개암	gae-am
coconut	코코넛	ko-ko-neot
pistachios	피스타치오	pi-seu-ta-chi-o

48. Bread. Sweets

bakers' confectionery (pastry)	과자류	gwa-ja-ryu
bread	빵	ppang
biscuits	쿠키	ku-ki
chocolate (n)	초콜릿	cho-kol-lit
chocolate (as adj)	초콜릿의	cho-kol-lis-ui
candy (wrapped)	사탕	sa-tang
cake (e.g. cupcake)	케이크	ke-i-keu
cake (e.g. birthday ~)	케이크	ke-i-keu
pie (e.g. apple ~)	파이	pa-i
filling (for cake, pie)	속	sok
jam (whole fruit jam)	잼	jaem
marmalade	마멀레이드	ma-meol-le-i-deu
wafers	와플	wa-peul
ice-cream	아이스크림	a-i-seu-keu-rim

49. Cooked dishes

course, dish	요리, 코스	yo-ri, ko-seu
cuisine	요리	yo-ri
recipe	요리법	yo-ri-beop
portion	분량	bul-lyang
salad	샐러드	sael-leo-deu
soup	수프	su-peu
clear soup (broth)	육수	yuk-su
sandwich (bread)	샌드위치	saen-deu-wi-chi

fried eggs	계란후라이	gye-ran-hu-ra-i
hamburger (beefburger)	햄버거	haem-beo-geo
beefsteak	비프스테이크	bi-peu-seu-te-i-keu

side dish	사이드 메뉴	sa-i-deu me-nyu
spaghetti	스파게티	seu-pa-ge-ti
mash	으깬 감자	eu-kkaen gam-ja
pizza	피자	pi-ja
porridge (oatmeal, etc.)	죽	juk
omelette	오믈렛	o-meul-let

boiled (e.g. ~ beef)	삶은	sal-meun
smoked (adj)	훈제된	hun-je-doen
fried (adj)	튀긴	twi-gin
dried (adj)	말린	mal-lin
frozen (adj)	얼린	eol-lin
pickled (adj)	초절인	cho-jeo-rin

sweet (sugary)	단	dan
salty (adj)	짠	jjan
cold (adj)	차가운	cha-ga-un
hot (adj)	뜨거운	tteu-geo-un
bitter (adj)	쓴	sseun
tasty (adj)	맛있는	man-nin-neun

to cook in boiling water	삶다	sam-da
to cook (dinner)	요리하다	yo-ri-ha-da
to fry (vt)	부치다	bu-chi-da
to heat up (food)	데우다	de-u-da

to salt (vt)	소금을 넣다	so-geu-meul leo-ta
to pepper (vt)	후추를 넣다	hu-chu-reul leo-ta
to grate (vt)	강판에 갈다	gang-pa-ne gal-da
peel (n)	껍질	kkeop-jil
to peel (vt)	껍질 벗기다	kkeop-jil beot-gi-da

50. Spices

salt	소금	so-geum
salty (adj)	짜	jja
to salt (vt)	소금을 넣다	so-geu-meul leo-ta

black pepper	후추	hu-chu
red pepper (milled ~)	고춧가루	go-chut-ga-ru
mustard	겨자	gyeo-ja
horseradish	고추냉이	go-chu-naeng-i

condiment	양념	yang-nyeom
spice	향료	hyang-nyo
sauce	소스	so-seu
vinegar	식초	sik-cho

| anise | 아니스 | a-ni-seu |
| basil | 바질 | ba-jil |

cloves	정향	jeong-hyang
ginger	생강	saeng-gang
coriander	고수	go-su
cinnamon	계피	gye-pi

sesame	깨	kkae
bay leaf	월계수잎	wol-gye-su-ip
paprika	파프리카	pa-peu-ri-ka
caraway	캐러웨이	kae-reo-we-i
saffron	사프란	sa-peu-ran

51. Meals

| food | 음식 | eum-sik |
| to eat (vi, vt) | 먹다 | meok-da |

breakfast	아침식사	a-chim-sik-sa
to have breakfast	아침을 먹다	a-chi-meul meok-da
lunch	점심식사	jeom-sim-sik-sa
to have lunch	점심을 먹다	jeom-si-meul meok-da
dinner	저녁식사	jeo-nyeok-sik-sa
to have dinner	저녁을 먹다	jeo-nyeo-geul meok-da

| appetite | 식욕 | si-gyok |
| Enjoy your meal! | 맛있게 드십시오! | man-nit-ge deu-sip-si-o! |

to open (~ a bottle)	열다	yeol-da
to spill (liquid)	엎지르다	eop-ji-reu-da
to spill out (vi)	쏟아지다	sso-da-ji-da

to boil (vi)	끓다	kkeul-ta
to boil (vt)	끓이다	kkeu-ri-da
boiled (~ water)	끓인	kkeu-rin
to chill, cool down (vt)	식히다	sik-i-da
to chill (vi)	식다	sik-da

| taste, flavour | 맛 | mat |
| aftertaste | 뒷 맛 | dwit mat |

to slim down (lose weight)	살을 빼다	sa-reul ppae-da
diet	다이어트	da-i-eo-teu
vitamin	비타민	bi-ta-min
calorie	칼로리	kal-lo-ri

| vegetarian (n) | 채식주의자 | chae-sik-ju-ui-ja |
| vegetarian (adj) | 채식주의의 | chae-sik-ju-ui-ui |

fats (nutrient)	지방	ji-bang
proteins	단백질	dan-baek-jil
carbohydrates	탄수화물	tan-su-hwa-mul

slice (of lemon, ham)	조각	jo-gak
piece (of cake, pie)	조각	jo-gak
crumb (of bread, cake, etc.)	부스러기	bu-seu-reo-gi

52. Table setting

spoon	숟가락	sut-ga-rak
knife	나이프	na-i-peu
fork	포크	po-keu

cup (e.g., coffee ~)	컵	keop
plate (dinner ~)	접시	jeop-si
saucer	받침 접시	bat-chim jeop-si
serviette	냅킨	naep-kin
toothpick	이쑤시개	i-ssu-si-gae

53. Restaurant

restaurant	레스토랑	re-seu-to-rang
coffee bar	커피숍	keo-pi-syop
pub, bar	바	ba
tearoom	카페, 티룸	ka-pe, ti-rum

waiter	웨이터	we-i-teo
waitress	웨이트리스	we-i-teu-ri-seu
barman	바텐더	ba-ten-deo

menu	메뉴판	me-nyu-pan
wine list	와인 메뉴	wa-in me-nyu
to book a table	테이블 예약을 하다	te-i-beul rye-ya-geul ha-da

course, dish	요리, 코스	yo-ri, ko-seu
to order (meal)	주문하다	ju-mun-ha-da
to make an order	주문을 하다	ju-mu-neul ha-da

aperitif	아페리티프	a-pe-ri-ti-peu
starter	애피타이저	ae-pi-ta-i-jeo
dessert, pudding	디저트	di-jeo-teu

bill	계산서	gye-san-seo
to pay the bill	계산하다	gye-san-ha-da
to give change	거스름돈을 주다	geo-seu-reum-do-neul ju-da
tip	팁	tip

Family, relatives and friends

54. Personal information. Forms

name (first name)	이름	i-reum
surname (last name)	성	seong
date of birth	생년월일	saeng-nyeon-wo-ril
place of birth	탄생지	tan-saeng-ji
nationality	국적	guk-jeok
place of residence	거소	geo-so
country	나라	na-ra
profession (occupation)	직업	ji-geop
gender, sex	성별	seong-byeol
height	키	ki
weight	몸무게	mom-mu-ge

55. Family members. Relatives

mother	어머니	eo-meo-ni
father	아버지	a-beo-ji
son	아들	a-deul
daughter	딸	ttal
younger daughter	작은딸	ja-geun-ttal
younger son	작은아들	ja-geun-a-deul
eldest daughter	맏딸	mat-ttal
eldest son	맏아들	ma-da-deul
brother	형제	hyeong-je
sister	자매	ja-mae
cousin (masc.)	사촌 형제	sa-chon hyeong-je
cousin (fem.)	사촌 자매	sa-chon ja-mae
mummy	엄마	eom-ma
dad, daddy	아빠	a-ppa
parents	부모	bu-mo
child	아이, 아동	a-i, a-dong
children	아이들	a-i-deul
grandmother	할머니	hal-meo-ni
grandfather	할아버지	ha-ra-beo-ji
grandson	손자	son-ja
granddaughter	손녀	son-nyeo
grandchildren	손자들	son-ja-deul
uncle	삼촌	sam-chon

| nephew | 조카 | jo-ka |
| niece | 조카딸 | jo-ka-ttal |

mother-in-law (wife's mother)	장모	jang-mo
father-in-law (husband's father)	시아버지	si-a-beo-ji
son-in-law (daughter's husband)	사위	sa-wi
stepmother	계모	gye-mo
stepfather	계부	gye-bu

infant	영아	yeong-a
baby (infant)	아기	a-gi
little boy, kid	꼬마	kko-ma

wife	아내	a-nae
husband	남편	nam-pyeon
spouse (husband)	배우자	bae-u-ja
spouse (wife)	배우자	bae-u-ja

married (masc.)	결혼한	gyeol-hon-han
married (fem.)	결혼한	gyeol-hon-han
single (unmarried)	미혼의	mi-hon-ui
bachelor	미혼 남자	mi-hon nam-ja
divorced (masc.)	이혼한	i-hon-han
widow	과부	gwa-bu
widower	홀아비	ho-ra-bi

relative	친척	chin-cheok
close relative	가까운 친척	ga-kka-un chin-cheok
distant relative	먼 친척	meon chin-cheok
relatives	친척들	chin-cheok-deul

orphan (boy or girl)	고아	go-a
guardian (of a minor)	후견인	hu-gyeon-in
to adopt (a boy)	입양하다	i-byang-ha-da
to adopt (a girl)	입양하다	i-byang-ha-da

56. Friends. Colleagues

friend (masc.)	친구	chin-gu
friend (fem.)	친구	chin-gu
friendship	우정	u-jeong
to be friends	사귀다	sa-gwi-da

pal (masc.)	벗	beot
pal (fem.)	벗	beot
partner	파트너	pa-teu-neo

chief (boss)	상사	sang-sa
superior (n)	윗사람	wit-sa-ram
subordinate (n)	부하	bu-ha
colleague	동료	dong-nyo

acquaintance (person)	아는 사람	a-neun sa-ram
fellow traveller	동행자	dong-haeng-ja
classmate	동급생	dong-geup-saeng

neighbour (masc.)	이웃	i-ut
neighbour (fem.)	이웃	i-ut
neighbours	이웃들	i-ut-deul

57. Man. Woman

woman	여자	yeo-ja
girl (young woman)	소녀, 아가씨	so-nyeo, a-ga-ssi
bride	신부	sin-bu

beautiful (adj)	아름다운	a-reum-da-un
tall (adj)	키가 큰	ki-ga keun
slender (adj)	날씬한	nal-ssin-han
short (adj)	키가 작은	ki-ga ja-geun

| blonde (n) | 블론드 여자 | beul-lon-deu yeo-ja |
| brunette (n) | 갈색머리 여성 | gal-saeng-meo-ri yeo-seong |

ladies' (adj)	여성의	yeo-seong-ui
virgin (girl)	처녀	cheo-nyeo
pregnant (adj)	임신한	im-sin-han

man (adult male)	남자	nam-ja
blonde haired man	블론드 남자	beul-lon-deu nam-ja
dark haired man	갈색머리 남자	gal-saeng-meo-ri nam-ja
tall (adj)	키가 큰	ki-ga keun
short (adj)	키가 작은	ki-ga ja-geun

rude (rough)	무례한	mu-rye-han
stocky (adj)	땅딸막한	ttang-ttal-mak-an
robust (adj)	강건한	gang-han
strong (adj)	강한	gang-han
strength	힘	him

plump, fat (adj)	뚱뚱한	ttung-ttung-han
swarthy (dark-skinned)	거무스레한	geo-mu-seu-re-han
slender (well-built)	날씬한	nal-ssin-han
elegant (adj)	우아한	u-a-han

58. Age

age	나이	na-i
youth (young age)	청년시절	cheong-nyeon-si-jeol
young (adj)	젊은	jeol-meun

younger (adj)	더 젊은	deo jeol-meun
older (adj)	더 나이 든	deo na-i deun
young man	젊은 분	jeol-meun bun

| teenager | 청소년 | cheong-so-nyeon |
| guy, fellow | 사내 | sa-nae |

| old man | 노인 | no-in |
| old woman | 노인 | no-in |

| adult (adj) | 어른 | eo-reun |
| middle-aged (adj) | 중년의 | jung-nyeo-nui |

| elderly (adj) | 나이 든 | na-i deun |
| old (adj) | 늙은 | neul-geun |

retirement	은퇴	eun-toe
to retire (from job)	은퇴하다	eun-toe-ha-da
retiree, pensioner	은퇴자	eun-toe-ja

59. Children

child	아이, 아동	a-i, a-dong
children	아이들	a-i-deul
twins	쌍둥이	ssang-dung-i

cradle	요람	yo-ram
rattle	딸랑이	ttal-lang-i
nappy	기저귀	gi-jeo-gwi

| dummy, comforter | 젖꼭지 | jeot-kkok-ji |
| pram | 유모차 | yu-mo-cha |

| nursery | 유치원 | yu-chi-won |
| babysitter | 애기보는 사람 | ae-gi-bo-neun sa-ram |

| childhood | 유년 | yu-nyeon |
| doll | 인형 | in-hyeong |

| toy | 장난감 | jang-nan-gam |
| construction set (toy) | 블록 장난감 | beul-lok jang-nan-gam |

well-bred (adj)	잘 교육받은	jal gyo-yuk-ba-deun
ill-bred (adj)	잘못 키운	jal-mot ki-un
spoilt (adj)	버릇없는	beo-reus-eom-neun

| to be naughty | 짓궂다 | jit-gut-da |
| mischievous (adj) | 장난기 있는 | jang-nan-gi in-neun |

| mischievousness | 장난기 | jang-nan-gi |
| mischievous child | 장난꾸러기 | jang-nan-kku-reo-gi |

| obedient (adj) | 말 잘 듣는 | mal jal deun-neun |
| disobedient (adj) | 반항적인 | ban-hang-jeo-gin |

docile (adj)	유순한	yu-sun-han
clever (intelligent)	영리한	yeong-ni-han
child prodigy	신동	sin-dong

60. Married couples. Family life

to kiss (vt)	키스하다	ki-seu-ha-da
to kiss (vi)	입을 맞추다	i-beul mat-chu-da
family (n)	가족	ga-jok
family (as adj)	가족의	ga-jo-gui
couple	부부	bu-bu
marriage (state)	결혼	gyeol-hon
hearth (home)	따뜻한 가정	tta-tteu-tan ga-jeong
dynasty	혈통	hyeol-tong
date	데이트	de-i-teu
kiss	키스	ki-seu
love (for sb)	사랑	sa-rang
to love (sb)	사랑하다	sa-rang-ha-da
beloved	사랑받는	sa-rang-ban-neun
tenderness	상냥함	sang-nyang-ham
tender (affectionate)	자상한	ja-sang-han
faithfulness	성실	seong-sil
faithful (adj)	성실한	seong-sil-han
care (attention)	배려	bae-ryeo
caring (~ father)	배려하는	bae-ryeo-ha-neun
newlyweds	신혼 부부	sin-hon bu-bu
honeymoon	허니문	heo-ni-mun
to get married (ab. woman)	결혼하다	gyeol-hon-ha-da
to get married (ab. man)	결혼하다	gyeol-hon-ha-da
wedding	결혼식	gyeol-hon-sik
anniversary	기념일	gi-nyeom-il
lover (masc.)	애인	ae-in
mistress (lover)	정부	jeong-bu
adultery	불륜	bul-lyun
to cheat on ... (commit adultery)	바람을 피우다	ba-ra-meul pi-u-da
jealous (adj)	질투하는	jil-tu-ha-neun
to be jealous	질투하다	jil-tu-ha-da
divorce	이혼	i-hon
to divorce (vi)	이혼하다	i-hon-ha-da
to quarrel (vi)	다투다	da-tu-da
to be reconciled (after an argument)	화해하다	hwa-hae-ha-da
together (adv)	같이	ga-chi
sex	섹스	sek-seu
happiness	행복	haeng-bok
happy (adj)	행복한	haeng-bok-an
misfortune (accident)	불행	bul-haeng
unhappy (adj)	불행한	bul-haeng-han

Character. Feelings. Emotions

61. Feelings. Emotions

feeling (emotion)	감정	gam-jeong
feelings	감정	gam-jeong
to feel (vt)	느끼다	neu-kki-da
hunger	배고픔	bae-go-peum
to be hungry	배가 고프다	bae-ga go-peu-da
thirst	목마름	mong-ma-reum
to be thirsty	목마르다	mong-ma-reu-da
sleepiness	졸음	jo-reum
to feel sleepy	졸리다	jol-li-da
tiredness	피로	pi-ro
tired (adj)	피곤한	pi-gon-han
to get tired	피곤하다	pi-gon-ha-da
mood (humour)	기분	gi-bun
boredom	지루함	ji-ru-ham
to be bored	심심하다	sim-sim-ha-da
seclusion	은둔 생활	eun-dun saeng-hwal
to seclude oneself	고적하게 살다	go-jeok-a-ge sal-da
to worry (make anxious)	걱정하게 만들다	geok-jeong-ha-ge man-deul-da
to be worried	걱정하다	geok-jeong-ha-da
worrying (n)	걱정	geok-jeong
anxiety	심려	sim-nyeo
preoccupied (adj)	사로잡힌	sa-ro-ja-pin
to be nervous	긴장하다	gin-jang-ha-da
to panic (vi)	공황 상태에 빠지다	gong-hwang sang-tae-e ppa-ji-da
hope	희망	hui-mang
to hope (vi, vt)	희망하다	hui-mang-ha-da
certainty	확실	hwak-sil
certain, sure (adj)	확실한	hwak-sil-han
uncertainty	불확실성	bul-hwak-sil-seong
uncertain (adj)	불확실한	bul-hwak-sil-han
drunk (adj)	취한	chwi-han
sober (adj)	술 취하지 않은	sul chwi-ha-ji a-neun
weak (adj)	약한	yak-an
happy (adj)	행복한	haeng-bok-an
to scare (vt)	겁주다	geop-ju-da
fury (madness)	격분	gyeok-bun
rage (fury)	격노	gyeong-no

depression	우울함	u-ul-ham
discomfort (unease)	불편함	bul-pyeon-ham
comfort	안락	al-lak
to regret (be sorry)	후회하다	hu-hoe-ha-da
regret	후회	hu-hoe
bad luck	불운	bu-run
sadness	슬픔	seul-peum

shame (remorse)	부끄러움	bu-kkeu-reo-um
gladness	기쁨, 반가움	gi-ppeum, ban-ga-um
enthusiasm, zeal	열광, 열성	yeol-gwang, yeol-seong
enthusiast	열광자	yeol-gwang-ja
to show enthusiasm	열의를 보이다	yeo-rui-reul bo-i-da

62. Character. Personality

character	성격	seong-gyeok
character flaw	성격결함	seong-gyeok-gyeol-ham
mind	마음	ma-eum
reason	이성	i-seong

conscience	양심	yang-sim
habit (custom)	습관	seup-gwan
ability (talent)	능력	neung-nyeok
can (e.g. ~ swim)	할 수 있다	hal su it-da

patient (adj)	참을성 있는	cha-meul-seong in-neun
impatient (adj)	참을성 없는	cha-meul-seong eom-neun
curious (inquisitive)	호기심이 많은	ho-gi-sim-i ma-neun
curiosity	호기심	ho-gi-sim

modesty	겸손	gyeom-son
modest (adj)	겸손한	gyeom-son-han
immodest (adj)	자만하는	ja-man-ha-neun

| lazy (adj) | 게으른 | ge-eu-reun |
| lazy person (masc.) | 게으름뱅이 | ge-eu-reum-baeng-i |

cunning (n)	교활	gyo-hwal
cunning (as adj)	교활한	gyo-hwal-han
distrust	불신	bul-sin
distrustful (adj)	불신하는	bul-sin-ha-neun

generosity	관대함	gwan-dae-ham
generous (adj)	관대한	gwan-dae-han
talented (adj)	재능이 있는	jae-neung-i in-neun
talent	재능	jae-neung

courageous (adj)	용감한	yong-gam-han
courage	용기	yong-gi
honest (adj)	정직한	jeong-jik-an
honesty	정직	jeong-jik
careful (cautious)	주의깊은	ju-ui-gi-peun
brave (courageous)	용감한	yong-gam-han

| serious (adj) | 진지한 | jin-ji-han |
| strict (severe, stern) | 엄한 | eom-han |

decisive (adj)	과단성 있는	gwa-dan-seong in-neun
indecisive (adj)	과단성 없는	gwa-dan-seong eom-neun
shy, timid (adj)	소심한	so-sim-han
shyness, timidity	소심	so-sim

confidence (trust)	신뢰	sil-loe
to believe (trust)	신뢰하다	sil-loe-ha-da
trusting (credulous)	잘 믿는	jal min-neun

sincerely (adv)	성실하게	seong-sil-ha-ge
sincere (adj)	성실한	seong-sil-han
sincerity	성실	seong-sil
open (person)	열린	yeol-lin

calm (adj)	차분한	cha-bun-han
frank (sincere)	솔직한	sol-jik-an
naïve (adj)	순진한	sun-jin-han
absent-minded (adj)	건망증이 심한	geon-mang-jeung-i sim-han
funny (odd)	웃긴	ut-gin

greed, stinginess	욕심	yok-sim
greedy, stingy (adj)	욕심 많은	yok-sim ma-neun
stingy (adj)	인색한	in-saek-an
evil (adj)	사악한	sa-a-kan
stubborn (adj)	고집이 센	go-ji-bi sen
unpleasant (adj)	불쾌한	bul-kwae-han

selfish person (masc.)	이기주의자	i-gi-ju-ui-ja
selfish (adj)	이기적인	i-gi-jeo-gin
coward	비겁한 자, 겁쟁이	bi-geo-pan ja, geop-jaeng-i
cowardly (adj)	비겁한	bi-geo-pan

63. Sleep. Dreams

to sleep (vi)	잠을 자다	ja-meul ja-da
sleep, sleeping	잠	jam
dream	꿈	kkum
to dream (in sleep)	꿈을 꾸다	kku-meul kku-da
sleepy (adj)	졸린	jol-lin

bed	침대	chim-dae
mattress	매트리스	mae-teu-ri-seu
blanket (eiderdown)	이불	i-bul
pillow	베개	be-gae
sheet	시트	si-teu

insomnia	불면증	bul-myeon-jeung
sleepless (adj)	불면의	bul-myeon-ui
sleeping pill	수면제	su-myeon-je
to take a sleeping pill	수면제를 먹다	su-myeon-je-reul meok-da
to feel sleepy	졸리다	jol-li-da

to yawn (vi)	하품하다	ha-pum-ha-da
to go to bed	잠자리에 들다	jam-ja-ri-e deul-da
to make up the bed	침대를 정리하다	chim-dae-reul jeong-ni-ha-da
to fall asleep	잠들다	jam-deul-da
nightmare	악몽	ang-mong
snore, snoring	코골기	ko-gol-gi
to snore (vi)	코를 골다	ko-reul gol-da
alarm clock	알람 시계	al-lam si-gye
to wake (vt)	깨우다	kkae-u-da
to wake up	깨다	kkae-da
to get up (vi)	일어나다	i-reo-na-da
to have a wash	세수하다	se-su-ha-da

64. Humour. Laughter. Gladness

humour (wit, fun)	유머	yu-meo
sense of humour	유머 감각	yu-meo gam-gak
to enjoy oneself	즐기다	jeul-gi-da
cheerful (merry)	명랑한	myeong-nang-han
merriment (gaiety)	즐거움	jeul-geo-um
smile	미소	mi-so
to smile (vi)	미소를 짓다	mi-so-reul jit-da
to start laughing	웃기 시작하다	ut-gi si-jak-a-da
to laugh (vi)	웃다	ut-da
laugh, laughter	웃음	us-eum
anecdote	일화	il-hwa
funny (anecdote, etc.)	웃긴	ut-gin
funny (odd)	웃긴	ut-gin
to joke (vi)	농담하다	nong-dam-ha-da
joke (verbal)	농담	nong-dam
joy (emotion)	기쁜, 즐거움	gi-ppeun, jeul-geo-um
to rejoice (vi)	기뻐하다	gi-ppeo-ha-da
joyful (adj)	기쁜	gi-ppeun

65. Discussion, conversation. Part 1

communication	의사소통	ui-sa-so-tong
to communicate	연락을 주고받다	yeol-la-geul ju-go-bat-da
conversation	대화	dae-hwa
dialogue	대화	dae-hwa
discussion (discourse)	논의	non-ui
dispute (debate)	언쟁	eon-jaeng
to dispute, to debate	언쟁하다	eon-jaeng-ha-da
interlocutor	대화 상대	dae-hwa sang-dae
topic (theme)	주제	ju-je

point of view	관점	gwan-jeom
opinion (point of view)	의견	ui-gyeon
speech (talk)	연설	yeon-seol

discussion (of a report, etc.)	의논	ui-non
to discuss (vt)	의논하다	ui-non-ha-da
talk (conversation)	대화	dae-hwa
to talk (to chat)	대화하다	i-ya-gi-ha-da
meeting (encounter)	회의	hoe-ui
to meet (vi, vt)	만나다	man-na-da

proverb	속담	sok-dam
saying	속담	sok-dam
riddle (poser)	수수께끼	su-su-kke-kki
to pose a riddle	수수께끼를 내다	su-su-kke-kki-reul lae-da
password	비밀번호	bi-mil-beon-ho
secret	비밀	bi-mil

oath (vow)	맹세	maeng-se
to swear (an oath)	맹세하다	maeng-se-ha-da
promise	약속	yak-sok
to promise (vt)	약속하다	yak-sok-a-da

advice (counsel)	조언	jo-eon
to advise (vt)	조언하다	jo-eon-ha-da
to listen to ... (obey)	··· 를 따르다	... reul tta-reu-da

news	소식	so-sik
sensation (news)	센세이션	sen-se-i-syeon
information (report)	정보	jeong-bo
conclusion (decision)	결론	gyeol-lon
voice	목소리	mok-so-ri
compliment	칭찬	ching-chan
kind (nice)	친절한	chin-jeol-han

word	단어	dan-eo
phrase	어구	eo-gu
answer	대답	dae-dap

| truth | 진리 | jil-li |
| lie | 거짓말 | geo-jin-mal |

thought	생각	saeng-gak
idea (inspiration)	관념	gwan-nyeom
fantasy	판타지	pan-ta-ji

66. Discussion, conversation. Part 2

respected (adj)	존경받는	jon-gyeong-ban-neun
to respect (vt)	존경하다	jon-gyeong-ha-da
respect	존경	jon-gyeong
Dear ... (letter)	친애하는 ···	chin-ae-ha-neun ...
to introduce (sb to sb)	소개하다	so-gae-ha-da
intention	의도	ui-do

to intend (have in mind)	의도하다	ui-do-ha-da
wish	바람	ba-ram
to wish (~ good luck)	바라다	ba-ra-da
surprise (astonishment)	놀라움	nol-la-um
to surprise (amaze)	놀라게 하다	nol-la-ge ha-da
to be surprised	놀라다	nol-la-da
to give (vt)	주다	ju-da
to take (get hold of)	잡다	jap-da
to give back	돌려주다	dol-lyeo-ju-da
to return (give back)	돌려주다	dol-lyeo-ju-da
to apologize (vi)	사과하다	sa-gwa-ha-da
apology	사과	sa-gwa
to forgive (vt)	용서하다	yong-seo-ha-da
to talk (speak)	말하다	mal-ha-da
to listen (vi)	듣다	deut-da
to hear out	끝까지 듣다	kkeut-kka-ji deut-da
to understand (vt)	이해하다	i-hae-ha-da
to show (to display)	보여주다	bo-yeo-ju-da
to look at ...	··· 를 보다	... reul bo-da
to call (yell for sb)	부르다	bu-reu-da
to disturb (vt)	방해하다	bang-hae-ha-da
to pass (to hand sth)	건네주다	geon-ne-ju-da
demand (request)	요청	yo-cheong
to request (ask)	부탁하다	bu-tak-a-da
demand (firm request)	요구	yo-gu
to demand (request firmly)	요구하다	yo-gu-ha-da
to tease (call names)	놀리다	nol-li-da
to mock (make fun of)	조롱하다	jo-rong-ha-da
mockery, derision	조롱, 조소	jo-rong, jo-so
nickname	별명	byeol-myeong
insinuation	암시	am-si
to insinuate (imply)	암시하다	am-si-ha-da
to mean (vt)	의미하다	ui-mi-ha-da
description	서술	seo-sul
to describe (vt)	서술하다	seo-sul-ha-da
praise (compliments)	칭찬	ching-chan
to praise (vt)	칭찬하다	ching-chan-ha-da
disappointment	실망	sil-mang
to disappoint (vt)	실망시키다	sil-mang-si-ki-da
to be disappointed	실망하다	sil-mang-ha-da
supposition	추측	chu-cheuk
to suppose (assume)	추측하다	chu-cheuk-a-da
warning (caution)	경고	gyeong-go
to warn (vt)	경고하다	gyeong-go-ha-da

67. Discussion, conversation. Part 3

to talk into (convince)	설득하다	seol-deu-ka-da
to calm down (vt)	진정시키다	jin-jeong-si-ki-da
silence (~ is golden)	침묵	chim-muk
to be silent (not speaking)	침묵을 지키다	chim-mu-geul ji-ki-da
to whisper (vi, vt)	속삭이다	sok-sa-gi-da
whisper	속삭임	sok-sa-gim
frankly, sincerely (adv)	솔직하게	sol-jik-a-ge
in my opinion ...	내 생각에 ⋯	nae saeng-ga-ge ...
detail (of the story)	세부	se-bu
detailed (adj)	자세한	ja-se-han
in detail (adv)	자세하게	ja-se-ha-ge
hint, clue	단서	dan-seo
to give a hint	힌트를 주다	hin-teu-reul ju-da
look (glance)	흘낏 봄	heul-kkit bom
to have a look	보다	bo-da
fixed (look)	고정된	go-jeong-doen
to blink (vi)	눈을 깜빡이다	nu-neul kkam-ppa-gi-da
to wink (vi)	눈짓하다	nun-ji-ta-da
to nod (in assent)	끄덕이다	kkeu-deo-gi-da
sigh	한숨	han-sum
to sigh (vi)	한숨을 쉬다	han-su-meul swi-da
to shudder (vi)	몸을 떨다	mo-meul tteol-da
gesture	손짓	son-jit
to touch (one's arm, etc.)	만지다	man-ji-da
to seize (e.g., ~ by the arm)	잡다	jap-da
to tap (on the shoulder)	톡 치다	tuk chi-da
Look out!	조심!	jo-sim!
Really?	정말?	jeong-mal?
Are you sure?	확실해요?	hwak-sil-hae-yo?
Good luck!	행운을 빕니다!	haeng-u-neul bim-ni-da!
I see!	알겠어요!	al-ge-seo-yo!
What a pity!	유감이에요!	yu-ga-mi-e-yo!

68. Agreement. Refusal

consent	동의	dong-ui
to consent (vi)	동의하다	dong-ui-ha-da
approval	찬성	chan-seong
to approve (vt)	찬성하다	chan-seong-ha-da
refusal	거절	geo-jeol
to refuse (vi, vt)	거절하다	geo-jeol-ha-da
Great!	좋아요!	jo-a-yo!
All right!	좋아요!	jo-a-yo!

Okay! (I agree)	그래요!	geu-rae-yo!
forbidden (adj)	금지된	geum-ji-doen
it's forbidden	금지되어 있다	geum-ji-doe-eo it-da
it's impossible	불가능하다	bul-ga-neung-ha-da
incorrect (adj)	틀린	teul-lin
to reject (~ a demand)	거부하다	geo-bu-ha-da
to support (cause, idea)	지지하다	ji-ji-ha-da
to accept (~ an apology)	받아들이다	ba-da-deu-ri-da
to confirm (vt)	확인해 주다	hwa-gin-hae ju-da
confirmation	확인	hwa-gin
permission	허락	heo-rak
to permit (vt)	허가하다	heo-ga-ha-da
decision	결정	gyeol-jeong
to say nothing	아무 말도 않다	a-mu mal-do an-ta
(hold one's tongue)		
condition (term)	조건	jo-geon
excuse (pretext)	핑계	ping-gye
praise (compliments)	칭찬	ching-chan
to praise (vt)	칭찬하다	ching-chan-ha-da

69. Success. Good luck. Failure

success	성공	seong-gong
successfully (adv)	성공적으로	seong-gong-jeo-geu-ro
successful (adj)	성공적인	seong-gong-jeo-gin
luck (good luck)	운	un
Good luck!	행운을 빕니다!	haeng-u-neul bim-ni-da!
lucky (e.g. ~ day)	운이 좋은	un-i jo-eun
lucky (fortunate)	운이 좋은	un-i jo-eun
failure	실패	sil-pae
misfortune	불운	bu-run
bad luck	불운	bu-run
unsuccessful (adj)	성공적이지 못한	seong-gong-jeo-gi-ji mo-tan
catastrophe	재난	jae-nan
pride	자존심	ja-jon-sim
proud (adj)	자존심 강한	ja-jon-sim gang-han
to be proud	득의만면이다	deu-gui-man-myeon-i-da
winner	승리자	seung-ni-ja
to win (vi)	이기다	i-gi-da
to lose (not win)	지다	ji-da
try	사실, 시도	sa-sil, si-do
to try (vi)	해보다	hae-bo-da
chance (opportunity)	기회	gi-hoe

70. Quarrels. Negative emotions

shout (scream)	고함	go-ham
to shout (vi)	소리치다	so-ri-chi-da
quarrel	싸움	ssa-um
to quarrel (vi)	다투다	da-tu-da
fight (squabble)	싸움	ssa-um
to make a scene	싸움을 하다	ssa-u-meul ha-da
conflict	갈등	gal-deung
misunderstanding	오해	o-hae
insult	모욕	mo-yok
to insult (vt)	모욕하다	mo-yok-a-da
insulted (adj)	모욕 당한	mo-yok dang-han
resentment	분노	bun-no
to offend (vt)	모욕하다	mo-yok-a-da
to take offence	약오르다	ya-go-reu-da
indignation	분개	bun-gae
to be indignant	분개하다	bun-gae-ha-da
complaint	불평	bul-pyeong
to complain (vi, vt)	불평하다	bul-pyeong-ha-da
apology	사과	sa-gwa
to apologize (vi)	사과하다	sa-gwa-ha-da
to beg pardon	용서를 빌다	yong-seo-reul bil-da
criticism	비판	bi-pan
to criticize (vt)	비판하다	bi-pan-ha-da
accusation (charge)	비난	bi-nan
to accuse (vt)	비난하다	bi-nan-ha-da
revenge	복수	bok-su
to avenge (get revenge)	복수하다	bok-su-ha-da
to pay back	갚아주다	ga-pa-ju-da
disdain	경멸	gyeong-myeol
to despise (vt)	경멸하다	gyeong-myeol-ha-da
hatred, hate	증오	jeung-o
to hate (vt)	증오하다	jeung-o-ha-da
nervous (adj)	긴장한	gin-jang-han
to be nervous	긴장하다	gin-jang-ha-da
angry (mad)	화가 난	hwa-ga nan
to make angry	화나게 하다	hwa-na-ge ha-da
humiliation	굴욕	gu-ryok
to humiliate (vt)	굴욕감을 주다	gu-ryok-ga-meul ju-da
to humiliate oneself	창피를 당하다	chang-pi-reul dang-ha-da
shock	충격	chung-gyeok
to shock (vt)	충격을 주다	chung-gyeo-geul ju-da
trouble (e.g. serious ~)	문제	mun-je
unpleasant (adj)	불쾌한	bul-kwae-han

fear (dread)	두려움	du-ryeo-um
terrible (storm, heat)	끔찍한	kkeum-jjik-an
scary (e.g. ~ story)	무서운	mu-seo-un
horror	공포	gong-po
awful (crime, news)	지독한	ji-dok-an

to cry (weep)	울다	ul-da
to start crying	울기 시작하다	ul-gi si-jak-a-da
tear	눈물	nun-mul

fault	잘못	jal-mot
guilt (feeling)	죄책감	joe-chaek-gam
dishonor (disgrace)	불명예	bul-myeong-ye
protest	항의	hang-ui
stress	스트레스	seu-teu-re-seu

to disturb (vt)	방해하다	bang-hae-ha-da
to be furious	화내다	hwa-nae-da
angry (adj)	화가 난	hwa-ga nan
to end (~ a relationship)	끝내다	kkeun-nae-da
to swear (at sb)	욕하다	yok-a-da

to scare (become afraid)	무서워하다	mu-seo-wo-ha-da
to hit (strike with hand)	치다	chi-da
to fight (street fight, etc.)	싸우다	ssa-u-da

to settle (a conflict)	해결하다	hae-gyeol-ha-da
discontented (adj)	불만족한	bul-kwae-han
furious (adj)	맹렬한	maeng-nyeol-han

| It's not good! | 그건 좋지 않아요! | geu-geon jo-chi a-na-yo! |
| It's bad! | 그건 나빠요! | geu-geon na-ppa-yo! |

Medicine

illness	병	byeong
to be ill	눕다	nup-da
health	건강	geon-gang
runny nose (coryza)	비염	bi-yeom
tonsillitis	편도염	pyeon-do-yeom
cold (illness)	감기	gam-gi
to catch a cold	감기에 걸리다	gam-gi-e geol-li-da
bronchitis	기관지염	gi-gwan-ji-yeom
pneumonia	폐렴	pye-ryeom
flu, influenza	독감	dok-gam
shortsighted (adj)	근시의	geun-si-ui
longsighted (adj)	원시의	won-si-ui
strabismus (crossed eyes)	사시	sa-si
squint-eyed (adj)	사시인	sa-si-in
cataract	백내장	baeng-nae-jang
glaucoma	녹내장	nong-nae-jang
stroke	뇌졸중	noe-jol-jung
heart attack	심장마비	sim-jang-ma-bi
myocardial infarction	심근경색증	sim-geun-gyeong-saek-jeung
paralysis	마비	ma-bi
to paralyse (vt)	마비되다	ma-bi-doe-da
allergy	알레르기	al-le-reu-gi
asthma	천식	cheon-sik
diabetes	당뇨병	dang-nyo-byeong
toothache	치통, 이앓이	chi-tong, i-a-ri
caries	충치	chung-chi
diarrhoea	설사	seol-sa
constipation	변비증	byeon-bi-jeung
stomach upset	배탈	bae-tal
food poisoning	식중독	sik-jung-dok
to get food poisoning	식중독에 걸리다	sik-jung-do-ge geol-li-da
arthritis	관절염	gwan-jeo-ryeom
rickets	구루병	gu-ru-byeong
rheumatism	류머티즘	ryu-meo-ti-jeum
gastritis	위염	wi-yeom
appendicitis	맹장염	maeng-jang-yeom
cholecystitis	담낭염	dam-nang-yeom

ulcer	궤양	gwe-yang
measles	홍역	hong-yeok
rubella (German measles)	풍진	pung-jin
jaundice	황달	hwang-dal
hepatitis	간염	gan-nyeom

schizophrenia	정신 분열증	jeong-sin bu-nyeol-jeung
rabies (hydrophobia)	광견병	gwang-gyeon-byeong
neurosis	신경증	sin-gyeong-jeung
concussion	뇌진탕	noe-jin-tang

cancer	암	am
sclerosis	경화증	gyeong-hwa-jeung
multiple sclerosis	다발성 경화증	da-bal-seong gyeong-hwa-jeung

alcoholism	알코올 중독	al-ko-ol jung-dok
alcoholic (n)	알코올 중독자	al-ko-ol jung-dok-ja
syphilis	매독	mae-dok
AIDS	에이즈	e-i-jeu

tumour	종양	jong-yang
malignant (adj)	악성의	ak-seong-ui
benign (adj)	양성의	yang-seong-ui

fever	열병	yeol-byeong
malaria	말라리아	mal-la-ri-a
gangrene	괴저	goe-jeo
seasickness	뱃멀미	baen-meol-mi
epilepsy	간질	gan-jil

epidemic	유행병	yu-haeng-byeong
typhus	발진티푸스	bal-jin-ti-pu-seu
tuberculosis	결핵	gyeol-haek
cholera	콜레라	kol-le-ra
plague (bubonic ~)	페스트	pe-seu-teu

72. Symptoms. Treatments. Part 1

symptom	증상	jeung-sang
temperature	체온	che-on
high temperature (fever)	열	yeol
pulse (heartbeat)	맥박	maek-bak

dizziness (vertigo)	현기증	hyeon-gi-jeung
hot (adj)	뜨거운	tteu-geo-un
shivering	전율	jeo-nyul
pale (e.g. ~ face)	창백한	chang-baek-an

cough	기침	gi-chim
to cough (vi)	기침을 하다	gi-chi-meul ha-da
to sneeze (vi)	재채기하다	jae-chae-gi-ha-da
faint	실신	sil-sin
to faint (vi)	실신하다	sil-sin-ha-da

bruise (hématome)	멍	meong
bump (lump)	혹	hok
to bang (bump)	부딪치다	bu-dit-chi-da
contusion (bruise)	타박상	ta-bak-sang
to get a bruise	타박상을 입다	ta-bak-sang-eul rip-da
to limp (vi)	절다	jeol-da
dislocation	탈구	tal-gu
to dislocate (vt)	탈구하다	tal-gu-ha-da
fracture	골절	gol-jeol
to have a fracture	골절하다	gol-jeol-ha-da
cut (e.g. paper ~)	베인	be-in
to cut oneself	베다	jeol-chang-eul rip-da
bleeding	출혈	chul-hyeol
burn (injury)	화상	hwa-sang
to get burned	데다	de-da
to prick (vt)	찌르다	jji-reu-da
to prick oneself	찔리다	jjil-li-da
to injure (vt)	다치다	da-chi-da
injury	부상	bu-sang
wound	부상	bu-sang
trauma	정신적 외상	jeong-sin-jeok goe-sang
to be delirious	망상을 겪다	mang-sang-eul gyeok-da
to stutter (vi)	말을 더듬다	ma-reul deo-deum-da
sunstroke	일사병	il-sa-byeong

73. Symptoms. Treatments. Part 2

pain, ache	통증	tong-jeung
splinter (in foot, etc.)	가시	ga-si
sweat (perspiration)	땀	ttam
to sweat (perspire)	땀이 나다	ttam-i na-da
vomiting	구토	gu-to
convulsions	경련	gyeong-nyeon
pregnant (adj)	임신한	im-sin-han
to be born	태어나다	tae-eo-na-da
delivery, labour	출산	chul-san
to deliver (~ a baby)	낳다	na-ta
abortion	낙태	nak-tae
breathing, respiration	호흡	ho-heup
in-breath (inhalation)	들숨	deul-sum
out-breath (exhalation)	날숨	nal-sum
to exhale (breathe out)	내쉬다	nae-swi-da
to inhale (vi)	들이쉬다	deu-ri-swi-da
disabled person	장애인	jang-ae-in
cripple	병신	byeong-sin

drug addict	마약 중독자	ma-yak jung-dok-ja
deaf (adj)	귀가 먼	gwi-ga meon
mute (adj)	벙어리인	beong-eo-ri-in
deaf mute (adj)	농아인	nong-a-in
mad, insane (adj)	미친	mi-chin
madman (demented person)	광인	gwang-in
madwoman	광인	gwang-in
to go insane	미치다	mi-chi-da
gene	유전자	yu-jeon-ja
immunity	면역성	myeo-nyeok-seong
hereditary (adj)	유전의	yu-jeon-ui
congenital (adj)	선천적인	seon-cheon-jeo-gin
virus	바이러스	ba-i-reo-seu
microbe	미생물	mi-saeng-mul
bacterium	세균	se-gyun
infection	감염	gam-nyeom

74. Symptoms. Treatments. Part 3

hospital	병원	byeong-won
patient	환자	hwan-ja
diagnosis	진단	jin-dan
cure	치료	chi-ryo
to get treatment	치료를 받다	chi-ryo-reul bat-da
to treat (~ a patient)	치료하다	chi-ryo-ha-da
to nurse (look after)	간호하다	gan-ho-ha-da
care (nursing ~)	간호	gan-ho
operation, surgery	수술	su-sul
to bandage (head, limb)	붕대를 감다	bung-dae-reul gam-da
bandaging	붕대	bung-dae
vaccination	예방주사	ye-bang-ju-sa
to vaccinate (vt)	접종하다	jeop-jong-ha-da
injection	주사	ju-sa
to give an injection	주사하다	ju-sa-ha-da
amputation	절단	jeol-dan
to amputate (vt)	절단하다	jeol-dan-ha-da
coma	혼수 상태	hon-su sang-tae
to be in a coma	혼수 상태에 있다	hon-su sang-tae-e it-da
intensive care	집중 치료	jip-jung chi-ryo
to recover (~ from flu)	회복하다	hoe-bok-a-da
condition (patient's ~)	상태	sang-tae
consciousness	의식	ui-sik
memory (faculty)	기억	gi-eok
to pull out (tooth)	빼다	ppae-da
filling	충전물	chung-jeon-mul

to fill (a tooth)	때우다	ttae-u-da
hypnosis	최면	choe-myeon
to hypnotize (vt)	최면을 걸다	choe-myeo-neul geol-da

75. Doctors

doctor	의사	ui-sa
nurse	간호사	gan-ho-sa
personal doctor	개인 의사	gae-in ui-sa

dentist	치과 의사	chi-gwa ui-sa
optician	안과 의사	an-gwa ui-sa
general practitioner	내과 의사	nae-gwa ui-sa
surgeon	외과 의사	oe-gwa ui-sa

psychiatrist	정신과 의사	jeong-sin-gwa ui-sa
paediatrician	소아과 의사	so-a-gwa ui-sa
psychologist	심리학자	sim-ni-hak-ja
gynaecologist	부인과 의사	bu-in-gwa ui-sa
cardiologist	심장병 전문의	sim-jang-byeong jeon-mun-ui

76. Medicine. Drugs. Accessories

medicine, drug	약	yak
remedy	약제	yak-je
prescription	처방	cheo-bang

tablet, pill	정제	jeong-je
ointment	연고	yeon-go
ampoule	앰풀	aem-pul
mixture, solution	혼합물	hon-ham-mul
syrup	물약	mul-lyak
capsule	알약	a-ryak
powder	가루약	ga-ru-yak

gauze bandage	거즈 붕대	geo-jeu bung-dae
cotton wool	솜	som
iodine	요오드	yo-o-deu

plaster	반창고	ban-chang-go
eyedropper	점안기	jeom-an-gi
thermometer	체온계	che-on-gye
syringe	주사기	ju-sa-gi

| wheelchair | 휠체어 | hwil-che-eo |
| crutches | 목발 | mok-bal |

painkiller	진통제	jin-tong-je
laxative	완하제	wan-ha-je
spirits (ethanol)	알코올	al-ko-ol
medicinal herbs	약초	yak-cho
herbal (~ tea)	약초의	yak-cho-ui

77. Smoking. Tobacco products

tobacco	담배	dam-bae
cigarette	담배	dam-bae
cigar	시가	si-ga
pipe	담뱃대	dam-baet-dae
packet (of cigarettes)	갑	gap
matches	성냥	seong-nyang
matchbox	성냥 갑	seong-nyang gap
lighter	라이터	ra-i-teo
ashtray	재떨이	jae-tteo-ri
cigarette case	담배 케이스	dam-bae ke-i-seu
cigarette holder	물부리	mul-bu-ri
filter (cigarette tip)	필터	pil-teo
to smoke (vi, vt)	피우다	pi-u-da
to light a cigarette	담배에 불을 붙이다	dam-bae-e bu-reul bu-chi-da
smoking	흡연	heu-byeon
smoker	흡연자	heu-byeon-ja
cigarette end	꽁초	kkong-cho
smoke, fumes	연기	yeon-gi
ash	재	jae

HUMAN HABITAT

City

78. City. Life in the city

city, town	도시	do-si
capital city	수도	su-do
village	마을	ma-eul
city map	도시 지도	do-si ji-do
city centre	시내	si-nae
suburb	근교	geun-gyo
suburban (adj)	근교의	geun-gyo-ui
environs (suburbs)	주변	ju-byeon
city block	한 구획	han gu-hoek
residential block (area)	동	dong
traffic	교통	gyo-tong
traffic lights	신호등	sin-ho-deung
public transport	대중교통	dae-jung-gyo-tong
crossroads	교차로	gyo-cha-ro
zebra crossing	횡단 보도	hoeng-dan bo-do
pedestrian subway	지하 보도	ji-ha bo-do
to cross (~ the street)	건너가다	geon-neo-ga-da
pedestrian	보행자	bo-haeng-ja
pavement	인도	in-do
bridge	다리	da-ri
embankment (river walk)	강변로	gang-byeon-no
allée (garden walkway)	길	gil
park	공원	gong-won
boulevard	대로	dae-ro
square	광장	gwang-jang
avenue (wide street)	가로	ga-ro
street	거리	geo-ri
side street	골목	gol-mok
dead end	막다른길	mak-da-reun-gil
house	집	jip
building	빌딩	bil-ding
skyscraper	고층 건물	go-cheung geon-mul
facade	전면	jeon-myeon
roof	지붕	ji-bung
window	창문	chang-mun

arch	아치	a-chi
column	기둥	gi-dung
corner	모퉁이	mo-tung-i

shop window	쇼윈도우	syo-win-do-u
signboard (store sign, etc.)	간판	gan-pan
poster (e.g., playbill)	포스터	po-seu-teo
advertising poster	광고 포스터	gwang-go po-seu-teo
hoarding	광고판	gwang-go-pan

rubbish	쓰레기	sseu-re-gi
rubbish bin	쓰레기통	sseu-re-gi-tong
rubbish dump	쓰레기장	sseu-re-gi-jang

telephone box	공중 전화	gong-jung jeon-hwa
lamppost	가로등	ga-ro-deung
bench (park ~)	벤치	ben-chi

police officer	경찰관	gyeong-chal-gwan
police	경찰	gyeong-chal
beggar	거지	geo-ji
homeless (n)	노숙자	no-suk-ja

79. Urban institutions

shop	가게, 상점	ga-ge, sang-jeom
chemist, pharmacy	약국	yak-guk
optician (spectacles shop)	안경 가게	an-gyeong ga-ge
shopping centre	쇼핑몰	syo-ping-mol
supermarket	슈퍼마켓	syu-peo-ma-ket

bakery	빵집	ppang-jip
baker	제빵사	je-ppang-sa
cake shop	제과점	je-gwa-jeom
grocery shop	식료품점	sing-nyo-pum-jeom
butcher shop	정육점	jeong-yuk-jeom

greengrocer	야채 가게	ya-chae ga-ge
market	시장	si-jang

coffee bar	커피숍	keo-pi-syop
restaurant	레스토랑	re-seu-to-rang
pub, bar	바	ba
pizzeria	피자 가게	pi-ja ga-ge

hairdresser	미장원	mi-jang-won
post office	우체국	u-che-guk
dry cleaners	드라이 클리닝	deu-ra-i keul-li-ning
photo studio	사진관	sa-jin-gwan

shoe shop	신발 가게	sin-bal ga-ge
bookshop	서점	seo-jeom
sports shop	스포츠용품 매장	seu-po-cheu-yong-pum mae-jang

clothes repair shop	옷 수선 가게	ot su-seon ga-ge
formal wear hire	의류 임대	ui-ryu im-dae
video rental shop	비디오 대여	bi-di-o dae-yeo

circus	서커스	seo-keo-seu
zoo	동물원	dong-mu-rwon
cinema	영화관	yeong-hwa-gwan
museum	박물관	bang-mul-gwan
library	도서관	do-seo-gwan

theatre	극장	geuk-jang
opera (opera house)	오페라극장	o-pe-ra-geuk-jang
nightclub	나이트 클럽	na-i-teu keul-leop
casino	카지노	ka-ji-no

mosque	모스크	mo-seu-keu
synagogue	유대교 회당	yu-dae-gyo hoe-dang
cathedral	대성당	dae-seong-dang
temple	사원, 신전	sa-won, sin-jeon
church	교회	gyo-hoe

college	단과대학	dan-gwa-dae-hak
university	대학교	dae-hak-gyo
school	학교	hak-gyo

prefecture	도, 현	do, hyeon
town hall	시청	si-cheong
hotel	호텔	ho-tel
bank	은행	eun-haeng

embassy	대사관	dae-sa-gwan
travel agency	여행사	yeo-haeng-sa
information office	안내소	an-nae-so
currency exchange	환전소	hwan-jeon-so

| underground, tube | 지하철 | ji-ha-cheol |
| hospital | 병원 | byeong-won |

| petrol station | 주유소 | ju-yu-so |
| car park | 주차장 | ju-cha-jang |

80. Signs

signboard (store sign, etc.)	간판	gan-pan
notice (door sign, etc.)	안내문	an-nae-mun
poster	포스터	po-seu-teo
direction sign	방향표시	bang-hyang-pyo-si
arrow (sign)	화살표	hwa-sal-pyo

caution	경고	gyeong-go
warning sign	경고판	gyeong-go-pan
to warn (vt)	경고하다	gyeong-go-ha-da
rest day (weekly ~)	휴일	hyu-il
timetable (schedule)	시간표	si-gan-pyo

opening hours	영업 시간	yeong-eop si-gan
WELCOME!	어서 오세요!	eo-seo o-se-yo!
ENTRANCE	입구	ip-gu
WAY OUT	출구	chul-gu
PUSH	미세요	mi-se-yo
PULL	당기세요	dang-gi-se-yo
OPEN	열림	yeol-lim
CLOSED	닫힘	da-chim
WOMEN	여성전용	yeo-seong-jeo-nyong
MEN	남성	nam-seong-jeo-nyong
DISCOUNTS	할인	ha-rin
SALE	세일	se-il
NEW!	신상품	sin-sang-pum
FREE	공짜	gong-jja
ATTENTION!	주의!	ju-ui!
NO VACANCIES	빈 방 없음	bin bang eop-seum
RESERVED	예약석	ye-yak-seok
ADMINISTRATION	관리부	gwal-li-bu
STAFF ONLY	직원 전용	ji-gwon jeo-nyong
BEWARE OF THE DOG!	개조심	gae-jo-sim
NO SMOKING	금연	geu-myeon
DO NOT TOUCH!	손 대지 마시오!	son dae-ji ma-si-o!
DANGEROUS	위험	wi-heom
DANGER	위험	wi-heom
HIGH VOLTAGE	고전압	go-jeon-ap
NO SWIMMING!	수영 금지	su-yeong geum-ji
OUT OF ORDER	수리중	su-ri-jung
FLAMMABLE	가연성 물자	ga-yeon-seong mul-ja
FORBIDDEN	금지	geum-ji
NO TRESPASSING!	출입 금지	chu-rip geum-ji
WET PAINT	칠 주의	chil ju-ui

81. Urban transport

bus, coach	버스	beo-seu
tram	전차	jeon-cha
trolleybus	트롤리 버스	teu-rol-li beo-seu
route (bus ~)	노선	no-seon
number (e.g. bus ~)	번호	beon-ho
to go by ...	··· 타고 가다	... ta-go ga-da
to get on (~ the bus)	타다	ta-da
to get off ...	··· 에서 내리다	... e-seo nae-ri-da
stop (e.g. bus ~)	정류장	jeong-nyu-jang
next stop	다음 정류장	da-eum jeong-nyu-jang

terminus	종점	jong-jeom
timetable	시간표	si-gan-pyo
to wait (vt)	기다리다	gi-da-ri-da
ticket	표	pyo
fare	요금	yo-geum
cashier (ticket seller)	계산원	gye-san-won
ticket inspection	검표	geom-pyo
ticket inspector	검표원	geom-pyo-won
to be late (for ...)	... 시간에 늦다	... si-gan-e neut-da
to miss (~ the train, etc.)	놓치다	no-chi-da
to be in a hurry	서두르다	seo-du-reu-da
taxi, cab	택시	taek-si
taxi driver	택시 운전 기사	taek-si un-jeon gi-sa
by taxi	택시로	taek-si-ro
taxi rank	택시 정류장	taek-si jeong-nyu-jang
to call a taxi	택시를 부르다	taek-si-reul bu-reu-da
to take a taxi	택시를 타다	taek-si-reul ta-da
traffic	교통	gyo-tong
traffic jam	교통 체증	gyo-tong che-jeung
rush hour	러시 아워	reo-si a-wo
to park (vi)	주차하다	ju-cha-ha-da
to park (vt)	주차하다	ju-cha-ha-da
car park	주차장	ju-cha-jang
underground, tube	지하철	ji-ha-cheol
station	역	yeok
to take the tube	지하철을 타다	ji-ha-cheo-reul ta-da
train	기차	gi-cha
train station	기차역	gi-cha-yeok

82. Sightseeing

monument	기념비	gi-nyeom-bi
fortress	요새	yo-sae
palace	궁전	gung-jeon
castle	성	seong
tower	탑	tap
mausoleum	영묘	yeong-myo
architecture	건축	geon-chuk
medieval (adj)	중세의	jung-se-ui
ancient (adj)	고대의	go-dae-ui
national (adj)	국가의	guk-ga-ui
famous (monument, etc.)	유명한	yu-myeong-han
tourist	관광객	gwan-gwang-gaek
guide (person)	가이드	ga-i-deu
excursion, sightseeing tour	견학, 관광	gyeon-hak, gwan-gwang
to show (vt)	보여주다	bo-yeo-ju-da

to tell (vt)	이야기하다	i-ya-gi-ha-da
to find (vt)	찾다	chat-da
to get lost (lose one's way)	길을 잃다	gi-reul ril-ta
map (e.g. underground ~)	노선도	no-seon-do
map (e.g. city ~)	지도	ji-do

souvenir, gift	기념품	gi-nyeom-pum
gift shop	기념품 가게	gi-nyeom-pum ga-ge
to take pictures	사진을 찍다	sa-ji-neul jjik-da
to have one's picture taken	사진을 찍다	sa-ji-neul jjik-da

83. Shopping

to buy (purchase)	사다	sa-da
shopping	구매	gu-mae
to go shopping	쇼핑하다	syo-ping-ha-da
shopping	쇼핑	syo-ping

| to be open (ab. shop) | 열리다 | yeol-li-da |
| to be closed | 닫다 | dat-da |

footwear, shoes	신발	sin-bal
clothes, clothing	옷	ot
cosmetics	화장품	hwa-jang-pum
food products	식품	sik-pum
gift, present	선물	seon-mul

| shop assistant (masc.) | 판매원 | pan-mae-won |
| shop assistant (fem.) | 여판매원 | yeo-pan-mae-won |

cash desk	계산대	gye-san-dae
mirror	거울	geo-ul
counter (shop ~)	계산대	gye-san-dae
fitting room	탈의실	ta-rui-sil

to try on	입어보다	i-beo-bo-da
to fit (ab. dress, etc.)	어울리다	eo-ul-li-da
to fancy (vt)	좋아하다	jo-a-ha-da

price	가격	ga-gyeok
price tag	가격표	ga-gyeok-pyo
to cost (vt)	값이 … 이다	gap-si … i-da
How much?	얼마?	eol-ma?
discount	할인	ha-rin

inexpensive (adj)	비싸지 않은	bi-ssa-ji a-neun
cheap (adj)	싼	ssan
expensive (adj)	비싼	bi-ssan
It's expensive	비쌉니다	bi-ssam-ni-da

hire (n)	임대	im-dae
to hire (~ a dinner jacket)	빌리다	bil-li-da
credit (trade credit)	신용	si-nyong
on credit (adv)	신용으로	si-nyong-eu-ro

84. Money

money	돈	don
currency exchange	환전	hwan-jeon
exchange rate	환율	hwa-nyul
cashpoint	현금 자동 지급기	hyeon-geum ja-dong ji-geup-gi
coin	동전	dong-jeon

| dollar | 달러 | dal-leo |
| euro | 유로 | yu-ro |

lira	리라	ri-ra
Deutschmark	마르크	ma-reu-keu
franc	프랑	peu-rang
pound sterling	파운드	pa-un-deu
yen	엔	en

debt	빚	bit
debtor	채무자	chae-mu-ja
to lend (money)	빌려주다	bil-lyeo-ju-da
to borrow (vi, vt)	빌리다	bil-li-da

bank	은행	eun-haeng
account	계좌	gye-jwa
to deposit into the account	계좌에 입금하다	ip-geum-ha-da
to withdraw (vt)	출금하다	chul-geum-ha-da

credit card	신용 카드	si-nyong ka-deu
cash	현금	hyeon-geum
cheque	수표	su-pyo
to write a cheque	수표를 끊다	su-pyo-reul kkeun-ta
chequebook	수표책	su-pyo-chaek

wallet	지갑	ji-gap
purse	동전지갑	dong-jeon-ji-gap
safe	금고	geum-go

heir	상속인	sang-so-gin
inheritance	유산	yu-san
fortune (wealth)	재산, 큰돈	jae-san, keun-don

lease	임대	im-dae
rent (money)	집세	jip-se
to rent (sth from sb)	임대하다	im-dae-ha-da

price	가격	ga-gyeok
cost	비용	bi-yong
sum	액수	aek-su

to spend (vt)	쓰다	sseu-da
expenses	출비를	chul-bi-reul
to economize (vi, vt)	절약하다	jeo-ryak-a-da
economical	경제적인	gyeong-je-jeo-gin
to pay (vi, vt)	지불하다	ji-bul-ha-da

payment	지불	ji-bul
change (give the ~)	거스름돈	geo-seu-reum-don

tax	세금	se-geum
fine	벌금	beol-geum
to fine (vt)	벌금을 부과하다	beol-geu-meul bu-gwa-ha-da

85. Post. Postal service

post office	우체국	u-che-guk
post (letters, etc.)	우편물	u-pyeon-mul
postman	우체부	u-che-bu
opening hours	영업 시간	yeong-eop si-gan

letter	편지	pyeon-ji
registered letter	등기 우편	deung-gi u-pyeon
postcard	엽서	yeop-seo
telegram	전보	jeon-bo
parcel	소포	so-po
money transfer	송금	song-geum

to receive (vt)	받다	bat-da
to send (vt)	보내다	bo-nae-da
sending	발송	bal-song

address	주소	ju-so
postcode	우편 번호	u-pyeon beon-ho
sender	발송인	bal-song-in
receiver	수신인	su-sin-in

name (first name)	이름	i-reum
surname (last name)	성	seong

postage rate	요금	yo-geum
standard (adj)	일반의	il-ba-nui
economical (adj)	경제적인	gyeong-je-jeo-gin

weight	무게	mu-ge
to weigh (~ letters)	무게를 달다	mu-ge-reul dal-da
envelope	봉투	bong-tu
postage stamp	우표	u-pyo

Dwelling. House. Home

86. House. Dwelling

house	집	jip
at home (adv)	집에	ji-be
yard	마당	ma-dang
fence (iron ~)	울타리	ul-ta-ri
brick (n)	벽돌	byeok-dol
brick (as adj)	벽돌의	byeok-do-rui
stone (n)	돌	dol
stone (as adj)	돌의	do-rui
concrete (n)	콘크리트	kon-keu-ri-teu
concrete (as adj)	콘크리트의	kon-keu-ri-teu-ui
new (new-built)	새로운	sae-ro-un
old (adj)	오래된	o-rae-doen
decrepit (house)	쓰러질듯한	sseu-reo-jil-deu-tan
modern (adj)	근대의	geun-dae-ui
multistorey (adj)	다층의	da-cheung-ui
tall (~ building)	높은	no-peun
floor, storey	층	cheung
single-storey (adj)	단층의	dan-cheung-ui
ground floor	일층	il-cheung
top floor	꼭대기층	kkok-dae-gi-cheung
roof	지붕	ji-bung
chimney	굴뚝	gul-ttuk
roof tiles	기와	gi-wa
tiled (adj)	기와를 얹은	gi-wa-reul reon-jeun
loft (attic)	다락	da-rak
window	창문	chang-mun
glass	유리	yu-ri
window ledge	창가	chang-ga
shutters	덧문	deon-mun
wall	벽	byeok
balcony	발코니	bal-ko-ni
downpipe	선홈통	seon-hom-tong
upstairs (to be ~)	위층으로	wi-cheung-eu-ro
to go upstairs	위층에 올라가다	wi-cheung-e ol-la-ga-da
to come down (the stairs)	내려오다	nae-ryeo-o-da
to move (to new premises)	이사가다	i-sa-ga-da

87. House. Entrance. Lift

entrance	입구	ip-gu
stairs (stairway)	계단	gye-dan
steps	단	dan
banisters	난간	nan-gan
lobby (hotel ~)	로비	ro-bi
postbox	우편함	u-pyeon-ham
waste bin	쓰레기통	sseu-re-gi-tong
refuse chute	쓰레기 활송 장치	sseu-re-gi hwal-song jang-chi
lift	엘리베이터	el-li-be-i-teo
goods lift	화물 엘리베이터	hwa-mul rel-li-be-i-teo
lift cage	엘리베이터 카	el-li-be-i-teo ka
to take the lift	엘리베이터를 타다	el-li-be-i-teo-reul ta-da
flat	아파트	a-pa-teu
residents (~ of a building)	주민	ju-min
neighbour (masc.)	이웃	i-ut
neighbour (fem.)	이웃	i-ut
neighbours	이웃들	i-ut-deul

88. House. Electricity

electricity	전기	jeon-gi
light bulb	전구	jeon-gu
switch	스위치	seu-wi-chi
fuse (plug fuse)	퓨즈	pyu-jeu
cable, wire (electric ~)	전선	jeon-seon
wiring	배선	bae-seon
electricity meter	전기 계량기	jeon-gi gye-ryang-gi
readings	판독값	pan-dok-gap

89. House. Doors. Locks

door	문	mun
gate (vehicle ~)	대문	dae-mun
handle, doorknob	손잡이	son-ja-bi
to unlock (unbolt)	빗장을 벗기다	bit-jang-eul beot-gi-da
to open (vt)	열다	yeol-da
to close (vt)	닫다	dat-da
key	열쇠	yeol-soe
bunch (of keys)	열쇠 꾸러미	yeol-soe kku-reo-mi
to creak (door, etc.)	삐걱거리다	ppi-geok-geo-ri-da
creak	삐걱거리는 소리	ppi-geok-geo-ri-neun so-ri
hinge (door ~)	경첩	gyeong-cheop
doormat	문 매트	mun mae-teu
door lock	자물쇠	ja-mul-soe

keyhole	열쇠 구멍	yeol-soe gu-meong
crossbar (sliding bar)	빗장	bit-jang
door latch	빗장걸이	bit-jang-geo-ri
padlock	맹꽁이 자물쇠	maeng-kkong-i ja-mul-soe

to ring (~ the door bell)	울리다	ul-li-da
ringing (sound)	벨소리	bel-so-ri
doorbell	벨	bel
doorbell button	초인종	cho-in-jong
knock (at the door)	노크	no-keu
to knock (vi)	두드리다	du-deu-ri-da

code	코드	ko-deu
combination lock	숫자 배합 자물쇠	sut-ja bae-hap ja-mul-soe
intercom	인터콤	in-teo-kom
number (on the door)	번호	beon-ho
doorplate	문패	mun-pae
peephole	문구멍	mun-gu-meong

90. Country house

village	마을	ma-eul
vegetable garden	채소밭	chae-so-bat
fence	울타리	ul-ta-ri
picket fence	말뚝 울타리	mal-ttuk gul-ta-ri
wicket gate	쪽문	jjong-mun

granary	곡창	gok-chang
cellar	지하 저장실	ji-ha jeo-jang-sil
shed (garden ~)	헛간	heot-gan
water well	우물	u-mul

stove (wood-fired ~)	화덕	hwa-deok
to stoke the stove	불을 지피다	bu-reul ji-pi-da
firewood	장작	jang-jak
log (firewood)	통나무	tong-na-mu

veranda	베란다	be-ran-da
deck (terrace)	테라스	te-ra-seu
stoop (front steps)	현관	hyeon-gwan
swing (hanging seat)	그네	geu-ne

91. Villa. Mansion

country house	시외 주택	si-oe ju-taek
country-villa	별장	byeol-jang
wing (~ of a building)	동	dong

garden	정원	jeong-won
park	공원	gong-won
conservatory (greenhouse)	열대온실	yeol-dae-on-sil
to look after (garden, etc.)	··· 을 맡다	... eul mat-da

swimming pool	수영장	su-yeong-jang
gym (home gym)	헬스장	hel-seu-jang
tennis court	테니스장	te-ni-seu-jang
home theater (room)	홈씨어터	hom-ssi-eo-teo
garage	차고	cha-go

| private property | 개인 소유물 | gae-in so-yu-mul |
| private land | 사유 토지 | sa-yu to-ji |

| warning (caution) | 경고 | gyeong-go |
| warning sign | 경고판 | gyeong-go-pan |

security	보안	bo-an
security guard	보안요원	bo-a-nyo-won
burglar alarm	도난 경보기	do-nan gyeong-bo-gi

92. Castle. Palace

castle	성	seong
palace	궁전	gung-jeon
fortress	요새	yo-sae
wall (round castle)	성벽	seong-byeok
tower	탑	tap
keep, donjon	내성	nae-seong

| portcullis | 내리닫이 쇠창살문 | nae-ri-da-ji soe-chang-sal-mun |

subterranean passage	지하 통로	ji-ha tong-no
moat	해자	hae-ja
chain	쇠사슬	soe-sa-seul
arrow loop	총안	chong-an

magnificent (adj)	장대한	jang-dae-han
majestic (adj)	장엄한	jang-eom-han
impregnable (adj)	난공불락의	nan-gong-bul-la-gui
medieval (adj)	중세의	jung-se-ui

93. Flat

flat	아파트	a-pa-teu
room	방	bang
bedroom	침실	chim-sil
dining room	식당	sik-dang
living room	거실	geo-sil
study (home office)	서재	seo-jae

entry room	곁방	gyeot-bang
bathroom	욕실	yok-sil
water closet	화장실	hwa-jang-sil
ceiling	천장	cheon-jang
floor	마루	ma-ru
corner	구석	gu-seok

94. Flat. Cleaning

to clean (vi, vt)	청소하다	cheong-so-ha-da
to put away (to stow)	치우다	chi-u-da
dust	먼지	meon-ji
dusty (adj)	먼지 투성이의	meon-ji tu-seong-i-ui
to dust (vt)	먼지를 떨다	meon-ji-reul tteol-da
vacuum cleaner	진공 청소기	jin-gong cheong-so-gi
to vacuum (vt)	진공 청소기로 청소하다	jin-gong cheong-so-gi-ro cheong-so-ha-da
to sweep (vi, vt)	쓸다	sseul-da
sweepings	쓸기	sseul-gi
order	정돈	jeong-don
disorder, mess	뒤죽박죽	dwi-juk-bak-juk
mop	대걸레	dae-geol-le
duster	행주	haeng-ju
short broom	빗자루	bit-ja-ru
dustpan	쓰레받기	sseu-re-bat-gi

95. Furniture. Interior

furniture	가구	ga-gu
table	식탁, 테이블	sik-tak, te-i-beul
chair	의자	ui-ja
bed	침대	chim-dae
sofa, settee	소파	so-pa
armchair	안락 의자	al-lak gui-ja
bookcase	책장	chaek-jang
shelf	책꽂이	chaek-kko-ji
wardrobe	옷장	ot-jang
coat rack (wall-mounted ~)	옷걸이	ot-geo-ri
coat stand	스탠드옷걸이	seu-taen-deu-ot-geo-ri
chest of drawers	서랍장	seo-rap-jang
coffee table	커피 테이블	keo-pi te-i-beul
mirror	거울	geo-ul
carpet	양탄자	yang-tan-ja
small carpet	러그	reo-geu
fireplace	벽난로	byeong-nan-no
candle	초	cho
candlestick	촛대	chot-dae
drapes	커튼	keo-teun
wallpaper	벽지	byeok-ji
blinds (jalousie)	블라인드	beul-la-in-deu
table lamp	테이블 램프	deung

wall lamp (sconce)	벽등	byeok-deung
standard lamp	플로어 스탠드	peul-lo-eo seu-taen-deu
chandelier	샹들리에	syang-deul-li-e

leg (of a chair, table)	다리	da-ri
armrest	팔걸이	pal-geo-ri
back (backrest)	등받이	deung-ba-ji
drawer	서랍	seo-rap

96. Bedding

bedclothes	침구	chim-gu
pillow	베개	be-gae
pillowslip	베갯잇	be-gaen-nit
duvet	이불	i-bul
sheet	시트	si-teu
bedspread	침대보	chim-dae-bo

97. Kitchen

kitchen	부엌	bu-eok
gas	가스	ga-seu
gas cooker	가스 레인지	ga-seu re-in-ji
electric cooker	전기 레인지	jeon-gi re-in-ji
oven	오븐	o-beun
microwave oven	전자 레인지	jeon-ja re-in-ji

refrigerator	냉장고	naeng-jang-go
freezer	냉동고	naeng-dong-go
dishwasher	식기 세척기	sik-gi se-cheok-gi

mincer	고기 분쇄기	go-gi bun-swae-gi
juicer	과즙기	gwa-jeup-gi
toaster	토스터	to-seu-teo
mixer	믹서기	mik-seo-gi

coffee machine	커피 메이커	keo-pi me-i-keo
coffee pot	커피 주전자	keo-pi ju-jeon-ja
coffee grinder	커피 그라인더	keo-pi geu-ra-in-deo

kettle	주전자	ju-jeon-ja
teapot	티팟	ti-pat
lid	뚜껑	ttu-kkeong
tea strainer	차거름망	cha-geo-reum-mang

spoon	숟가락	sut-ga-rak
teaspoon	티스푼	ti-seu-pun
soup spoon	숟가락	sut-ga-rak
fork	포크	po-keu
knife	칼	kal
tableware (dishes)	식기	sik-gi
plate (dinner ~)	접시	jeop-si

saucer	받침 접시	bat-chim jeop-si
shot glass	소주잔	so-ju-jan
glass (tumbler)	유리잔	yu-ri-jan
cup	컵	keop
sugar bowl	설탕그릇	seol-tang-geu-reut
salt cellar	소금통	so-geum-tong
pepper pot	후추통	hu-chu-tong
butter dish	버터 접시	beo-teo jeop-si
stock pot (soup pot)	냄비	naem-bi
frying pan (skillet)	프라이팬	peu-ra-i-paen
ladle	국자	guk-ja
colander	체	che
tray (serving ~)	쟁반	jaeng-ban
bottle	병	byeong
jar (glass)	유리병	yu-ri-byeong
tin (can)	캔, 깡통	kaen, kkang-tong
bottle opener	병따개	byeong-tta-gae
tin opener	깡통 따개	kkang-tong tta-gae
corkscrew	코르크 마개 뽑이	ko-reu-keu ma-gae ppo-bi
filter	필터	pil-teo
to filter (vt)	여과하다	yeo-gwa-ha-da
waste (food ~, etc.)	쓰레기	sseu-re-gi
waste bin (kitchen ~)	쓰레기통	sseu-re-gi-tong

98. Bathroom

bathroom	욕실	yok-sil
water	물	mul
tap	수도꼭지	su-do-kkok-ji
hot water	온수	on-su
cold water	냉수	naeng-su
toothpaste	치약	chi-yak
to clean one's teeth	이를 닦다	i-reul dak-da
to shave (vi)	깎다	kkak-da
shaving foam	면도 크림	myeon-do keu-rim
razor	면도기	myeon-do-gi
to wash (one's hands, etc.)	씻다	ssit-da
to have a bath	목욕하다	mo-gyok-a-da
shower	샤워	sya-wo
to have a shower	샤워하다	sya-wo-ha-da
bath	욕조	yok-jo
toilet (toilet bowl)	변기	byeon-gi
sink (washbasin)	세면대	se-myeon-dae
soap	비누	bi-nu
soap dish	비누 그릇	bi-nu geu-reut

sponge	스펀지	seu-peon-ji
shampoo	샴푸	syam-pu
towel	수건	su-geon
bathrobe	목욕가운	mo-gyok-ga-un

laundry (laundering)	빨래	ppal-lae
washing machine	세탁기	se-tak-gi
to do the laundry	빨래하다	ppal-lae-ha-da
washing powder	가루세제	ga-ru-se-je

99. Household appliances

TV, telly	텔레비전	tel-le-bi-jeon
tape recorder	카세트 플레이어	ka-se-teu peul-le-i-eo
video	비디오테이프 녹화기	bi-di-o-te-i-peu nok-wa-gi
radio	라디오	ra-di-o
player (CD, MP3, etc.)	플레이어	peul-le-i-eo

video projector	프로젝터	peu-ro-jek-teo
home cinema	홈씨어터	hom-ssi-eo-teo
DVD player	디비디 플레이어	di-bi-di peul-le-i-eo
amplifier	앰프	aem-peu
video game console	게임기	ge-im-gi

video camera	캠코더	kaem-ko-deo
camera (photo)	카메라	ka-me-ra
digital camera	디지털 카메라	di-ji-teol ka-me-ra

vacuum cleaner	진공 청소기	jin-gong cheong-so-gi
iron (e.g. steam ~)	다리미	da-ri-mi
ironing board	다림질 판	da-rim-jil pan

telephone	전화	jeon-hwa
mobile phone	휴대폰	hyu-dae-pon
typewriter	타자기	ta-ja-gi
sewing machine	재봉틀	jae-bong-teul

microphone	마이크	ma-i-keu
headphones	헤드폰	he-deu-pon
remote control (TV)	원격 조종	won-gyeok jo-jong

CD, compact disc	씨디	ssi-di
cassette, tape	테이프	te-i-peu
vinyl record	레코드 판	re-ko-deu pan

100. Repairs. Renovation

renovations	수리를	su-ri-reul
to renovate (vt)	수리를 하다	su-ri-reul ha-da
to repair, to fix (vt)	보수하다	bo-su-ha-da
to put in order	정리하다	jeong-ni-ha-da
to redo (do again)	다시 하다	da-si ha-da

paint	페인트	pe-in-teu
to paint (~ a wall)	페인트를 칠하다	pe-in-teu-reul chil-ha-da
house painter	페인트공	pe-in-teu-gong
paintbrush	붓	but

| whitewash | 백색 도료 | baek-saek do-ryo |
| to whitewash (vt) | 백색 도료를 칠하다 | baek-saek do-ryo-reul chil-ha-da |

wallpaper	벽지	byeok-ji
to wallpaper (vt)	벽지를 붙이다	byeok-ji-reul bu-chi-da
varnish	니스	ni-seu
to varnish (vt)	니스를 칠하다	ni-seu-reul chil-ha-da

101. Plumbing

water	물	mul
hot water	온수	on-su
cold water	냉수	naeng-su
tap	수도꼭지	su-do-kkok-ji

drop (of water)	물방울	mul-bang-ul
to drip (vi)	방울져 떨어지다	bang-ul-jyeo tteo-reo-ji-da
to leak (ab. pipe)	새다	sae-da
leak (pipe ~)	누출	nu-chul
puddle	웅덩이	ung-deong-i

pipe	관, 파이프	gwan, pa-i-peu
valve (e.g., ball ~)	밸브	bael-beu
to be clogged up	막히다	mak-i-da

tools	공구	gong-gu
adjustable spanner	멍키렌치	meong-ki-ren-chi
to unscrew (lid, filter, etc.)	열리다	yeol-li-da
to screw (tighten)	돌려서 조이다	dol-lyeo-seo jo-i-da

to unclog (vt)	··· 를 뚫다	… reul ttul-ta
plumber	배관공	bae-gwan-gong
basement	지하실	ji-ha-sil
sewerage (system)	하수도	ha-su-do

102. Fire. Conflagration

fire (accident)	불	bul
flame	화염	hwa-yeom
spark	불똥	bul-ttong
smoke (from fire)	연기	yeon-gi
torch (flaming stick)	횃불	hwaet-bul
campfire	모닥불	mo-dak-bul

| petrol | 휘발유, 가솔린 | hwi-ba-ryu, ga-sol-lin |
| paraffin | 등유 | deung-yu |

flammable (adj)	가연성의	ga-yeon-seong-ui
explosive (adj)	폭발성의	pok-bal-seong-ui
NO SMOKING	금연	geu-myeon

safety	안전	an-jeon
danger	위험	wi-heom
dangerous (adj)	위험한	wi-heom-han

to catch fire	불이 붙다	bu-ri but-da
explosion	폭발	pok-bal
to set fire	방화하다	bang-hwa-ha-da
arsonist	방화범	bang-hwa-beom
arson	방화	bang-hwa

to blaze (vi)	활활 타다	hwal-hwal ta-da
to burn (be on fire)	타다	ta-da
to burn down	불에 타다	bu-re ta-da

firefighter, fireman	소방관	so-bang-gwan
fire engine	소방차	so-bang-cha
fire brigade	소방대	so-bang-dae

fire hose	소방 호스	so-bang ho-seu
fire extinguisher	소화기	so-hwa-gi
helmet	헬멧	hel-met
siren	사이렌	sa-i-ren

to cry (for help)	소리치다	so-ri-chi-da
to call for help	도와 달라고 외치다	do-wa dal-la-go oe-chi-da
rescuer	구조자	gu-jo-ja
to rescue (vt)	구조하다	gu-jo-ha-da

to arrive (vi)	도착하다	do-chak-a-da
to extinguish (vt)	끄다	kkeu-da
water	물	mul
sand	모래	mo-rae

ruins (destruction)	폐허	pye-heo
to collapse (building, etc.)	붕괴되다	bung-goe-doe-da
to fall down (vi)	무너지다	mu-neo-ji-da
to cave in (ceiling, floor)	무너지다	mu-neo-ji-da

| piece of debris | 파편 | pa-pyeon |
| ash | 재 | jae |

| to suffocate (die) | 질식하다 | jil-sik-a-da |
| to be killed (perish) | 사망하다 | sa-mang-ha-da |

HUMAN ACTIVITIES

Job. Business. Part 1

103. **Office. Working in the office**

office (company ~)	사무실	sa-mu-sil
office (director's ~)	사무실	sa-mu-sil
reception desk	접수처	jeop-su-cheo
secretary	비서	bi-seo
director	사장	sa-jang
manager	매니저	mae-ni-jeo
accountant	회계사	hoe-gye-sa
employee	직원	ji-gwon
furniture	가구	ga-gu
desk	책상	chaek-sang
desk chair	책상 의자	chaek-sang ui-ja
coat stand	스탠드옷걸이	seu-taen-deu-ot-geo-ri
computer	컴퓨터	keom-pyu-teo
printer	프린터	peu-rin-teo
fax machine	팩스기	paek-seu-gi
photocopier	복사기	bok-sa-gi
paper	종이	jong-i
office supplies	사무용품	sa-mu-yong-pum
mouse mat	마우스 패드	ma-u-seu pae-deu
sheet of paper	한 장	han jang
binder	바인더	ba-in-deo
catalogue	카탈로그	ka-tal-lo-geu
phone directory	전화번호부	jeon-hwa-beon-ho-bu
documentation	문서	mun-seo
brochure (e.g. 12 pages ~)	브로셔	beu-ro-syeo
leaflet (promotional ~)	전단	jeon-dan
sample	샘플	saem-peul
training meeting	수련회를	su-ryeon-hoe-reul
meeting (of managers)	회의	hoe-ui
lunch time	점심시간	jeom-sim-si-gan
to make a copy	사본을 만들다	sa-bo-neul man-deul-da
to make multiple copies	복사하다	bok-sa-ha-da
to receive a fax	팩스를 받다	paek-seu-reul bat-da
to send a fax	팩스를 보내다	paek-seu-reul bo-nae-da
to call (by phone)	전화하다	jeon-hwa-ha-da
to answer (vt)	대답하다	dae-da-pa-da

to put through	연결해 주다	yeon-gyeol-hae ju-da
to arrange, to set up	마련하다	ma-ryeon-ha-da
to demonstrate (vt)	전시하다	jeon-si-ha-da
to be absent	결석하다	gyeol-seok-a-da
absence	결근	gyeol-geun

104. Business processes. Part 1

occupation	직업	ji-geop
firm	회사	hoe-sa
company	회사	hoe-sa
corporation	사단 법인	sa-dan beo-bin
enterprise	업체	eop-che
agency	에이전시	e-i-jeon-si

agreement (contract)	약정	yak-jeong
contract	계약	gye-yak
deal	거래	geo-rae
order (to place an ~)	주문	ju-mun
terms (of the contract)	조건	jo-geon

wholesale (adv)	도매로	do-mae-ro
wholesale (adj)	도매의	do-mae-ui
wholesale (n)	도매	do-mae
retail (adj)	소매의	so-mae-ui
retail (n)	소매	so-mae

competitor	경쟁자	gyeong-jaeng-ja
competition	경쟁	gyeong-jaeng
to compete (vi)	경쟁하다	gyeong-jaeng-ha-da

| partner (associate) | 파트너 | pa-teu-neo |
| partnership | 파트너십 | pa-teu-neo-sip |

crisis	위기	wi-gi
bankruptcy	파산	pa-san
to go bankrupt	파산하다	pa-san-ha-da
difficulty	어려움	eo-ryeo-um
problem	문제	mun-je
catastrophe	재난	jae-nan

economy	경기, 경제	gyeong-gi, gyeong-je
economic (~ growth)	경제의	gyeong-je-ui
economic recession	경기침체	gyeong-gi-chim-che

| goal (aim) | 목표 | mok-pyo |
| task | 임무 | im-mu |

to trade (vi)	거래하다	geo-rae-ha-da
network (distribution ~)	네트워크	ne-teu-wo-keu
inventory (stock)	재고	jae-go
range (assortment)	세트	se-teu
leader (leading company)	리더	ri-deo
large (~ company)	규모가 큰	gyu-mo-ga keun

monopoly	독점	dok-jeom
theory	이론	i-ron
practice	실천	sil-cheon
experience (in my ~)	경험	gyeong-heom
trend (tendency)	경향	gyeong-hyang
development	개발	gae-bal

105. Business processes. Part 2

profit (foregone ~)	수익, 이익	su-ik, i-ik
profitable (~ deal)	수익성이 있는	su-ik-seong-i in-neun
delegation (group)	대표단	dae-pyo-dan
salary	급여, 월급	geu-byeo, wol-geup
to correct (an error)	고치다	go-chi-da
business trip	출장	chul-jang
commission	수수료	su-su-ryo
to control (vt)	제어하다	je-eo-ha-da
conference	회의	hoe-ui
licence	면허증	myeon-heo-jeung
reliable (~ partner)	믿을 만한	mi-deul man-han
initiative (undertaking)	시작	si-jak
norm (standard)	표준	pyo-jun
circumstance	상황	sang-hwang
duty (of an employee)	의무	ui-mu
organization (company)	조직	jo-jik
organization (process)	준비	jun-bi
organized (adj)	조직된	jo-jik-doen
cancellation	취소	chwi-so
to cancel (call off)	취소하다	chwi-so-ha-da
report (official ~)	보고서	bo-go-seo
patent	특허	teuk-eo
to patent (obtain patent)	특허를 받다	teuk-eo-reul bat-da
to plan (vt)	계획하다	gye-hoek-a-da
bonus (money)	보너스	bo-neo-seu
professional (adj)	전문가의	jeon-mun-ga-ui
procedure	절차	jeol-cha
to examine (contract, etc.)	조사하다	jo-sa-ha-da
calculation	계산	gye-san
reputation	평판	pyeong-pan
risk	위험	wi-heom
to manage, to run	운영하다	u-nyeong-ha-da
information (report)	정보	jeong-bo
property	소유	so-yu
union	연합	yeon-hap
life insurance	생명 보험	saeng-myeong bo-heom
to insure (vt)	보험에 들다	bo-heom-e deul-da

insurance	보험	bo-heom
auction (~ sale)	경매	gyeong-mae
to notify (inform)	통지하다	tong-ji-ha-da
management (process)	주관	ju-gwan
service (~ industry)	서비스	seo-bi-seu
forum	포럼	po-reom
to function (vi)	기능하다	gi-neung-ha-da
stage (phase)	단계	dan-gye
legal (~ services)	법률상의	beom-nyul-sang-ui
lawyer (legal advisor)	법률고문	beom-nyul-go-mun

106. Production. Works

plant	공장	gong-jang
factory	공장	gong-jang
workshop	작업장	ja-geop-jang
works, production site	현장	hyeon-jang
industry (manufacturing)	산업, 공업	san-eop, gong-eop
industrial (adj)	산업의	san-eo-bui
heavy industry	중공업	jung-gong-eop
light industry	경공업	gyeong-gong-eop
products	제품	je-pum
to produce (vt)	제조하다	je-jo-ha-da
raw materials	원재료	won-jae-ryo
foreman (construction ~)	작업반장	ja-geop-ban-jang
workers team (crew)	작업반	ja-geop-ban
worker	노동자	no-dong-ja
working day	근무일	geun-mu-il
pause (rest break)	휴식	hyu-sik
meeting	회의	hoe-ui
to discuss (vt)	의논하다	ui-non-ha-da
plan	계획	gye-hoek
to fulfil the plan	계획을 수행하다	gye-hoe-geul su-haeng-ha-da
rate of output	생산량	saeng-sal-lyang
quality	품질	pum-jil
control (checking)	관리	gwal-li
quality control	품질 관리	pum-jil gwal-li
workplace safety	산업안전	sa-neo-ban-jeon
discipline	규율	gyu-yul
violation (of safety rules, etc.)	위반	wi-ban
to violate (rules)	위반하다	wi-ban-ha-da
strike	파업	pa-eop
striker	파업자	pa-eop-ja
to be on strike	파업하다	pa-eo-pa-da
trade union	노동조합	no-dong-jo-hap
to invent (machine, etc.)	발명하다	bal-myeong-ha-da

invention	발명	bal-myeong
research	연구	yeon-gu
to improve (make better)	개선하다	gae-seon-ha-da
technology	기술	gi-sul
technical drawing	건축 도면	geon-chuk do-myeon

load, cargo	화물	hwa-mul
loader (person)	하역부	ha-yeok-bu
to load (vehicle, etc.)	싣다	sit-da
loading (process)	적재	jeok-jae

| to unload (vi, vt) | 짐을 부리다 | ji-meul bu-ri-da |
| unloading | 짐부리기 | jim-bu-ri-gi |

transport	운송	un-song
transport company	운송 회사	un-song hoe-sa
to transport (vt)	운송하다	un-song-ha-da

wagon	화차	hwa-cha
tank (e.g., oil ~)	탱크	taeng-keu
lorry	트럭	teu-reok

| machine tool | 공작 기계 | gong-jak gi-gye |
| mechanism | 기계 장치 | gi-gye jang-chi |

industrial waste	산업폐기물	san-eop-pye-gi-mul
packing (process)	포장	po-jang
to pack (vt)	포장하다	po-jang-ha-da

107. Contract. Agreement

contract	계약	gye-yak
agreement	약정	yak-jeong
addendum	별첨	byeol-cheom

| to sign a contract | 계약에 서명하다 | gye-ya-ge seo-myeong-ha-da |
| signature | 서명 | seo-myeong |

| to sign (vt) | 서명하다 | seo-myeong-ha-da |
| seal (stamp) | 도장 | do-jang |

| subject of the contract | 계약 내용 | gye-yak nae-yong |
| clause | 항 | hang |

| parties (in contract) | 양측 | yang-cheuk |
| legal address | 법인 주소 | beo-bin ju-so |

| to violate the contract | 계약을 위반하다 | gye-ya-geul rwi-ban-ha-da |
| commitment (obligation) | 의무 | ui-mu |

responsibility	책임	chae-gim
force majeure	불가항력	bul-ga-hang-nyeok
dispute	분쟁	bun-jaeng
penalties	제재	je-jae

108. Import & Export

import	수입	su-ip
importer	수입업자	su-i-beop-ja
to import (vt)	수입하다	su-i-pa-da
import (as adj.)	수입의	su-i-bui
exporter	수출업자	su-chu-reop-ja
to export (vt)	수출하다	su-chul-ha-da
goods (merchandise)	상품	sang-pum
consignment, lot	탁송물	tak-song-mul
weight	무게	mu-ge
volume	부피	bu-pi
cubic metre	입방 미터	ip-bang mi-teo
manufacturer	생산자	saeng-san-ja
transport company	운송 회사	un-song hoe-sa
container	컨테이너	keon-te-i-neo
border	국경	guk-gyeong
customs	세관	se-gwan
customs duty	관세	gwan-se
customs officer	세관원	se-gwan-won
smuggling	밀수입	mil-su-ip
contraband (smuggled goods)	밀수품	mil-su-pum

109. Finances

share, stock	주식	ju-sik
bond (certificate)	채권	chae-gwon
promissory note	어음	eo-eum
stock exchange	증권거래소	jeung-gwon-geo-rae-so
stock price	주가	ju-ga
to go down (become cheaper)	내리다	nae-ri-da
to go up (become more expensive)	오르다	o-reu-da
controlling interest	지배 지분	ji-bae ji-bun
investment	투자	tu-ja
to invest (vt)	투자하다	tu-ja-ha-da
percent	퍼센트	peo-sen-teu
interest (on investment)	이자	i-ja
profit	수익, 이익	su-ik, i-ik
profitable (adj)	수익성이 있는	su-ik-seong-i in-neun
tax	세금	se-geum
currency (foreign ~)	통화	tong-hwa

national (adj)	국가의	guk-ga-ui
exchange (currency ~)	환전	hwan-jeon

accountant	회계사	hoe-gye-sa
accounting	회계	hoe-gye

bankruptcy	파산	pa-san
collapse, ruin	붕괴	bung-goe
ruin	파산	pa-san
to be ruined (financially)	파산하다	pa-san-ha-da
inflation	인플레이션	in-peul-le-i-syeon
devaluation	평가절하	pyeong-ga-jeol-ha

capital	자본	ja-bon
income	소득	so-deuk
turnover	총매출액	chong-mae-chu-raek
resources	재원을	jae-wo-neul
monetary resources	재정 자원을	jae-jeong ja-wo-neul
to reduce (expenses)	줄이다	ju-ri-da

110. Marketing

marketing	마케팅	ma-ke-ting
market	시장	si-jang
market segment	시장 분야	si-jang bu-nya
product	제품	je-pum
goods (merchandise)	상품	sang-pum

trademark	트레이드마크	teu-re-i-deu-ma-keu
logotype	로고	ro-go
logo	로고	ro-go

demand	수요	su-yo
supply	공급	gong-geup
need	필요	pi-ryo
consumer	소비자	so-bi-ja

analysis	분석	bun-seok
to analyse (vt)	분석하다	bun-seok-a-da
positioning	포지셔닝	po-ji-syeo-ning
to position (vt)	포지셔닝하다	po-ji-syeo-ning-ha-da

price	가격	ga-gyeok
pricing policy	가격 정책	ga-gyeok jeong-chaek
price formation	가격 형성	ga-gyeok yeong-seong

111. Advertising

advertising	광고	gwang-go
to advertise (vt)	광고하다	gwang-go-ha-da
budget	예산	ye-san
ad, advertisement	광고	gwang-go

TV advertising	텔레비전 광고	tel-le-bi-jeon gwang-go
radio advertising	라디오 광고	ra-di-o gwang-go
outdoor advertising	옥외 광고	o-goe gwang-go

mass medias	매체	mae-che
periodical (n)	정기 간행물	jeong-gi gan-haeng-mul
image (public appearance)	이미지	i-mi-ji

| slogan | 슬로건 | seul-lo-geon |
| motto (maxim) | 표어 | pyo-eo |

campaign	캠페인	kaem-pe-in
advertising campaign	광고 캠페인	gwang-go kaem-pe-in
target group	공략 대상	gong-nyak dae-sang

business card	명함	myeong-ham
leaflet (promotional ~)	전단	jeon-dan
brochure (e.g. 12 pages ~)	브로셔	beu-ro-syeo
pamphlet	팜플렛	pam-peul-let
newsletter	회보	hoe-bo

signboard (store sign, etc.)	간판	gan-pan
poster	포스터	po-seu-teo
hoarding	광고판	gwang-go-pan

112. Banking

| bank | 은행 | eun-haeng |
| branch (of a bank) | 지점 | ji-jeom |

| consultant | 행원 | haeng-won |
| manager (director) | 지배인 | ji-bae-in |

bank account	은행계좌	eun-haeng-gye-jwa
account number	계좌 번호	gye-jwa beon-ho
current account	당좌	dang-jwa
deposit account	보통 예금	bo-tong ye-geum

to open an account	계좌를 열다	gye-jwa-reul ryeol-da
to close the account	계좌를 해지하다	gye-jwa-reul hae-ji-ha-da
to deposit into the account	계좌에 입금하다	ip-geum-ha-da
to withdraw (vt)	출금하다	chul-geum-ha-da

deposit	저금	jeo-geum
to make a deposit	입금하다	ip-geum-ha-da
wire transfer	송금	song-geum
to wire, to transfer	송금하다	song-geum-ha-da

| sum | 액수 | aek-su |
| How much? | 얼마? | eol-ma? |

signature	서명	seo-myeong
to sign (vt)	서명하다	seo-myeong-ha-da
credit card	신용 카드	si-nyong ka-deu

code (PIN code)	비밀번호	bi-mil-beon-ho
credit card number	신용 카드 번호	si-nyong ka-deu beon-ho
cashpoint	현금 자동 지급기	hyeon-geum ja-dong ji-geup-gi
cheque	수표	su-pyo
to write a cheque	수표를 끊다	su-pyo-reul kkeun-ta
chequebook	수표책	su-pyo-chaek
loan (bank ~)	대출	dae-chul
to apply for a loan	대출 신청하다	dae-chul sin-cheong-ha-da
to get a loan	대출을 받다	dae-chu-reul bat-da
to give a loan	대출하다	dae-chul-ha-da
guarantee	담보	dam-bo

113. Telephone. Phone conversation

telephone	전화	jeon-hwa
mobile phone	휴대폰	hyu-dae-pon
answerphone	자동 응답기	ja-dong eung-dap-gi
to call (by phone)	전화하다	jeon-hwa-ha-da
call, ring	통화	tong-hwa
to dial a number	번호로 걸다	beon-ho-ro geol-da
Hello!	여보세요!	yeo-bo-se-yo!
to ask (vt)	묻다	mut-da
to answer (vi, vt)	전화를 받다	jeon-hwa-reul bat-da
to hear (vt)	듣다	deut-da
well (adv)	잘	jal
not well (adv)	좋지 않은	jo-chi a-neun
noises (interference)	잡음	ja-beum
receiver	수화기	su-hwa-gi
to pick up (~ the phone)	전화를 받다	jeon-hwa-reul bat-da
to hang up (~ the phone)	전화를 끊다	jeon-hwa-reul kkeun-ta
busy (engaged)	통화 중인	tong-hwa jung-in
to ring (ab. phone)	울리다	ul-li-da
telephone book	전화 번호부	jeon-hwa beon-ho-bu
local (adj)	시내의	si-nae-ui
trunk (e.g. ~ call)	장거리의	jang-geo-ri-ui
international (adj)	국제적인	guk-je-jeo-gin

114. Mobile telephone

mobile phone	휴대폰	hyu-dae-pon
display	화면	hwa-myeon
button	버튼	beo-teun
SIM card	SIM 카드	SIM ka-deu

battery	건전지	geon-jeon-ji
to be flat (battery)	나가다	na-ga-da
charger	충전기	chung-jeon-gi
menu	메뉴	me-nyu
settings	설정	seol-jeong
tune (melody)	벨소리	bel-so-ri
to select (vt)	선택하다	seon-taek-a-da
calculator	계산기	gye-san-gi
voice mail	자동 응답기	ja-dong eung-dap-gi
alarm clock	알람 시계	al-lam si-gye
contacts	연락처	yeol-lak-cheo
SMS (text message)	문자 메시지	mun-ja me-si-ji
subscriber	가입자	ga-ip-ja

115. Stationery

ballpoint pen	볼펜	bol-pen
fountain pen	만년필	man-nyeon-pil
pencil	연필	yeon-pil
highlighter	형광펜	hyeong-gwang-pen
felt-tip pen	사인펜	sa-in-pen
notepad	공책	gong-chaek
diary	수첩	su-cheop
ruler	자	ja
calculator	계산기	gye-san-gi
rubber	지우개	ji-u-gae
drawing pin	압정	ap-jeong
paper clip	클립	keul-lip
glue	접착제	jeop-chak-je
stapler	호치키스	ho-chi-ki-seu
hole punch	펀치	peon-chi
pencil sharpener	연필깎이	yeon-pil-kka-kki

116. Various kinds of documents

account (report)	보고	bo-go
agreement	약정	yak-jeong
application form	신청서	sin-cheong-seo
authentic (adj)	진본의	jin-bo-nui
badge (identity tag)	명찰	myeong-chal
business card	명함	myeong-ham
certificate (~ of quality)	인증서	in-jeung-seo
cheque (e.g. draw a ~)	수표	su-pyo
bill (in restaurant)	계산서	gye-san-seo

constitution	헌법	heon-beop
contract (agreement)	계약	gye-yak
copy	사본	sa-bon
copy (of a contract, etc.)	사본	sa-bon
customs declaration	세관신고서	se-gwan-sin-go-seo
document	서류	seo-ryu
driving licence	운전 면허증	un-jeon myeon-heo-jeung
addendum	별첨	byeol-cheom
form	서식	seo-sik
ID card (e.g., warrant card)	신분증	sin-bun-jeung
inquiry (request)	문의서	mun-ui-seo
invitation card	초대장	cho-dae-jang
invoice	송장	song-jang
law	법	beop
letter (mail)	편지	pyeon-ji
letterhead	용지	yong-ji
list (of names, etc.)	목록	mong-nok
manuscript	원고	won-go
newsletter	회보	hoe-bo
note (short letter)	쪽지	jjok-ji
pass (for worker, visitor)	출입증	chu-rip-jeung
passport	여권	yeo-gwon
permit	허가증	heo-ga-jeung
curriculum vitae, CV	이력서	i-ryeok-seo
debt note, IOU	차용증서	cha-yong-jeung-seo
receipt (for purchase)	영수증	yeong-su-jeung
till receipt	영수증	yeong-su-jeung
report (mil.)	보고	bo-go
to show (ID, etc.)	보여주다	bo-yeo-ju-da
to sign (vt)	서명하다	seo-myeong-ha-da
signature	서명	seo-myeong
seal (stamp)	도장	do-jang
text	문서	mun-seo
ticket (for entry)	표	pyo
to cross out	그어 지우다	geu-eo ji-u-da
to fill in (~ a form)	작성하다	jak-seong-ha-da
waybill (shipping invoice)	선적 송장	seon-jeok song-jang
will (testament)	유언	yu-eon

117. Kinds of business

accounting services	회계 서비스	hoe-gye seo-bi-seu
advertising	광고	gwang-go
advertising agency	광고 회사	gwang-go hoe-sa
air-conditioners	에어컨	e-eo-keon
airline	항공사	hang-gong-sa
alcoholic beverages	주류	ju-ryu

antiques (antique dealers)	골동품	gol-dong-pum
art gallery (contemporary ~)	미술관	mi-sul-gwan
audit services	회계 감사	hoe-gye gam-sa
banking industry	금융업계	geu-myung-eop-gye
beauty salon	미장원	mi-jang-won
bookshop	서점	seo-jeom
brewery	맥주 양조장	maek-ju yang-jo-jang
business centre	비즈니스 센터	bi-jeu-ni-seu sen-teo
business school	비즈니스 스쿨	bi-jeu-ni-seu seu-kul
casino	카지노	ka-ji-no
chemist, pharmacy	약국	yak-guk
cinema	영화관	yeong-hwa-gwan
construction	건설	geon-seol
consulting	컨설팅	keon-seol-ting
dental clinic	치과 병원	chi-gwa byeong-won
design	디자인	di-ja-in
dry cleaners	드라이 클리닝	deu-ra-i keul-li-ning
employment agency	직업 소개소	ji-geop so-gae-so
financial services	재무 서비스	jae-mu seo-bi-seu
food products	식품	sik-pum
furniture (e.g. house ~)	가구	ga-gu
clothing, garment	옷	ot
hotel	호텔	ho-tel
ice-cream	아이스크림	a-i-seu-keu-rim
industry (manufacturing)	산업, 공업	san-eop, gong-eop
insurance	보험	bo-heom
Internet	인터넷	in-teo-net
investments (finance)	투자	tu-ja
jeweller	보석 상인	bo-seok sang-in
jewellery	보석	bo-seok
laundry (shop)	세탁소	se-tak-so
legal adviser	법률컨설팅	beom-nyul-keon-seol-ting
light industry	경공업	gyeong-gong-eop
magazine	잡지	jap-ji
medicine	의학	ui-hak
museum	박물관	bang-mul-gwan
news agency	통신사	tong-sin-sa
newspaper	신문	sin-mun
nightclub	나이트 클럽	na-i-teu keul-leop
oil (petroleum)	석유	seo-gyu
courier services	문서 송달 회사	mun-seo song-dal hoe-sa
pharmaceutics	의약	ui-yak
printing (industry)	인쇄산업	in-swae-san-eop
pub	바	ba
publishing house	출판사	chul-pan-sa
radio (~ station)	라디오	ra-di-o
real estate	부동산	bu-dong-san

restaurant	레스토랑	re-seu-to-rang
security company	보안 회사	bo-an hoe-sa
shop	가게, 상점	ga-ge, sang-jeom
sport	스포츠	seu-po-cheu
stock exchange	증권거래소	jeung-gwon-geo-rae-so
supermarket	슈퍼마켓	syu-peo-ma-ket
swimming pool (public ~)	수영장	su-yeong-jang
tailor shop	양복점	yang-bok-jeom
television	텔레비전	tel-le-bi-jeon
theatre	극장	geuk-jang
trade (commerce)	거래	geo-rae
transport companies	운송	un-song
travel	관광산업	gwan-gwang-sa-neop
undertakers	장례식장	jang-nye-sik-jang
veterinary surgeon	수의사	su-ui-sa
warehouse	창고	chang-go
waste collection	쓰레기 수거	sseu-re-gi su-geo

Job. Business. Part 2

118. Show. Exhibition

exhibition, show	전시회	jeon-si-hoe
trade show	상품 전시회	sang-pum jeon-si-hoe
participation	참가	cham-ga
to participate (vi)	참가하다	cham-ga-ha-da
participant (exhibitor)	참가자	cham-ga-ja
director	대표이사	dae-pyo-i-sa
organizers' office	조직위원회	jo-ji-gwi-won-hoe
organizer	조직위원회	jo-ji-gwi-won-hoe
to organize (vt)	조직하다	jo-jik-a-da
participation form	참가 신청서	cham-ga sin-cheong-seo
to fill in (vt)	작성하다	jak-seong-ha-da
details	상세	sang-se
information	정보	jeong-bo
price (cost, rate)	가격	ga-gyeok
including	포함하여	po-ham-ha-yeo
to include (vt)	포함하다	po-ham-ha-da
to pay (vi, vt)	지불하다	ji-bul-ha-da
registration fee	등록비	deung-nok-bi
entrance	입구	ip-gu
pavilion, hall	전시실	jeon-si-sil
to register (vt)	등록하다	deung-nok-a-da
badge (identity tag)	명찰	myeong-chal
stand	부스	bu-seu
to reserve, to book	예약하다	ye-yak-a-da
display case	진열장	ji-nyeol-jang
spotlight	스포트라이트	seu-po-teu-ra-i-teu
design	디자인	di-ja-in
to place (put, set)	배치하다	bae-chi-ha-da
distributor	배급업자	bae-geu-beop-ja
supplier	공급자	gong-geup-ja
country	나라	na-ra
foreign (adj)	외국의	oe-gu-gui
product	제품	je-pum
association	협회	hyeo-poe
conference hall	회의장	hoe-ui-jang
congress	회의	hoe-ui

contest (competition)	컨테스트	keon-te-seu-teu
visitor (attendee)	방문객	bang-mun-gaek
to visit (attend)	방문하다	bang-mun-ha-da
customer	고객	go-gaek

119. Mass Media

newspaper	신문	sin-mun
magazine	잡지	jap-ji
press (printed media)	언론	eon-non
radio	라디오	ra-di-o
radio station	라디오 방송국	ra-di-o bang-song-guk
television	텔레비전	tel-le-bi-jeon
presenter, host	진행자	jin-haeng-ja
newsreader	아나운서	a-na-un-seo
commentator	해설가	hae-seol-ga
journalist	저널리스트	jeo-neol-li-seu-teu
correspondent (reporter)	특파원	teuk-pa-won
press photographer	사진 기자	sa-jin gi-ja
reporter	리포터	ri-po-teo
editor	편집자	pyeon-jip-ja
editor-in-chief	편집장	pyeon-jip-jang
to subscribe (to ...)	... 를 구독하다	... reul gu-dok-a-da
subscription	구독	gu-dok
subscriber	구독자	gu-dok-ja
to read (vi, vt)	읽다	ik-da
reader	독자	dok-ja
circulation (of a newspaper)	발행 부수	bal-haeng bu-su
monthly (adj)	월간의	wol-ga-nui
weekly (adj)	주간의	ju-ga-nui
issue (edition)	호	ho
new (~ issue)	최신의	choe-si-nui
headline	헤드라인	he-deu-ra-in
short article	짧은 기사	jjal-beun gi-sa
column (regular article)	칼럼	kal-leom
article	기사	gi-sa
page	페이지	pe-i-ji
reportage, report	보도	bo-do
event (happening)	사건	sa-geon
sensation (news)	센세이션	sen-se-i-syeon
scandal	스캔들	seu-kaen-deul
scandalous (adj)	스캔들의	seu-kaen-deu-rui
great (~ scandal)	엄청난	eom-cheong-nan
programme (e.g. cooking ~)	쇼	syo
interview	인터뷰	in-teo-byu
live broadcast	라이브 방송	ra-i-beu bang-song
channel	채널	chae-neol

120. Agriculture

agriculture	농업	nong-eop
peasant (masc.)	소작농	so-jang-nong
peasant (fem.)	소작농	so-jang-nong
farmer	농부	nong-bu
tractor	트랙터	teu-raek-teo
combine, harvester	콤바인	kom-ba-in
plough	쟁기	jaeng-gi
to plough (vi, vt)	땅을 갈다	ttang-eul gal-da
ploughland	한 쟁기의 땅	han jaeng-gi-ui ttang
furrow (in field)	고랑	go-rang
to sow (vi, vt)	뿌리다	ppu-ri-da
seeder	파종기	pa-jong-gi
sowing (process)	씨뿌리기	pa-jong
scythe	긴 낫	gin nat
to mow, to scythe	낫질하다	nat-jil-ha-da
spade (tool)	삽	sap
to till (vt)	갈다	gal-da
hoe	호미	ho-mi
to hoe, to weed	풀을 뽑다	pu-reul ppop-da
weed (plant)	잡초	jap-cho
watering can	물뿌리개	mul-ppu-ri-gae
to water (plants)	물을 주다	mu-reul ju-da
watering (act)	살수	sal-su
pitchfork	쇠스랑	soe-seu-rang
rake	갈퀴	gal-kwi
fertiliser	비료	bi-ryo
to fertilise (vt)	비료를 주다	bi-ryo-reul ju-da
manure (fertiliser)	거름	geo-reum
field	밭	bat
meadow	풀밭	pul-bat
vegetable garden	채소밭	chae-so-bat
orchard (e.g. apple ~)	과수원	gwa-su-won
to graze (vt)	방목하다	bang-mo-ka-da
herdsman	목동	mok-dong
pasture	목초지	mok-cho-ji
cattle breeding	목축	mok-chuk
sheep farming	목양	mo-gyang
plantation	농원	nong-won
row (garden bed ~s)	이랑	i-rang
hothouse	온실	on-sil

| drought (lack of rain) | 가뭄 | ga-mum |
| dry (~ summer) | 건조한 | geon-jo-han |

| cereal crops | 곡류 | gong-nyu |
| to harvest, to gather | 수확하다 | su-hwak-a-da |

miller (person)	제분업자	je-bun-eop-ja
mill (e.g. gristmill)	제분소	je-bun-so
to grind (grain)	제분하다	je-bun-ha-da
flour	밀가루	mil-ga-ru
straw	짚	jip

121. Building. Building process

building site	공사장	gong-sa-jang
to build (vt)	건설하다	geon-seol-ha-da
building worker	공사장 인부	gong-sa-jang in-bu

project	프로젝트	peu-ro-jek-teu
architect	건축가	geon-chuk-ga
worker	노동자	no-dong-ja

foundations (of a building)	기초	gi-cho
roof	지붕	ji-bung
foundation pile	기초 말뚝	gi-cho mal-ttuk
wall	벽	byeok

| reinforcing bars | 철근 | cheol-geun |
| scaffolding | 비계 | bi-gye |

| concrete | 콘크리트 | kon-keu-ri-teu |
| granite | 화강암 | hwa-gang-am |

| stone | 돌 | dol |
| brick | 벽돌 | byeok-dol |

sand	모래	mo-rae
cement	시멘트	si-men-teu
plaster (for walls)	회반죽	hoe-ban-juk
to plaster (vt)	회반죽을 칠하다	hoe-ban-ju-geul chil-ha-da
paint	페인트	pe-in-teu

| to paint (~ a wall) | 페인트를 칠하다 | pe-in-teu-reul chil-ha-da |
| barrel | 통 | tong |

crane	크레인	keu-re-in
to lift, to hoist (vt)	올리다	ol-li-da
to lower (vt)	내리다	nae-ri-da

bulldozer	불도저	bul-do-jeo
excavator	굴착기	gul-chak-gi
scoop, bucket	굴삭기 버킷	beo-kit
to dig (excavate)	파다	pa-da
hard hat	안전모	an-jeon-mo

122. Science. Research. Scientists

science	과학	gwa-hak
scientific (adj)	과학의	gwa-ha-gui
scientist	과학자	gwa-hak-ja
theory	이론	i-ron
axiom	공리	gong-ni
analysis	분석	bun-seok
to analyse (vt)	분석하다	bun-seok-a-da
argument (strong ~)	주장	ju-jang
substance (matter)	물질	mul-jil
hypothesis	가설	ga-seol
dilemma	딜레마	dil-le-ma
dissertation	학위 논문	ha-gwi non-mun
dogma	도그마	do-geu-ma
doctrine	학설	hak-seol
research	연구	yeon-gu
to research (vt)	연구하다	yeon-gu-ha-da
tests (laboratory ~)	실험	sil-heom
laboratory	연구실	yeon-gu-sil
method	방법	bang-beop
molecule	분자	bun-ja
monitoring	감시	gam-si
discovery (act, event)	발견	bal-gyeon
postulate	공준	gong-jun
principle	원칙	won-chik
forecast	예상	ye-sang
to forecast (vt)	예상하다	ye-sang-ha-da
synthesis	종합	jong-hap
trend (tendency)	경향	gyeong-hyang
theorem	정리	jeong-ni
teachings	가르침	ga-reu-chim
fact	사실	sa-sil
expedition	탐험	tam-heom
experiment	실험	sil-heom
academician	아카데미 회원	a-ka-de-mi hoe-won
bachelor (e.g. ~ of Arts)	학사	hak-sa
doctor (PhD)	박사	bak-sa
Associate Professor	부교수	bu-gyo-su
Master (e.g. ~ of Arts)	석사	seok-sa
professor	교수	gyo-su

Professions and occupations

Job search. Dismissal

job	직업	ji-geop
personnel	직원	ji-gwon
career	경력	gyeong-nyeok
prospects (chances)	전망	jeon-mang
skills (mastery)	숙달	suk-dal
selection (screening)	선발	seon-bal
employment agency	직업 소개소	ji-geop so-gae-so
curriculum vitae, CV	이력서	i-ryeok-seo
job interview	면접	myeon-jeop
vacancy	결원	gyeo-rwon
salary, pay	급여, 월급	geu-byeo, wol-geup
fixed salary	고정급	go-jeong-geup
pay, compensation	급료	geum-nyo
position (job)	직위	ji-gwi
duty (of an employee)	의무	ui-mu
range of duties	업무범위	eom-mu-beom-wi
busy (I'm ~)	바쁜	ba-ppeun
to fire (dismiss)	해고하다	hae-go-ha-da
dismissal	해고	hae-go
unemployment	실업	si-reop
unemployed (n)	실업자	si-reop-ja
retirement	은퇴	eun-toe
to retire (from job)	은퇴하다	eun-toe-ha-da

124. Business people

director	사장	sa-jang
manager (director)	지배인	ji-bae-in
boss	상사	sang-sa
superior	상사	sang-sa
superiors	상사	sang-sa
president	회장	hoe-jang
chairman	의장	ui-jang
deputy (substitute)	부 ⋯	bu ...
assistant	조수	jo-su
secretary	비서	bi-seo

personal assistant	개인 비서	gae-in bi-seo
businessman	사업가	sa-eop-ga
entrepreneur	사업가	sa-eop-ga
founder	설립자	seol-lip-ja
to found (vt)	설립하다	seol-li-pa-da
founding member	설립자	seol-lip-ja
partner	파트너	pa-teu-neo
shareholder	주주	ju-ju
millionaire	백만장자	baeng-man-jang-ja
billionaire	억만장자	eong-man-jang-ja
owner, proprietor	소유자	so-yu-ja
landowner	토지 소유자	to-ji so-yu-ja
client	고객	go-gaek
regular client	단골	dan-gol
buyer (customer)	구매자	gu-mae-ja
visitor	방문객	bang-mun-gaek
professional (n)	전문가	jeon-mun-ga
expert	전문가	jeon-mun-ga
specialist	전문가	jeon-mun-ga
banker	은행가	eun-haeng-ga
broker	브로커	beu-ro-keo
cashier	계산원	gye-san-won
accountant	회계사	hoe-gye-sa
security guard	보안요원	bo-a-nyo-won
investor	투자가	tu-ja-ga
debtor	채무자	chae-mu-ja
creditor	빚쟁이	bit-jaeng-i
borrower	차용인	cha-yong-in
importer	수입업자	su-i-beop-ja
exporter	수출업자	su-chu-reop-ja
manufacturer	생산자	saeng-san-ja
distributor	배급업자	bae-geu-beop-ja
middleman	중간상인	jung-gan-sang-in
consultant	컨설턴트	keon-seol-teon-teu
sales representative	판매 대리인	pan-mae dae-ri-in
agent	중개인	jung-gae-in
insurance agent	보험설계사	bo-heom-seol-gye-sa

125. Service professions

cook	요리사	yo-ri-sa
chef (kitchen chef)	주방장	ju-bang-jang
baker	제빵사	je-ppang-sa
barman	바텐더	ba-ten-deo

| waiter | 웨이터 | we-i-teo |
| waitress | 웨이트리스 | we-i-teu-ri-seu |

lawyer, barrister	변호사	byeon-ho-sa
lawyer (legal expert)	법률고문	beom-nyul-go-mun
notary public	공증인	gong-jeung-in

electrician	전기 기사	jeon-gi gi-sa
plumber	배관공	bae-gwan-gong
carpenter	목수	mok-su

masseur	안마사	an-ma-sa
masseuse	안마사	an-ma-sa
doctor	의사	ui-sa

taxi driver	택시 운전 기사	taek-si un-jeon gi-sa
driver	운전 기사	un-jeon gi-sa
delivery man	배달원	bae-da-rwon

chambermaid	객실 청소부	gaek-sil cheong-so-bu
security guard	보안요원	bo-a-nyo-won
flight attendant (fem.)	승무원	seung-mu-won

schoolteacher	선생님	seon-saeng-nim
librarian	사서	sa-seo
translator	번역가	beo-nyeok-ga
interpreter	통역가	tong-yeok-ga
guide	가이드	ga-i-deu

hairdresser	미용사	mi-yong-sa
postman	우체부	u-che-bu
salesman (store staff)	점원	jeom-won

gardener	정원사	jeong-won-sa
domestic servant	하인	ha-in
maid (female servant)	하녀	ha-nyeo
cleaner (cleaning lady)	청소부	cheong-so-bu

126. Military professions and ranks

private	일병	il-byeong
sergeant	병장	byeong-jang
lieutenant	중위	jung-wi
captain	대위	dae-wi

major	소령	so-ryeong
colonel	대령	dae-ryeong
general	장군	jang-gun
marshal	원수	won-su
admiral	제독	je-dok

military (n)	군인	gun-in
soldier	군인	gun-in
officer	장교	jang-gyo

commander	사령관	sa-ryeong-gwan
border guard	국경 수비대원	guk-gyeong su-bi-dae-won
radio operator	무선 기사	mu-seon gi-sa
scout (searcher)	정찰병	jeong-chal-byeong
pioneer (sapper)	공병대원	gong-byeong-dae-won
marksman	사수	sa-su
navigator	항법사	hang-beop-sa

127. Officials. Priests

| king | 왕 | wang |
| queen | 여왕 | yeo-wang |

| prince | 왕자 | wang-ja |
| princess | 공주 | gong-ju |

| czar | 차르 | cha-reu |
| czarina | 여황제 | yeo-hwang-je |

president	대통령	dae-tong-nyeong
Secretary (minister)	장관	jang-gwan
prime minister	총리	chong-ni
senator	상원의원	sang-won-ui-won

diplomat	외교관	oe-gyo-gwan
consul	영사	yeong-sa
ambassador	대사	dae-sa
counselor (diplomatic officer)	고문관	go-mun-gwan

official, functionary (civil servant)	공무원	gong-mu-won
prefect	도지사, 현감	do-ji-sa, hyeon-gam
mayor	시장	si-jang

| judge | 판사 | pan-sa |
| prosecutor | 검사 | geom-sa |

missionary	선교사	seon-gyo-sa
monk	수도사	su-do-sa
abbot	수도원장	su-do-won-jang
rabbi	랍비	rap-bi

vizier	고관	go-gwan
shah	샤	sya
sheikh	셰이크	sye-i-keu

128. Agricultural professions

beekeeper	양봉가	yang-bong-ga
shepherd	목동	mok-dong
agronomist	농학자	nong-hak-ja
cattle breeder	목축업자	mok-chu-geop-ja

veterinary surgeon	수의사	su-ui-sa
farmer	농부	nong-bu
winemaker	포도주 제조자	po-do-ju je-jo-ja
zoologist	동물학자	dong-mul-hak-ja
cowboy	카우보이	ka-u-bo-i

129. Art professions

| actor | 배우 | bae-u |
| actress | 여배우 | yeo-bae-u |

| singer (masc.) | 가수 | ga-su |
| singer (fem.) | 여가수 | yeo-ga-su |

| dancer (masc.) | 무용가 | mu-yong-ga |
| dancer (fem.) | 여성 무용가 | yeo-seong mu-yong-ga |

| performer (masc.) | 공연자 | gong-yeon-ja |
| performer (fem.) | 여성 공연자 | yeo-seong gong-yeon-ja |

musician	음악가	eum-ak-ga
pianist	피아니스트	pi-a-ni-seu-teu
guitar player	기타 연주자	gi-ta yeon-ju-ja

conductor (orchestra ~)	지휘자	ji-hwi-ja
composer	작곡가	jak-gok-ga
impresario	기획자	gi-hoek-ja

film director	영화감독	yeong-hwa-gam-dok
producer	제작자	je-jak-ja
scriptwriter	시나리오 작가	si-na-ri-o jak-ga
critic	미술 비평가	mi-sul bi-pyeong-ga

writer	작가	jak-ga
poet	시인	si-in
sculptor	조각가	jo-gak-ga
artist (painter)	화가	hwa-ga

juggler	저글러	jeo-geul-leo
clown	어릿광대	eo-rit-gwang-dae
acrobat	곡예사	go-gye-sa
magician	마술사	ma-sul-sa

130. Various professions

doctor	의사	ui-sa
nurse	간호사	gan-ho-sa
psychiatrist	정신과 의사	jeong-sin-gwa ui-sa
dentist	치과 의사	chi-gwa ui-sa
surgeon	외과 의사	oe-gwa ui-sa
astronaut	우주비행사	u-ju-bi-haeng-sa
astronomer	천문학자	cheon-mun-hak-ja

driver (of a taxi, etc.)	운전 기사	un-jeon gi-sa
train driver	기관사	gi-gwan-sa
mechanic	정비공	jeong-bi-gong
miner	광부	gwang-bu
worker	노동자	no-dong-ja
locksmith	자물쇠공	ja-mul-soe-gong
joiner (carpenter)	목수	mok-su
turner (lathe operator)	선반공	seon-ban-gong
building worker	공사장 인부	gong-sa-jang in-bu
welder	용접공	yong-jeop-gong
professor (title)	교수	gyo-su
architect	건축가	geon-chuk-ga
historian	역사학자	yeok-sa-hak-ja
scientist	과학자	gwa-hak-ja
physicist	물리학자	mul-li-hak-ja
chemist (scientist)	화학자	hwa-hak-ja
archaeologist	고고학자	go-go-hak-ja
geologist	지질학자	ji-jil-hak-ja
researcher (scientist)	연구원	yeon-gu-won
babysitter	애기보는 사람	ae-gi-bo-neun sa-ram
teacher, educator	교사	gyo-sa
editor	편집자	pyeon-jip-ja
editor-in-chief	편집장	pyeon-jip-jang
correspondent	통신원	tong-sin-won
typist (fem.)	타이피스트	ta-i-pi-seu-teu
designer	디자이너	di-ja-i-neo
computer expert	컴퓨터 전문가	keom-pyu-teo jeon-mun-ga
programmer	프로그래머	peu-ro-geu-rae-meo
engineer (designer)	엔지니어	en-ji-ni-eo
sailor	선원	seon-won
seaman	수부	su-bu
rescuer	구조자	gu-jo-ja
firefighter	소방관	so-bang-gwan
police officer	경찰관	gyeong-chal-gwan
watchman	경비원	gyeong-bi-won
detective	형사	hyeong-sa
customs officer	세관원	se-gwan-won
bodyguard	경호원	gyeong-ho-won
prison officer	간수	gan-su
inspector	감독관	gam-dok-gwan
sportsman	스포츠맨	seu-po-cheu-maen
trainer, coach	코치	ko-chi
butcher	정육점 주인	jeong-yuk-jeom ju-in
cobbler (shoe repairer)	구둣방	gu-dut-bang
merchant	상인	sang-in
loader (person)	하역부	ha-yeok-bu

| fashion designer | 패션 디자이너 | pae-syeon di-ja-i-neo |
| model (fem.) | 모델 | mo-del |

131. Occupations. Social status

| schoolboy | 남학생 | nam-hak-saeng |
| student (college ~) | 대학생 | dae-hak-saeng |

philosopher	철학자	cheol-hak-ja
economist	경제 학자	gyeong-je hak-ja
inventor	발명가	bal-myeong-ga

unemployed (n)	실업자	si-reop-ja
retiree, pensioner	은퇴자	eun-toe-ja
spy, secret agent	비밀요원	bi-mi-ryo-won

prisoner	죄수	joe-su
striker	파업자	pa-eop-ja
bureaucrat	관료	gwal-lyo
traveller (globetrotter)	여행자	yeo-haeng-ja

| gay, homosexual (n) | 동성애자 | dong-seong-ae-ja |
| hacker | 해커 | hae-keo |

bandit	산적	san-jeok
hit man, killer	살인 청부업자	sa-rin cheong-bu-eop-ja
drug addict	마약 중독자	ma-yak jung-dok-ja
drug dealer	마약 밀매자	ma-yak mil-mae-ja
prostitute (fem.)	매춘부	mae-chun-bu
pimp	포주	po-ju

sorcerer	마법사	ma-beop-sa
sorceress (evil ~)	여자 마법사	yeo-ja ma-beop-sa
pirate	해적	hae-jeok
slave	노예	no-ye
samurai	사무라이	sa-mu-ra-i
savage (primitive)	야만인	ya-man-in

Sports

sportsman	스포츠맨	seu-po-cheu-maen
kind of sport	스포츠 종류	seu-po-cheu jong-nyu
basketball	농구	nong-gu
basketball player	농구 선수	nong-gu seon-su
baseball	야구	ya-gu
baseball player	야구 선수	ya-gu seon-su
football	축구	chuk-gu
football player	축구 선수	chuk-gu seon-su
goalkeeper	골키퍼	gol-ki-peo
ice hockey	하키	ha-ki
ice hockey player	하키 선수	ha-ki seon-su
volleyball	배구	bae-gu
volleyball player	배구 선수	bae-gu seon-su
boxing	권투	gwon-tu
boxer	권투 선수	gwon-tu seon-su
wrestling	레슬링	re-seul-ling
wrestler	레슬링 선수	re-seul-ling seon-su
karate	가라테	ga-ra-te
karate fighter	가라테 선수	ga-ra-te seon-su
judo	유도	yu-do
judo athlete	유도 선수	yu-do seon-su
tennis	테니스	te-ni-seu
tennis player	테니스 선수	te-ni-seu seon-su
swimming	수영	su-yeong
swimmer	수영 선수	su-yeong seon-su
fencing	펜싱	pen-sing
fencer	펜싱 선수	pen-sing seon-su
chess	체스	che-seu
chess player	체스 선수	che-seu seon-su
alpinism	등산	deung-san
alpinist	등산가	deung-san-ga
running	달리기	dal-li-gi

runner	달리기 선수	dal-li-gi seon-su
athletics	육상 경기	yuk-sang gyeong-gi
athlete	선수	seon-su

| horse riding | 승마 | seung-ma |
| horse rider | 승마 선수 | seung-ma seon-su |

figure skating	피겨 스케이팅	pi-gyeo seu-ke-i-ting
figure skater (masc.)	피겨 스케이팅 선수	pi-gyeo seu-ke-i-ting seon-su
figure skater (fem.)	피겨 스케이팅 선수	pi-gyeo seu-ke-i-ting seon-su

| powerlifting | 역도 | yeok-do |
| powerlifter | 역도 선수 | yeok-do seon-su |

| car racing | 자동차 경주 | ja-dong-cha gyeong-ju |
| racer (driver) | 카레이서 | ka-re-i-seo |

| cycling | 자전거경기 | ja-jeon-geo-gyeong-gi |
| cyclist | 자전거 선수 | ja-jeon-geo seon-su |

long jump	멀리뛰기	meol-li-ttwi-gi
pole vaulting	장대 높이뛰기	jang-dae no-pi-ttwi-gi
jumper	뛰기선수	ttwi-gi-seon-su

133. Kinds of sports. Miscellaneous

American football	미식 축구	mi-sik chuk-gu
badminton	배드민턴	bae-deu-min-teon
biathlon	바이애슬론	ba-i-ae-seul-lon
billiards	당구	dang-gu

bobsleigh	봅슬레이	bop-seul-le-i
bodybuilding	보디빌딩	bo-di-bil-ding
water polo	수구	su-gu
handball	핸드볼	haen-deu-bol
golf	골프	gol-peu

rowing	조정	jo-jeong
scuba diving	스쿠버다이빙	seu-ku-beo-da-i-bing
cross-country skiing	크로스컨트리 스키	keu-ro-seu-keon-teu-ri seu-ki
table tennis (ping-pong)	탁구	tak-gu

sailing	요트타기	yo-teu-ta-gi
rally	랠리	rael-li
rugby	럭비	reok-bi
snowboarding	스노보드	seu-no-bo-deu
archery	양궁	yang-gung

134. Gym

| barbell | 역기 | yeok-gi |
| dumbbells | 아령 | a-ryeong |

training machine	운동 기구	un-dong gi-gu
exercise bicycle	헬스자전거	hel-seu-ja-jeon-geo
treadmill	러닝 머신	reo-ning meo-sin

horizontal bar	철봉	cheol-bong
parallel bars	평행봉	pyeong-haeng-bong
vault (vaulting horse)	안마	an-ma
mat (exercise ~)	매트	mae-teu

| aerobics | 에어로빅 | e-eo-ro-bik |
| yoga | 요가 | yo-ga |

135. Ice hockey

ice hockey	하키	ha-ki
ice hockey player	하키 선수	ha-ki seon-su
to play ice hockey	하키를 하다	ha-ki-reul ha-da
ice	얼음	eo-reum

puck	하키 퍽	ha-ki peok
ice hockey stick	하키 스틱	ha-ki seu-tik
ice skates	스케이트	seu-ke-i-teu

| board (ice hockey rink ~) | 사이드보드 | sa-i-deu-bo-deu |
| shot | 슛 | syut |

goaltender	골키퍼	gol-ki-peo
goal (score)	득점	deuk-jeom
to score a goal	골을 넣다	go-reul leo-ta

| period | 피리어드 | pi-ri-eo-deu |
| substitutes bench | 후보 선수 대기석 | hu-bo seon-su dae-gi-seok |

136. Football

football	축구	chuk-gu
football player	축구 선수	chuk-gu seon-su
to play football	축구를 하다	chuk-gu-reul ha-da

major league	메이저 리그	me-i-jeo ri-geu
football club	축구클럽	chuk-gu-keul-leop
coach	코치	ko-chi
owner, proprietor	구단주	gu-dan-ju

team	팀	tim
team captain	주장	ju-jang
player	선수	seon-su
substitute	후보 선수	hu-bo seon-su

forward	포워드	po-wo-deu
centre forward	센터 포워드	sen-teo po-wo-deu
scorer	득점자	deuk-jeom-ja

defender, back	수비수	su-bi-su
midfielder, halfback	미드필더	mi-deu-pil-deo
match	경기	gyeong-gi
to meet (vi, vt)	만나다	man-na-da
final	결승전	gyeol-seung-jeon
semi-final	준결승전	jun-gyeol-seung-jeon
championship	선수권	seon-su-gwon
period, half	경기 시간	gyeong-gi si-gan
first period	전반전	jeon-ban-jeon
half-time	하프 타임	ha-peu ta-im
goal	골	gol
goalkeeper	골키퍼	gol-ki-peo
goalpost	골대	gol-dae
crossbar	크로스바	keu-ro-seu-ba
net	골망	gol-mang
to concede a goal	골을 내주다	go-reul lae-ju-da
ball	공	gong
pass	패스	pae-seu
kick	슛	syut
to kick (~ the ball)	슛을 하다	syus-eul ha-da
free kick (direct ~)	프리킥	peu-ri-kik
corner kick	코너킥	ko-neo-kik
attack	공격	gong-gyeok
counterattack	반격	ban-gyeok
combination	조합	jo-hap
referee	주심, 심판	ju-sim, sim-pan
to blow the whistle	휘슬을 불다	hwi-seu-reul bul-da
whistle (sound)	휘슬, 호각	hwi-seul
foul, misconduct	반칙	ban-chik
to commit a foul	반칙을 하다	ban-chi-geul ha-da
to send off	퇴장시키다	toe-jang-si-ki-da
yellow card	옐로카드	yel-lo-ka-deu
red card	레드카드	re-deu-ka-deu
disqualification	실격	sil-gyeok
to disqualify (vt)	실격시키다	sil-gyeok-si-ki-da
penalty kick	페널티킥	pe-neol-ti-kik
wall	수비벽	su-bi-byeok
to score (vi, vt)	득점하다	deuk-jeom-ha-da
goal (score)	득점	deuk-jeom
to score a goal	득점하다	deuk-jeom-ha-da
substitution	선수교체	seon-su-gyo-che
to replace (a player)	교체하다	gyo-che-ha-da
rules	규칙	gyu-chik
tactics	전술	jeon-sul
stadium	경기장	gyeong-gi-jang
terrace	관람석	gwal-lam-seok

| fan, supporter | 서포터 | seo-po-teo |
| to shout (vi) | 소리 치다 | so-ri chi-da |

| scoreboard | 스코어보드 | ho-gak |
| score | 점수 | jeom-su |

defeat	패배	pae-bae
to lose (not win)	지다	ji-da
draw	무승부	mu-seung-bu
to draw (vi)	무승부로 끝나다	mu-seung-bu-ro kkeun-na-da

victory	승리	seung-ni
to win (vi, vt)	이기다	i-gi-da
champion	챔피언	chaem-pi-eon
best (adj)	최고의	choe-go-ui
to congratulate (vt)	축하하다	chuk-a-ha-da

| commentator | 해설가 | hae-seol-ga |
| to commentate (vt) | 실황 방송을 하다 | sil-hwang bang-song-eul ha-da |

| broadcast | 방송 | bang-song |

137. Alpine skiing

skis	스키	seu-ki
to ski (vi)	스키를 타다	seu-ki-reul ta-da
mountain-ski resort	스키 리조트	seu-ki ri-jo-teu
ski lift	리프트	ri-peu-teu

ski poles	스키 폴	seu-ki pol
slope	슬로프	seul-lo-peu
slalom	슬랄롬	seul-lal-lom

138. Tennis. Golf

golf	골프	gol-peu
golf club	골프채	gol-peu-chae
golfer	골퍼	gol-peo

hole	홀	hol
club	골프채	gol-peu-chae
golf trolley	골프백카트	gol-peu-baek-ka-teu

| tennis | 테니스 | te-ni-seu |
| tennis court | 테니스장 | te-ni-seu-jang |

| serve | 서브 | seo-beu |
| to serve (vt) | 서브하다 | seo-beu-ha-da |

racket	라켓	ra-ket
net	네트	ne-teu
ball	공	gong

139. Chess

chess	체스	che-seu
chessmen	체스의 말	che-seu-ui mal
chess player	체스 선수	che-seu seon-su
chessboard	체스판	che-seu-pan
chessman	체스의 말	che-seu-ui mal
White (white pieces)	백	baek
Black (black pieces)	흑	heuk
pawn	폰	pon
bishop	비숍	bi-syop
knight	나이트	na-i-teu
rook	룩	ruk
queen	퀸	kwin
king	킹	king
move	두기	du-gi
to move (vi, vt)	말을 옮기다	ma-reul rom-gi-da
to sacrifice (vt)	희생시키다	hui-saeng-si-ki-da
castling	캐슬링	kae-seul-ling
check	체크	che-keu
checkmate	체크메이트	che-keu-me-i-teu
chess tournament	체스 토너먼트	che-seu to-neo-meon-teu
Grand Master	그랜드 마스터	geu-raen-deu ma-seu-teo
combination	조합	jo-hap
game (in chess)	판	pan
draughts	체커	che-keo

140. Boxing

boxing	권투	gwon-tu
fight (bout)	회전	hoe-jeon
round (in boxing)	라운드	ra-un-deu
ring	링	ring
gong	공	gong
punch	펀치	peon-chi
knockdown	녹다운	nok-da-un
knockout	녹아웃	no-ga-ut
to knock out	녹아웃 시키다	no-ga-ut si-ki-da
boxing glove	권투 글러브	gwon-tu geul-leo-beu
referee	부심	bu-sim
lightweight	라이트급	ra-i-teu-geup
middleweight	미들급	mi-deul-geup
heavyweight	헤비급	he-bi-geup

141. Sports. Miscellaneous

Olympic Games	올림픽	ol-lim-pik
winner	승리자	seung-ni-ja
to be winning	이기고 있다	i-gi-go it-da
to win (vi)	이기다	i-gi-da
leader	선두	seon-du
to lead (vi)	선두를 달리다	seon-du-reul dal-li-da
first place	일등	il-deung
second place	준우승	seu-ko-eo-bo-deu
third place	3위	sam-wi
medal	메달	me-dal
trophy	트로피	teu-ro-pi
prize cup (trophy)	우승컵	u-seung-keop
prize (in game)	상	sang
main prize	최고 상품	choe-go sang-pum
record	기록	gi-rok
to set a record	기록을 세우다	gi-ro-geul se-u-da
final	결승전	gyeol-seung-jeon
final (adj)	마지막의	ma-ji-ma-gui
champion	챔피언	chaem-pi-eon
championship	선수권	seon-su-gwon
stadium	경기장	gyeong-gi-jang
terrace	관람석	gwal-lam-seok
fan, supporter	서포터	seo-po-teo
opponent, rival	상대	sang-dae
start (start line)	출발점	chul-bal-jeom
finish line	결승점	gyeol-seung-jeom
defeat	패배	pae-bae
to lose (not win)	지다	ji-da
referee	심판	sim-pan
jury (judges)	배심원단	bae-si-mwon-dan
score	점수	jeom-su
draw	무승부	mu-seung-bu
to draw (vi)	무승부로 끝나다	mu-seung-bu-ro kkeun-na-da
point	점수	jeom-su
result (final score)	결과	gyeol-gwa
half-time	하프 타임	ha-peu ta-im
doping	도핑	do-ping
to penalise (vt)	처벌하다	cheo-beol-ha-da
to disqualify (vt)	실격시키다	sil-gyeok-si-ki-da
apparatus	기구	gi-gu
javelin	투창	tu-chang

shot (metal ball)	포환	po-hwan
ball (snooker, etc.)	공	gong
aim (target)	목표	mok-pyo
target	과녁	gwa-nyeok
to shoot (vi)	쏘다	sso-da
accurate (~ shot)	정확한	jeong-hwak-an
trainer, coach	코치	ko-chi
to train (sb)	훈련하다	hul-lyeon-ha-da
to train (vi)	훈련하다	hul-lyeon-ha-da
training	훈련	hul-lyeon
gym	헬스장	hel-seu-jang
exercise (physical)	운동, 연습	un-dong, yeon-seup
warm-up (athlete ~)	워밍업	wo-ming-eop

Education

school	학교	hak-gyo
headmaster	교장	gyo-jang
student (m)	남학생	nam-hak-saeng
student (f)	여학생	yeo-hak-saeng
schoolboy	남학생	nam-hak-saeng
schoolgirl	여학생	yeo-hak-saeng
to teach (sb)	가르치다	ga-reu-chi-da
to learn (language, etc.)	배우다	bae-u-da
to learn by heart	암기하다	am-gi-ha-da
to learn (~ to count, etc.)	배우다	bae-u-da
to be at school	재학 중이다	jae-hak jung-i-da
to go to school	학교에 가다	hak-gyo-e ga-da
alphabet	알파벳	al-pa-bet
subject (at school)	과목	gwa-mok
classroom	교실	gyo-sil
lesson	수업	su-eop
playtime, break	쉬는 시간	swi-neun si-gan
school bell	수업종	su-eop-jong
school desk	학교 책상	hak-gyo chaek-sang
blackboard	칠판	chil-pan
mark	성적	seong-jeok
good mark	좋은 성적	jo-eun seong-jeok
bad mark	나쁜 성적	na-ppeun seong-jeok
to give a mark	성적을 매기다	seong-jeo-geul mae-gi-da
mistake, error	실수	sil-su
to make mistakes	실수하다	sil-su-ha-da
to correct (an error)	고치다	go-chi-da
crib	커닝 페이퍼	keo-ning pe-i-peo
homework	숙제	suk-je
exercise (in education)	연습 문제	yeon-seup mun-je
to be present	출석하다	chul-seok-a-da
to be absent	결석하다	gyeol-seok-a-da
to punish (vt)	처벌하다	cheo-beol-ha-da
punishment	벌	beol
conduct (behaviour)	처신	cheo-sin
school report	성적표	seong-jeok-pyo

pencil	연필	yeon-pil
rubber	지우개	ji-u-gae
chalk	분필	bun-pil
pencil case	필통	pil-tong

schoolbag	책가방	chaek-ga-bang
pen	펜	pen
exercise book	노트	no-teu
textbook	교과서	gyo-gwa-seo
compasses	컴퍼스	keom-peo-seu

| to make technical drawings | 제도하다 | je-do-ha-da |
| technical drawing | 건축 도면 | geon-chuk do-myeon |

poem	시	si
by heart (adv)	외워서	oe-wo-seo
to learn by heart	암기하다	am-gi-ha-da

| school holidays | 학교 방학 | bang-hak |
| to be on holiday | 방학 중이다 | bang-hak jung-i-da |

test (at school)	필기 시험	pil-gi si-heom
essay (composition)	논술	non-sul
dictation	받아쓰기 시험	ba-da-sseu-gi si-heom

exam (examination)	시험	si-heom
to do an exam	시험을 보다	si-heo-meul bo-da
experiment (e.g., chemistry ~)	실험	sil-heom

143. College. University

academy	아카데미	a-ka-de-mi
university	대학교	dae-hak-gyo
faculty (e.g., ~ of Medicine)	교수진	gyo-su-jin

student (masc.)	대학생	dae-hak-saeng
student (fem.)	여대생	yeo-dae-saeng
lecturer (teacher)	강사	gang-sa

| lecture hall, room | 교실 | gyo-sil |
| graduate | 졸업생 | jo-reop-saeng |

| diploma | 졸업증 | jo-reop-jeung |
| dissertation | 학위 논문 | ha-gwi non-mun |

| study (report) | 연구 | yeon-gu |
| laboratory | 연구실 | yeon-gu-sil |

| lecture | 강의 | gang-ui |
| coursemate | 대학 동급생 | dae-hak dong-geup-saeng |

| scholarship, bursary | 장학금 | jang-hak-geum |
| academic degree | 학위 | ha-gwi |

144. Sciences. Disciplines

mathematics	수학	su-hak
algebra	대수학	dae-su-hak
geometry	기하학	gi-ha-hak
astronomy	천문학	cheon-mun-hak
biology	생물학	saeng-mul-hak
geography	지리학	ji-ri-hak
geology	지질학	ji-jil-hak
history	역사학	yeok-sa-hak
medicine	의학	ui-hak
pedagogy	교육학	gyo-yuk-ak
law	법학	beo-pak
physics	물리학	mul-li-hak
chemistry	화학	hwa-hak
philosophy	철학	cheol-hak
psychology	심리학	sim-ni-hak

145. Writing system. Orthography

grammar	문법	mun-beop
vocabulary	어휘	eo-hwi
phonetics	음성학	eum-seong-hak
noun	명사	myeong-sa
adjective	형용사	hyeong-yong-sa
verb	동사	dong-sa
adverb	부사	bu-sa
pronoun	대명사	dae-myeong-sa
interjection	감탄사	gam-tan-sa
preposition	전치사	jeon-chi-sa
root	어근	eo-geun
ending	어미	eo-mi
prefix	접두사	jeop-du-sa
syllable	음절	eum-jeol
suffix	접미사	jeom-mi-sa
stress mark	강세	gang-se
apostrophe	아포스트로피	a-po-seu-teu-ro-pi
full stop	마침표	ma-chim-pyo
comma	쉼표	swim-pyo
semicolon	세미콜론	se-mi-kol-lon
colon	콜론	kol-lon
ellipsis	말줄임표	mal-ju-rim-pyo
question mark	물음표	mu-reum-pyo
exclamation mark	느낌표	neu-kkim-pyo

inverted commas	따옴표	tta-om-pyo
in inverted commas	따옴표 안에	tta-om-pyo a-ne
parenthesis	괄호	gwal-ho
in parenthesis	괄호 속에	gwal-ho so-ge

hyphen	하이픈	ha-i-peun
dash	대시	jul-pyo
space (between words)	공백 문자	gong-baek mun-ja

letter	글자	geul-ja
capital letter	대문자	dae-mun-ja

vowel (n)	모음	mo-eum
consonant (n)	자음	ja-eum

sentence	문장	mun-jang
subject	주어	ju-eo
predicate	서술어	seo-su-reo

line	줄	jul
on a new line	줄을 바꾸어	ju-reul ba-kku-eo
paragraph	단락	dal-lak

word	단어	dan-eo
group of words	문구	mun-gu
expression	표현	pyo-hyeon
synonym	동의어	dong-ui-eo
antonym	반의어	ban-ui-eo

rule	규칙	gyu-chik
exception	예외	ye-oe
correct (adj)	맞는	man-neun

conjugation	활용	hwa-ryong
declension	어형 변화	eo-hyeong byeon-hwa
nominal case	격	gyeok
question	질문	jil-mun
to underline (vt)	밑줄을 긋다	mit-ju-reul geut-da
dotted line	점선	jeom-seon

146. Foreign languages

language	언어	eon-eo
foreign language	외국어	oe-gu-geo
to study (vt)	공부하다	gong-bu-ha-da
to learn (language, etc.)	배우다	bae-u-da

to read (vi, vt)	읽다	ik-da
to speak (vi, vt)	말하다	mal-ha-da
to understand (vt)	이해하다	i-hae-ha-da
to write (vt)	쓰다	sseu-da

fast (adv)	빨리	ppal-li
slowly (adv)	천천히	cheon-cheon-hi

fluently (adv)	유창하게	yu-chang-ha-ge
rules	규칙	gyu-chik
grammar	문법	mun-beop
vocabulary	어휘	eo-hwi
phonetics	음성학	eum-seong-hak
textbook	교과서	gyo-gwa-seo
dictionary	사전	sa-jeon
teach-yourself book	자습서	ja-seup-seo
phrasebook	회화집	hoe-hwa-jip
cassette, tape	테이프	te-i-peu
videotape	비디오테이프	bi-di-o-te-i-peu
CD, compact disc	씨디	ssi-di
DVD	디비디	di-bi-di
alphabet	알파벳	al-pa-bet
to spell (vt)	… 의 철자이다	… ui cheol-ja-i-da
pronunciation	발음	ba-reum
accent	악센트	ak-sen-teu
with an accent	사투리로	sa-tu-ri-ro
without an accent	억양 없이	eo-gyang eop-si
word	단어	dan-eo
meaning	의미	ui-mi
course (e.g. a French ~)	강좌	gang-jwa
to sign up	등록하다	deung-nok-a-da
teacher	강사	gang-sa
translation (process)	번역	beo-nyeok
translation (text, etc.)	번역	beo-nyeok
translator	번역가	beo-nyeok-ga
interpreter	통역가	tong-yeok-ga
polyglot	수개 국어를 말하는 사람	su-gae gu-geo-reul mal-ha-neun sa-ram
memory	기억력	gi-eong-nyeok

147. Fairy tale characters

Father Christmas	산타클로스	san-ta-keul-lo-seu
mermaid	인어	in-eo
magician, wizard	마법사	ma-beop-sa
fairy	요정	yo-jeong
magic (adj)	마법의	ma-beo-bui
magic wand	마술 지팡이	ma-sul ji-pang-i
fairy tale	동화	dong-hwa
miracle	기적	gi-jeok
dwarf	난쟁이	nan-jaeng-i
to turn into …	… 으로 변하다	… eu-ro byeon-ha-da

ghost	유령, 귀신	yu-ryeong, gwi-sin
phantom	유령	yu-ryeong
monster	괴물	goe-mul
dragon	용	yong
giant	거인	geo-in

148. Zodiac Signs

Aries	양자리	yang-ja-ri
Taurus	황소자리	hwang-so-ja-ri
Gemini	쌍둥이자리	ssang-dung-i-ja-ri
Cancer	게자리	ge-ja-ri
Leo	사자자리	sa-ja-ja-ri
Virgo	처녀자리	cheo-nyeo-ja-ri
Libra	천칭자리	cheon-ching-ja-ri
Scorpio	전갈자리	jeon-gal-ja-ri
Sagittarius	궁수자리	gung-su-ja-ri
Capricorn	염소자리	yeom-so-ja-ri
Aquarius	물병자리	mul-byeong-ja-ri
Pisces	물고기자리	mul-go-gi-ja-ri
character	성격	seong-gyeok
character traits	성격특성	seong-gyeok-teuk-seong
behaviour	행동	haeng-dong
to tell fortunes	점치다	jeom-chi-da
fortune-teller	점쟁이	jeom-jaeng-i
horoscope	천궁도	cheon-gung-do

Arts

theatre	극장	geuk-jang
opera	오페라	o-pe-ra
operetta	오페레타	o-pe-re-ta
ballet	발레	bal-le

theatre poster	포스터, 벽보	po-seu-teo, byeok-bo
theatre company	공연단	gong-yeon-dan
tour	순회	sun-hoe
to be on tour	투어를 가다	tu-eo-reul ga-da
to rehearse (vi, vt)	리허설 하다	ri-heo-seol ha-da
rehearsal	리허설	ri-heo-seol
repertoire	레퍼토리	re-peo-to-ri

performance	공연	gong-yeon
theatrical show	연극 공연	yeon-geuk gong-yeon
play	연극	yeon-geuk

ticket	표, 입장권	pyo, ip-jang-gwon
booking office	매표소	mae-pyo-so
lobby, foyer	로비	ro-bi
coat check (cloakroom)	휴대품 보관소	hyu-dae-pum bo-gwan-so
cloakroom ticket	보관소 꼬리표	bo-gwan-so kko-ri-pyo
binoculars	오페라 글라스	o-pe-ra geul-la-seu
usher	좌석 안내원	jwa-seok gan-nae-won

stalls (orchestra seats)	일반 객석	il-ban gaek-seok
balcony	발코니석	bal-ko-ni-seok
dress circle	특등석	teuk-deung-seok
box	특별석	teuk-byeol-seok
row	열	yeol
seat	자리	ja-ri

audience	청중	cheong-jung
spectator	관중	gwan-jung
to clap (vi, vt)	박수하다	bak-su-ha-da
applause	박수	bak-su
ovation	박수 갈채	bak-su gal-chae

stage	무대	mu-dae
curtain	커튼	keo-teun
scenery	무대 배경	mu-dae bae-gyeong
backstage	백스테이지	baek-seu-te-i-ji

scene (e.g. the last ~)	장면	jang-myeon
act	막	mak
interval	막간	mak-gan

150. Cinema

actor	배우	bae-u
actress	여배우	yeo-bae-u
film	영화	yeong-hwa
episode	부작	bu-jak
detective film	탐정 영화	tam-jeong yeong-hwa
action film	액션 영화	aek-syeon nyeong-hwa
adventure film	모험 영화	mo-heom myeong-hwa
science fiction film	공상과학영화	SF yeong-hwa
horror film	공포 영화	gong-po yeong-hwa
comedy film	코미디 영화	ko-mi-di yeong-hwa
melodrama	멜로드라마	mel-lo-deu-ra-ma
drama	드라마	deu-ra-ma
fictional film	극영화	geu-gyeong-hwa
documentary	다큐멘터리	da-kyu-men-teo-ri
cartoon	만화영화	man-hwa-yeong-hwa
silent films	무성영화	mu-seong-yeong-hwa
role (part)	역할	yeok-al
leading role	주역	ju-yeok
to play (vi, vt)	연기하다	yeon-gi-ha-da
film star	영화 스타	yeong-hwa seu-ta
well-known (adj)	유명한	yu-myeong-han
famous (adj)	유명한	yu-myeong-han
popular (adj)	인기 있는	in-gi in-neun
script (screenplay)	시나리오	si-na-ri-o
scriptwriter	시나리오 작가	si-na-ri-o jak-ga
film director	영화감독	yeong-hwa-gam-dok
producer	제작자	je-jak-ja
assistant	보조자	bo-jo-ja
cameraman	카메라맨	ka-me-ra-maen
stuntman	스턴트 맨	seu-teon-teu maen
to shoot a film	영화를 촬영하다	yeong-hwa-reul chwa-ryeong-ha-da
audition, screen test	오디션	o-di-syeon
shooting	촬영	chwa-ryeong
film crew	영화 제작팀	yeong-hwa je-jak-tim
film set	영화 세트	yeong-hwa se-teu
camera	카메라	ka-me-ra
cinema	영화관	yeong-hwa-gwan
screen (e.g. big ~)	스크린	seu-keu-rin
to show a film	영화를 상영하다	yeong-hwa-reul sang-yeong-ha-da
soundtrack	사운드트랙	sa-un-deu-teu-raek
special effects	특수 효과	teuk-su hyo-gwa

subtitles	자막	ja-mak
credits	엔딩 크레딧	en-ding keu-re-dit
translation	번역	beo-nyeok

151. Painting

art	예술	ye-sul
fine arts	미술	mi-sul
art gallery	미술관	mi-sul-gwan
art exhibition	미술 전시회	mi-sul jeon-si-hoe

painting (art)	회화	hoe-hwa
graphic art	그래픽 아트	geu-rae-pik ga-teu
abstract art	추상파	chu-sang-pa
impressionism	인상파	in-sang-pa

picture (painting)	그림	geu-rim
drawing	선화	seon-hwa
poster	포스터	po-seu-teo

illustration (picture)	삽화	sa-pwa
miniature	세밀화	se-mil-hwa
copy (of painting, etc.)	복제품	bok-je-pum
reproduction	복사	bok-sa

mosaic	모자이크	mo-ja-i-keu
stained glass window	스테인드 글라스	seu-te-in-deu geul-la-seu
fresco	프레스코화	peu-re-seu-ko-hwa
engraving	판화	pan-hwa

bust (sculpture)	흉상	hyung-sang
sculpture	조각	jo-gak
statue	조상	jo-sang
plaster of Paris	석고	seok-go
plaster (as adj)	석고의	seok-go-ui

portrait	초상화	cho-sang-hwa
self-portrait	자화상	ja-hwa-sang
landscape painting	풍경화	pung-gyeong-hwa
still life	정물화	jeong-mul-hwa
caricature	캐리커처	kae-ri-keo-cheo

paint	물감	mul-gam
watercolor paint	수채 물감	su-chae mul-gam
oil (paint)	유화 물감	yu-hwa mul-gam
pencil	연필	yeon-pil
Indian ink	먹물	meong-mul
charcoal	목탄	mok-tan

| to draw (vi, vt) | 그리다 | geu-ri-da |
| to paint (vi, vt) | 그리다 | geu-ri-da |

| to pose (vi) | 포즈를 취하다 | po-jeu-reul chwi-ha-da |
| artist's model (masc.) | 화가의 모델 | hwa-ga-ui mo-del |

artist's model (fem.)	화가의 모델	hwa-ga-ui mo-del
artist (painter)	화가	hwa-ga
work of art	미술 작품	mi-sul jak-pum
masterpiece	걸작	geol-jak
studio (artist's workroom)	작업실	ja-geop-sil

canvas (cloth)	캔버스	kaen-beo-seu
easel	이젤	i-jel
palette	팔레트	pal-le-teu

frame (picture ~, etc.)	액자	aek-ja
restoration	복원	bo-gwon
to restore (vt)	복원하다	bo-gwon-ha-da

152. Literature & Poetry

literature	문학	mun-hak
author (writer)	작가	jak-ga
pseudonym	필명	pil-myeong

book	책	chaek
volume	권	gwon
table of contents	목차	mok-cha
page	페이지	pe-i-ji
main character	주인공	ju-in-gong
autograph	사인	sa-in

short story	단편 소설	dan-pyeon so-seol
story (novella)	소설	so-seol
novel	장편 소설	jang-pyeon so-seol
work (writing)	작품	jak-pum
fable	우화	u-hwa
detective novel	추리 소설	chu-ri so-seol

poem (verse)	시	si
poetry	시	si
poem (epic, ballad)	서사시	seo-sa-si
poet	시인	si-in

fiction	픽션	pik-syeon
science fiction	공상과학소설	gong-sang-gwa-hak-so-seol
adventures	모험 소설	mo-heom so-seol
educational literature	교육 문학	gyo-yuk mun-hak
children's literature	아동 문학	a-dong mun-hak

153. Circus

circus	서커스	seo-keo-seu
travelling circus	순회 서커스	sun-hoe seo-keo-seu
programme	프로그램	peu-ro-geu-raem
performance	공연	gong-yeon
act (circus ~)	공연	gong-yeon

circus ring	무대	mu-dae
pantomime (act)	판토마임	pan-to-ma-im
clown	어릿광대	eo-rit-gwang-dae

acrobat	곡예사	go-gye-sa
acrobatics	곡예	go-gye
gymnast	체조선수	che-jo-seon-su
acrobatic gymnastics	체조	che-jo
somersault	공중제비	gong-jung-je-bi

strongman	힘 자랑하는 사나이	him ja-rang-ha-neun sa-na-i
tamer (e.g., lion ~)	조련사	jo-ryeon-sa
rider (circus horse ~)	곡마사	gong-ma-sa
assistant	조수	jo-su

stunt	묘기	myo-gi
magic trick	마술	ma-sul
conjurer, magician	마술사	ma-sul-sa

juggler	저글러	jeo-geul-leo
to juggle (vi, vt)	저글링 하다	jeo-geul-ling ha-da
animal trainer	조련사	jo-ryeon-sa
animal training	조련	jo-ryeon
to train (animals)	가르치다	ga-reu-chi-da

154. Music. Pop music

music	음악	eum-ak
musician	음악가	eum-ak-ga
musical instrument	악기	ak-gi
to play ...	··· 을 연주하다	... eul ryeon-ju-ha-da

guitar	기타	gi-ta
violin	바이올린	ba-i-ol-lin
cello	첼로	chel-lo
double bass	콘트라베이스	kon-teu-ra-be-i-seu
harp	하프	ha-peu

piano	피아노	pi-a-no
grand piano	그랜드 피아노	geu-raen-deu pi-a-no
organ	오르간	o-reu-gan

wind instruments	관악기	gwan-ak-gi
oboe	오보에	o-bo-e
saxophone	색소폰	saek-so-pon
clarinet	클라리넷	keul-la-ri-net
flute	플루트	peul-lu-teu
trumpet	트럼펫	teu-reom-pet

| accordion | 아코디언 | a-ko-di-eon |
| drum | 북 | buk |

| duo | 이중주 | i-jung-ju |
| trio | 삼중주 | sam-jung-ju |

quartet	사중주	sa-jung-ju
choir	합창단	hap-chang-dan
orchestra	오케스트라	o-ke-seu-teu-ra

pop music	대중 음악	dae-jung eum-ak
rock music	록 음악	rok geu-mak
rock group	록 그룹	rok geu-rup
jazz	재즈	jae-jeu

| idol | 아이돌 | a-i-dol |
| admirer, fan | 팬 | paen |

concert	콘서트	kon-seo-teu
symphony	교향곡	gyo-hyang-gok
composition	작품	jak-pum
to compose (write)	작곡하다	jak-gok-a-da

singing (n)	노래	no-rae
song	노래	no-rae
tune (melody)	멜로디	mel-lo-di
rhythm	리듬	ri-deum
blues	블루스	beul-lu-seu

sheet music	악보	ak-bo
baton	지휘봉	ji-hwi-bong
bow	활	hwal
string	현	hyeon
case (e.g. guitar ~)	케이스	ke-i-seu

Rest. Entertainment. Travel

155. Trip. Travel

tourism, travel	관광	gwan-gwang
tourist	관광객	gwan-gwang-gaek
trip, voyage	여행	yeo-haeng
adventure	모험	mo-heom
trip, journey	여행	yeo-haeng
holiday	휴가	hyu-ga
to be on holiday	휴가 중이다	hyu-ga jung-i-da
rest	휴양	hyu-yang
train	기차	gi-cha
by train	기차로	gi-cha-ro
aeroplane	비행기	bi-haeng-gi
by aeroplane	비행기로	bi-haeng-gi-ro
by car	자동차로	ja-dong-cha-ro
by ship	배로	bae-ro
luggage	짐, 수하물	jim, su-ha-mul
suitcase	여행 가방	yeo-haeng ga-bang
luggage trolley	수하물 카트	su-ha-mul ka-teu
passport	여권	yeo-gwon
visa	비자	bi-ja
ticket	표	pyo
air ticket	비행기표	bi-haeng-gi-pyo
guidebook	여행 안내서	yeo-haeng an-nae-seo
map (tourist ~)	지도	ji-do
area (rural ~)	지역	ji-yeok
place, site	곳	got
exotica (n)	이국	i-guk
exotic (adj)	이국적인	i-guk-jeo-gin
amazing (adj)	놀라운	nol-la-un
group	무리	mu-ri
excursion, sightseeing tour	견학, 관광	gyeon-hak, gwan-gwang
guide (person)	가이드	ga-i-deu

156. Hotel

hotel	호텔	ho-tel
motel	모텔	mo-tel
three-star (~ hotel)	3성급	sam-seong-geub

| five-star | 5성급 | o-seong-geub |
| to stay (in a hotel, etc.) | 머무르다 | meo-mu-reu-da |

room	객실	gaek-sil
single room	일인실	i-rin-sil
double room	더블룸	deo-beul-lum
to book a room	방을 예약하다	bang-eul rye-yak-a-da

| half board | 하숙 | ha-suk |
| full board | 식사 제공 | sik-sa je-gong |

with bath	욕조가 있는	yok-jo-ga in-neun
with shower	샤워가 있는	sya-wo-ga in-neun
satellite television	위성 텔레비전	wi-seong tel-le-bi-jeon
air-conditioner	에어컨	e-eo-keon
towel	수건	su-geon
key	열쇠	yeol-soe

administrator	관리자	gwal-li-ja
chambermaid	객실 청소부	gaek-sil cheong-so-bu
porter	포터	po-teo
doorman	도어맨	do-eo-maen

restaurant	레스토랑	re-seu-to-rang
pub, bar	바	ba
breakfast	아침식사	a-chim-sik-sa
dinner	저녁식사	jeo-nyeok-sik-sa
buffet	뷔페	bwi-pe

| lobby | 로비 | ro-bi |
| lift | 엘리베이터 | el-li-be-i-teo |

| DO NOT DISTURB | 방해하지 마세요 | bang-hae-ha-ji ma-se-yo |
| NO SMOKING | 금연 | geu-myeon |

157. Books. Reading

book	책	chaek
author	저자	jeo-ja
writer	작가	jak-ga
to write (~ a book)	쓰다	sseu-da

reader	독자	dok-ja
to read (vi, vt)	읽다	ik-da
reading (activity)	독서	dok-seo

| silently (to oneself) | 묵독 (~을 하다) | muk-dok |
| aloud (adv) | 큰소리로 | keun-so-ri-ro |

to publish (vt)	발행하다	bal-haeng-ha-da
publishing (process)	발행	bal-haeng
publisher	출판인	chul-pan-in
publishing house	출판사	chul-pan-sa
to come out (be released)	출간되다	chul-gan-doe-da

| release (of a book) | 발표 | bal-pyo |
| print run | 인쇄 부수 | in-swae bu-su |

| bookshop | 서점 | seo-jeom |
| library | 도서관 | do-seo-gwan |

story (novella)	소설	so-seol
short story	단편 소설	dan-pyeon so-seol
novel	장편 소설	jang-pyeon so-seol
detective novel	추리 소설	chu-ri so-seol

memoirs	회상록	hoe-sang-nok
legend	전설	jeon-seol
myth	신화	sin-hwa

poetry, poems	시	si
autobiography	자서전	ja-seo-jeon
selected works	선집	seon-jip
science fiction	공상과학소설	gong-sang-gwa-hak-so-seol

title	제목	je-mok
introduction	서문	seo-mun
title page	속표지	sok-pyo-ji

chapter	장	jang
extract	발췌	bal-chwe
episode	장면	jang-myeon

plot (storyline)	줄거리	jul-geo-ri
contents	내용	nae-yong
table of contents	목차	mok-cha
main character	주인공	ju-in-gong

volume	권	gwon
cover	표지	pyo-ji
binding	장정	jang-jeong
bookmark	서표	seo-pyo

page	페이지	pe-i-ji
to page through	페이지를 넘기다	pe-i-ji-reul leom-gi-da
margins	여백	yeo-baek
annotation (marginal note, etc.)	주석	ju-seok
footnote	각주	gak-ju

text	본문	bon-mun
type, fount	활자, 서체	hwal-ja, seo-che
misprint, typo	오타	o-ta

translation	번역	beo-nyeok
to translate (vt)	번역하다	beo-nyeok-a-da
original (n)	원본	won-bon

famous (adj)	유명한	yu-myeong-han
unknown (not famous)	잘 알려지지 않은	jal ral-lyeo-ji-ji a-neun
interesting (adj)	재미있는	jae-mi-in-neun

bestseller	베스트셀러	be-seu-teu-sel-leo
dictionary	사전	sa-jeon
textbook	교과서	gyo-gwa-seo
encyclopedia	백과사전	baek-gwa-sa-jeon

158. Hunting. Fishing

hunting	사냥	sa-nyang
to hunt (vi, vt)	사냥하다	sa-nyang-ha-da
hunter	사냥꾼	sa-nyang-kkun

to shoot (vi)	쏘다	sso-da
rifle	장총	jang-chong
bullet (shell)	탄환	tan-hwan
shot (lead balls)	산탄	san-tan

steel trap	덫	deot
snare (for birds, etc.)	덫	deot
to lay a steel trap	덫을 놓다	deo-cheul lo-ta

poacher	밀렵자	mil-lyeop-ja
game (in hunting)	사냥감	sa-nyang-gam
hound dog	사냥개	sa-nyang-gae
safari	사파리	sa-pa-ri
mounted animal	박제	bak-je

fisherman	낚시꾼	nak-si-kkun
fishing (angling)	낚시	nak-si
to fish (vi)	낚시질하다	nak-si-jil-ha-da

fishing rod	낚싯대	nak-sit-dae
fishing line	낚싯줄	nak-sit-jul
hook	바늘	ba-neul

| float | 찌 | jji |
| bait | 미끼 | mi-kki |

| to cast a line | 낚싯줄을 던지다 | nak-sit-ju-reul deon-ji-da |
| to bite (ab. fish) | 미끼를 물다 | mi-kki-reul mul-da |

| catch (of fish) | 어획고 | eo-hoek-go |
| ice-hole | 얼음구멍 | eo-reum-gu-meong |

fishing net	그물	geu-mul
boat	보트	bo-teu
to net (to fish with a net)	그물로 잡다	geu-mul-lo jap-da

| to cast[throw] the net | 그물을 던지다 | geu-mu-reul deon-ji-da |
| to haul the net in | 그물을 끌어당기다 | geu-mu-reul kkeu-reo-dang-gi-da |

whaler (person)	포경선원	po-gyeong-seon-won
whaleboat	포경선	po-gyeong-seon
harpoon	작살	jak-sal

159. Games. Billiards

billiards	당구	dang-gu
billiard room, hall	당구장	dang-gu-jang
ball (snooker, etc.)	공	gong
to pocket a ball	공을 넣다	gong-eul leo-ta
cue	큐	kyu
pocket	구멍	gu-meong

160. Games. Playing cards

diamonds	스페이드	seu-pe-i-deu
spades	스페이드	seu-pe-i-deu
hearts	하트	ha-teu
clubs	클럽	keul-leop
ace	에이스	e-i-seu
king	왕	wang
queen	퀸	kwin
jack, knave	잭	jaek
playing card	카드	ka-deu
cards	카드	ka-deu
trump	으뜸패	eu-tteum-pae
pack of cards	카드 한 벌	ka-deu han beol
to deal (vi, vt)	돌리다	dol-li-da
to shuffle (cards)	카드를 섞다	ka-deu-reul seok-da
lead, turn (n)	차례	cha-rye
cardsharp	카드 판의 사기꾼	ka-deu pan-ui sa-gi-kkun

161. Casino. Roulette

casino	카지노	ka-ji-no
roulette (game)	룰렛	rul-let
bet	내기	nae-gi
to place bets	돈을 걸다	do-neul geol-da
red	적색	jeok-saek
black	흑색	heuk-saek
to bet on red	레드에 돈을 걸다	re-deu-e do-neul geol-da
to bet on black	블랙에 돈을 걸다	beul-lae-ge do-neul geol-da
croupier (dealer)	딜러	dil-leo
rules (~ of the game)	규칙	gyu-chik
chip	칩	chip
to win (vi, vt)	돈을 따다	do-neul tta-da
win (winnings)	딴 돈	ttan don
to lose (~ 100 dollars)	잃다	il-ta

loss (losses)	손해	son-hae
player	플레이어	peul-le-i-eo
blackjack (card game)	블랙잭	beul-laek-jaek
craps (dice game)	크랩 게임	keu-raep ge-im
fruit machine	슬롯머신	seul-lon-meo-sin

162. Rest. Games. Miscellaneous

to stroll (vi, vt)	산책하다	san-chaek-a-da
stroll (leisurely walk)	산책	san-chaek
car ride	드라이브	deu-ra-i-beu
adventure	모험	mo-heom
picnic	소풍, 피크닉	so-pung, pi-keu-nik

game (chess, etc.)	게임	ge-im
player	선수	seon-su
game (one ~ of chess)	게임	ge-im

collector (e.g. philatelist)	수집가	su-jip-ga
to collect (stamps, etc.)	수집하다	su-ji-pa-da
collection	수집	su-jip

crossword puzzle	크로스워드	keu-ro-seu-wo-deu
racecourse (hippodrome)	경마장	gyeong-ma-jang
disco (discotheque)	클럽	keul-leop

| sauna | 사우나 | sa-u-na |
| lottery | 복권 | bok-gwon |

camping trip	캠핑	kaem-ping
camp	캠프	kaem-peu
tent (for camping)	텐트	ten-teu
compass	나침반	na-chim-ban
camper	야영객	ya-yeong-gaek

to watch (film, etc.)	시청하다	si-cheong-ha-da
viewer	시청자	si-cheong-ja
TV show (TV program)	방송 프로그램	bang-song peu-ro-geu-raem

163. Photography

| camera (photo) | 카메라 | ka-me-ra |
| photo, picture | 사진 | sa-jin |

photographer	사진 작가	sa-jin jak-ga
photo studio	사진관	sa-jin-gwan
photo album	사진 앨범	sa-jin ael-beom

camera lens	카메라 렌즈	ka-me-ra ren-jeu
telephoto lens	망원 렌즈	mang-won len-jeu
filter	필터	pil-teo
lens	렌즈	ren-jeu

optics (high-quality ~)	렌즈	ren-jeu
diaphragm (aperture)	조리개	jo-ri-gae
exposure time (shutter speed)	셔터 속도	syeo-teo sok-do
viewfinder	파인더	pa-in-deo
digital camera	디지털 카메라	di-ji-teol ka-me-ra
tripod	삼각대	sam-gak-dae
flash	플래시	peul-lae-si
to photograph (vt)	사진을 찍다	sa-ji-neul jjik-da
to take pictures	사진을 찍다	sa-ji-neul jjik-da
to have one's picture taken	사진을 찍다	sa-ji-neul jjik-da
focus	포커스	po-keo-seu
to focus	초점을 맞추다	cho-jeo-meul mat-chu-da
sharp, in focus (adj)	선명한	seon-myeong-han
sharpness	선명성	seon-myeong-seong
contrast	대비	dae-bi
contrast (as adj)	대비의	dae-bi-ui
picture (photo)	사진	sa-jin
negative (n)	음화	eum-hwa
film (a roll of ~)	사진 필름	sa-jin pil-leum
frame (still)	한 장면	han jang-myeon
to print (photos)	인화하다	in-hwa-ha-da

164. Beach. Swimming

beach	해변, 바닷가	hae-byeon, ba-dat-ga
sand	모래	mo-rae
deserted (beach)	황량한	hwang-nyang-han
suntan	선탠	seon-taen
to get a tan	선탠을 하다	seon-tae-neul ha-da
tanned (adj)	햇볕에 탄	haet-byeo-te tan
sunscreen	자외선 차단제	ja-oe-seon cha-dan-je
bikini	비키니	bi-ki-ni
swimsuit, bikini	수영복	su-yeong-bok
swim trunks	수영복	su-yeong-bok
swimming pool	수영장	su-yeong-jang
to swim (vi)	수영하다	su-yeong-ha-da
shower	샤워	sya-wo
to change (one's clothes)	옷을 갈아입다	os-eul ga-ra-ip-da
towel	수건	su-geon
boat	보트	bo-teu
motorboat	모터보트	mo-teo-bo-teu
water ski	수상 스키	su-sang seu-ki
pedalo	수상 자전거	su-sang ja-jeon-geo

| surfing | 서핑 | seo-ping |
| surfer | 서퍼 | seo-peo |

scuba set	스쿠버 장비	seu-ku-beo jang-bi
flippers (swim fins)	오리발	o-ri-bal
mask (diving ~)	잠수마스크	jam-su-ma-seu-keu
diver	잠수부	jam-su-bu
to dive (vi)	잠수하다	jam-su-ha-da
underwater (adv)	수중	su-jung

beach umbrella	파라솔	pa-ra-sol
beach chair (sun lounger)	선베드	seon-be-deu
sunglasses	선글라스	seon-geul-la-seu
air mattress	에어 매트	e-eo mae-teu

| to play (amuse oneself) | 놀다 | nol-da |
| to go for a swim | 수영하다 | su-yeong-ha-da |

beach ball	비치볼	bi-chi-bol
to inflate (vt)	부풀리다	bu-pul-li-da
inflatable, air (adj)	부풀릴 수 있는	bu-pul-lil su in-neun

wave	파도	pa-do
buoy (line of ~s)	부표	bu-pyo
to drown (ab. person)	익사하다	ik-sa-ha-da

to save, to rescue	구조하다	gu-jo-ha-da
life jacket	구명조끼	gu-myeong-jo-kki
to observe, to watch	지켜보다	ji-kyeo-bo-da
lifeguard	구조원	gu-jo-won

TECHNICAL EQUIPMENT. TRANSPORT

Technical equipment

165. Computer

computer	컴퓨터	keom-pyu-teo
notebook, laptop	노트북	no-teu-buk
to turn on	켜다	kyeo-da
to turn off	끄다	kkeu-da
keyboard	키보드	ki-bo-deu
key	키	ki
mouse	마우스	ma-u-seu
mouse mat	마우스 패드	ma-u-seu pae-deu
button	버튼	beo-teun
cursor	커서	keo-seo
monitor	모니터	mo-ni-teo
screen	화면, 스크린	hwa-myeon
hard disk	하드 디스크	ha-deu di-seu-keu
hard disk capacity	하드 디스크 용량	ha-deu di-seu-keu yong-nyang
memory	메모리	me-mo-ri
random access memory	램	raem
file	파일	pa-il
folder	폴더	pol-deo
to open (vt)	열다	yeol-da
to close (vt)	닫다	dat-da
to save (vt)	저장하다	jeo-jang-ha-da
to delete (vt)	삭제하다	sak-je-ha-da
to copy (vt)	복사하다	bok-sa-ha-da
to sort (vt)	정렬하다	jeong-nyeol-ha-da
to transfer (copy)	전송하다	jeon-song-ha-da
programme	프로그램	peu-ro-geu-raem
software	소프트웨어	so-peu-teu-we-eo
programmer	프로그래머	peu-ro-geu-rae-meo
to program (vt)	프로그램을 작성하다	peu-ro-geu-rae-meul jak-seong-ha-da
hacker	해커	hae-keo
password	비밀번호	bi-mil-beon-ho
virus	바이러스	ba-i-reo-seu

to find, to detect	발견하다	bal-gyeon-ha-da
byte	바이트	ba-i-teu
megabyte	메가바이트	me-ga-ba-i-teu

| data | 데이터 | de-i-teo |
| database | 데이터베이스 | de-i-teo-be-i-seu |

cable (USB, etc.)	케이블	ke-i-beul
to disconnect (vt)	연결해제하다	yeon-gyeol-hae-je-ha-da
to connect (sth to sth)	연결하다	yeon-gyeol-ha-da

166. Internet. E-mail

Internet	인터넷	in-teo-net
browser	브라우저	beu-ra-u-jeo
search engine	검색 엔진	geom-saek gen-jin
provider	인터넷 서비스 제공자	in-teo-net seo-bi-seu je-gong-ja

webmaster	웹마스터	wem-ma-seu-teo
website	웹사이트	wep-sa-i-teu
web page	웹페이지	wep-pe-i-ji

| address (e-mail ~) | 주소 | ju-so |
| address book | 주소록 | ju-so-rok |

| postbox | 우편함 | u-pyeon-ham |
| post | 메일 | me-il |

message	메시지	me-si-ji
sender	발송인	bal-song-in
to send (vt)	보내다	bo-nae-da
sending (of mail)	발송	bal-song
receiver	수신인	su-sin-in
to receive (vt)	받다	bat-da

| correspondence | 서신 교환 | seo-sin gyo-hwan |
| to correspond (vi) | 편지를 주고 받다 | pyeon-ji-reul ju-go bat-da |

file	파일	pa-il
to download (vt)	다운받다	da-un-bat-da
to create (vt)	창조하다	chang-jo-ha-da
to delete (vt)	삭제하다	sak-je-ha-da
deleted (adj)	삭제된	sak-je-doen

connection (ADSL, etc.)	연결	yeon-gyeol
speed	속도	sok-do
access	접속	jeop-sok
port (e.g. input ~)	포트	po-teu

connection (make a ~)	연결	yeon-gyeol
to connect to ... (vi)	··· 에 연결하다	... e yeon-gyeol-ha-da
to select (vt)	선택하다	seon-taek-a-da
to search (for ...)	··· 를 검색하다	... reul geom-saek-a-da

167. Electricity

electricity	전기	jeon-gi
electric, electrical (adj)	전기의	jeon-gi-ui
electric power station	발전소	bal-jeon-so
energy	에너지	e-neo-ji
electric power	전력	jeol-lyeok
light bulb	전구	jeon-gu
torch	손전등	son-jeon-deung
street light	가로등	ga-ro-deung
light	전깃불	jeon-git-bul
to turn on	켜다	kyeo-da
to turn off	끄다	kkeu-da
to turn off the light	불을 끄다	bu-reul kkeu-da
to burn out (vi)	끊어지다	kkeu-neo-ji-da
short circuit	쇼트	syo-teu
broken wire	절단	jeol-dan
contact (electrical ~)	접촉	jeop-chok
light switch	스위치	seu-wi-chi
socket outlet	소켓	so-ket
plug	플러그	peul-leo-geu
extension lead	연장 코드	yeon-jang ko-deu
fuse	퓨즈	pyu-jeu
cable, wire	전선	jeon-seon
wiring	배선	bae-seon
ampere	암페어	am-pe-eo
amperage	암페어수	am-pe-eo-su
volt	볼트	bol-teu
voltage	전압	jeon-ap
electrical device	전기기구	jeon-gi-gi-gu
indicator	센서	sen-seo
electrician	전기 기사	jeon-gi gi-sa
to solder (vt)	납땜하다	nap-ttaem-ha-da
soldering iron	납땜인두	nap-ttaem-in-du
electric current	전류	jeol-lyu

168. Tools

tool, instrument	공구	gong-gu
tools	공구	gong-gu
equipment (factory ~)	장비	jang-bi
hammer	망치	mang-chi
screwdriver	나사돌리개	na-sa-dol-li-gae
axe	도끼	do-kki

saw	톱	top
to saw (vt)	톱을 켜다	to-beul kyeo-da
plane (tool)	대패	dae-pae
to plane (vt)	대패질하다	dae-pae-jil-ha-da
soldering iron	납땜인두	nap-ttaem-in-du
to solder (vt)	납땜하다	nap-ttaem-ha-da

file (tool)	줄	jul
carpenter pincers	집게	jip-ge
combination pliers	펜치	pen-chi
chisel	끌	kkeul

drill bit	드릴 비트	deu-ril bi-teu
electric drill	전동 드릴	jeon-dong deu-ril
to drill (vi, vt)	뚫다	ttul-ta

| knife | 칼, 나이프 | kal, na-i-peu |
| blade | 칼날 | kal-lal |

sharp (blade, etc.)	날카로운	nal-ka-ro-un
dull, blunt (adj)	무딘	mu-din
to get blunt (dull)	무뎌지다	mu-dyeo-ji-da
to sharpen (vt)	갈다	gal-da

bolt	볼트	bol-teu
nut	너트	neo-teu
thread (of a screw)	나사산	na-sa-san
wood screw	나사못	na-sa-mot

| nail | 못 | mot |
| nailhead | 못대가리 | mot-dae-ga-ri |

ruler (for measuring)	자	ja
tape measure	줄자	jul-ja
spirit level	수준기	su-jun-gi
magnifying glass	돋보기	dot-bo-gi

measuring instrument	계측기	gye-cheuk-gi
to measure (vt)	측정하다	cheuk-jeong-ha-da
scale (temperature ~, etc.)	눈금	nun-geum
readings	판독값	pan-dok-gap

| compressor | 컴프레서 | keom-peu-re-seo |
| microscope | 현미경 | hyeon-mi-gyeong |

pump (e.g. water ~)	펌프	peom-peu
robot	로봇	ro-bot
laser	레이저	re-i-jeo

spanner	스패너	seu-pae-neo
adhesive tape	스카치 테이프	seu-ka-chi te-i-peu
glue	접착제	jeop-chak-je

sandpaper	사포	sa-po
magnet	자석	ja-seok
gloves	장갑	jang-gap

rope	밧줄	bat-jul
cord	끈	kkeun
wire (e.g. telephone ~)	전선	jeon-seon
cable	케이블	ke-i-beul

sledgehammer	슬레지해머	seul-le-ji-hae-meo
prybar	쇠지레	soe-ji-re
ladder	사다리	sa-da-ri
stepladder	접사다리	jeop-sa-da-ri

to screw (tighten)	돌려서 조이다	dol-lyeo-seo jo-i-da
to unscrew (lid, filter, etc.)	열리다	yeol-li-da
to tighten (e.g. with a clamp)	조이다	jo-i-da
to glue, to stick	붙이다	bu-chi-da
to cut (vt)	자르다	ja-reu-da

malfunction (fault)	고장	go-jang
repair (mending)	수리	su-ri
to repair, to fix (vt)	보수하다	bo-su-ha-da
to adjust (machine, etc.)	조절하다	jo-jeol-ha-da

to check (to examine)	확인하다	hwa-gin-ha-da
checking	확인	hwa-gin
readings	판독값	pan-dok-gap

| reliable, solid (machine) | 믿을 만한 | mi-deul man-han |
| complex (adj) | 복잡한 | bok-ja-pan |

to rust (get rusted)	녹이 슬다	no-gi seul-da
rusty (adj)	녹이 슨	no-gi seun
rust	녹	nok

Transport

aeroplane	비행기	bi-haeng-gi
air ticket	비행기표	bi-haeng-gi-pyo
airline	항공사	hang-gong-sa
airport	공항	gong-hang
supersonic (adj)	초음속의	cho-eum-so-gui
pilot	비행사	bi-haeng-sa
stewardess	승무원	seung-mu-won
navigator	항법사	hang-beop-sa
wings	날개	nal-gae
tail	꼬리	kko-ri
cockpit	조종석	jo-jong-seok
engine	엔진	en-jin
undercarriage (landing gear)	착륙 장치	chang-nyuk jang-chi
turbine	터빈	teo-bin
propeller	추진기	chu-jin-gi
black box	블랙박스	beul-laek-bak-seu
yoke (control column)	조종간	jo-jong-gan
fuel	연료	yeol-lyo
safety card	안전 안내서	an-jeon an-nae-seo
oxygen mask	산소 마스크	san-so ma-seu-keu
uniform	제복	je-bok
lifejacket	구명조끼	gu-myeong-jo-kki
parachute	낙하산	nak-a-san
takeoff	이륙	i-ryuk
to take off (vi)	이륙하다	i-ryuk-a-da
runway	활주로	hwal-ju-ro
visibility	시계	si-gye
flight (act of flying)	비행	bi-haeng
altitude	고도	go-do
air pocket	에어 포켓	e-eo po-ket
seat	자리	ja-ri
headphones	헤드폰	he-deu-pon
folding tray (tray table)	접는 테이블	jeom-neun te-i-beul
airplane window	창문	chang-mun
aisle	통로	tong-no

170. Train

train	기차, 열차	gi-cha, nyeol-cha
commuter train	통근 열차	tong-geun nyeol-cha
express train	급행 열차	geu-paeng yeol-cha
diesel locomotive	디젤 기관차	di-jel gi-gwan-cha
steam locomotive	증기 기관차	jeung-gi gi-gwan-cha
coach, carriage	객차	gaek-cha
buffet car	식당차	sik-dang-cha
rails	레일	re-il
railway	철도	cheol-do
sleeper (track support)	침목	chim-mok
platform (railway ~)	플랫폼	peul-laet-pom
platform (~ 1, 2, etc.)	길	gil
semaphore	신호기	sin-ho-gi
station	역	yeok
train driver	기관사	gi-gwan-sa
porter (of luggage)	포터	po-teo
carriage attendant	차장	cha-jang
passenger	승객	seung-gaek
ticket inspector	검표원	geom-pyo-won
corridor (in train)	통로	tong-no
emergency brake	비상 브레이크	bi-sang beu-re-i-keu
compartment	침대차	chim-dae-cha
berth	침대	chim-dae
upper berth	윗침대	wit-chim-dae
lower berth	아래 침대	a-rae chim-dae
bed linen, bedding	침구	chim-gu
ticket	표	pyo
timetable	시간표	si-gan-pyo
information display	안내 전광판	an-nae jeon-gwang-pan
to leave, to depart	떠난다	tteo-na-da
departure (of a train)	출발	chul-bal
to arrive (ab. train)	도착하다	do-chak-a-da
arrival	도착	do-chak
to arrive by train	기차로 도착하다	gi-cha-ro do-chak-a-da
to get on the train	기차에 타다	gi-cha-e ta-da
to get off the train	기차에서 내리다	gi-cha-e-seo nae-ri-da
train crash	기차 사고	gi-cha sa-go
steam locomotive	증기 기관차	jeung-gi gi-gwan-cha
stoker, fireman	화부	hwa-bu
firebox	화실	hwa-sil
coal	석탄	seok-tan

171. Ship

ship	배	bae
vessel	배	bae
steamship	증기선	jeung-gi-seon
riverboat	강배	gang-bae
cruise ship	크루즈선	keu-ru-jeu-seon
cruiser	순양함	su-nyang-ham
yacht	요트	yo-teu
tugboat	예인선	ye-in-seon
sailing ship	범선	beom-seon
brigantine	쌍돛대 범선	ssang-dot-dae beom-seon
ice breaker	쇄빙선	swae-bing-seon
submarine	잠수함	jam-su-ham
boat (flat-bottomed ~)	보트	bo-teu
dinghy (lifeboat)	종선	jong-seon
lifeboat	구조선	gu-jo-seon
motorboat	모터보트	mo-teo-bo-teu
captain	선장	seon-jang
seaman	수부	su-bu
sailor	선원	seon-won
crew	승무원	seung-mu-won
boatswain	갑판장	gap-pan-jang
cook	요리사	yo-ri-sa
ship's doctor	선의	seon-ui
deck	갑판	gap-pan
mast	돛대	dot-dae
sail	돛	dot
hold	화물칸	hwa-mul-kan
bow (prow)	이물	i-mul
stern	고물	go-mul
oar	노	no
screw propeller	스크루	seu-keu-ru
cabin	선실	seon-sil
wardroom	사관실	sa-gwan-sil
engine room	엔진실	en-jin-sil
radio room	무전실	mu-jeon-sil
wave (radio)	전파	jeon-pa
spyglass	망원경	mang-won-gyeong
bell	종	jong
flag	기	gi
hawser (mooring ~)	밧줄	bat-jul
knot (bowline, etc.)	매듭	mae-deup

| deckrails | 난간 | nan-gan |
| gangway | 사다리 | sa-da-ri |

anchor	닻	dat
to weigh anchor	닻을 올리다	da-cheul rol-li-da
to drop anchor	닻을 내리다	da-cheul lae-ri-da
anchor chain	닻줄	dat-jul

port (harbour)	항구	hang-gu
quay, wharf	부두	bu-du
to berth (moor)	정박시키다	jeong-bak-si-ki-da
to cast off	출항하다	chul-hang-ha-da

trip, voyage	여행	yeo-haeng
cruise (sea trip)	크루즈	keu-ru-jeu
course (route)	항로	hang-no
route (itinerary)	노선	no-seon

fairway (safe water channel)	항로	hang-no
shallows	얕은 곳	ya-teun got
to run aground	좌초하다	jwa-cho-ha-da

storm	폭풍우	pok-pung-u
signal	신호	sin-ho
to sink (vi)	가라앉다	ga-ra-an-da
SOS (distress signal)	조난 신호	jo-nan sin-ho
ring buoy	구명부환	gu-myeong-bu-hwan

172. Airport

airport	공항	gong-hang
aeroplane	비행기	bi-haeng-gi
airline	항공사	hang-gong-sa
air traffic controller	관제사	gwan-je-sa

departure	출발	chul-bal
arrival	도착	do-chak
to arrive (by plane)	도착하다	do-chak-a-da

| departure time | 출발시간 | chul-bal-si-gan |
| arrival time | 도착시간 | do-chak-si-gan |

| to be delayed | 연기되다 | yeon-gi-doe-da |
| flight delay | 항공기 지연 | hang-gong-gi ji-yeon |

information board	안내 전광판	an-nae jeon-gwang-pan
information	정보	jeong-bo
to announce (vt)	알리다	al-li-da
flight (e.g. next ~)	비행편	bi-haeng-pyeon
customs	세관	se-gwan
customs officer	세관원	se-gwan-won
customs declaration	세관신고서	se-gwan-sin-go-seo
to fill in the declaration	세관 신고서를 작성하다	se-gwan sin-go-seo-reul jak-seong-ha-da

passport control	여권 검사	yeo-gwon geom-sa
luggage	짐, 수하물	jim, su-ha-mul
hand luggage	휴대 가능 수하물	hyu-dae ga-neung su-ha-mul
luggage trolley	수하물 카트	su-ha-mul ka-teu

landing	착륙	chang-nyuk
landing strip	활주로	hwal-ju-ro
to land (vi)	착륙하다	chang-nyuk-a-da
airstair (passenger stair)	승강계단	seung-gang-gye-dan

check-in	체크인	che-keu-in
check-in counter	체크인 카운터	che-keu-in ka-un-teo
to check-in (vi)	체크인하다	che-keu-in-ha-da
boarding card	탑승권	tap-seung-gwon
departure gate	탑승구	tap-seung-gu

transit	트랜싯, 환승	teu-raen-sit, hwan-seung
to wait (vt)	기다리다	gi-da-ri-da
departure lounge	공항 라운지	gong-hang na-un-ji
to see off	배웅하다	bae-ung-ha-da
to say goodbye	작별인사를 하다	jak-byeo-rin-sa-reul ha-da

173. Bicycle. Motorcycle

bicycle	자전거	ja-jeon-geo
scooter	스쿠터	seu-ku-teo
motorbike	오토바이	o-to-ba-i

to go by bicycle	자전거로 가다	ja-jeon-geo-ro ga-da
handlebars	핸들	haen-deul
pedal	페달	pe-dal
brakes	브레이크	beu-re-i-keu
bicycle seat (saddle)	안장	an-jang

pump	펌프	peom-peu
pannier rack	짐 선반	jim seon-ban
front lamp	라이트	ra-i-teu
helmet	헬멧	hel-met

wheel	바퀴	ba-kwi
mudguard	펜더	pen-deo
rim	테	te
spoke	바퀴살	ba-kwi-sal

Cars

| car | 자동차 | ja-dong-cha |
| sports car | 스포츠카 | seu-po-cheu-ka |

limousine	리무진	ri-mu-jin
off-road vehicle	오프로드 카	o-peu-ro-deu ka
drophead coupé (convertible)	오픈카	o-peun-ka
minibus	승합차	seung-hap-cha

| ambulance | 응급차 | eung-geup-cha |
| snowplough | 제설차 | je-seol-cha |

lorry	트럭	teu-reok
road tanker	유조차	yu-jo-cha
van (small truck)	유개 화물차	yu-gae hwa-mul-cha
tractor unit	트랙터	teu-raek-teo
trailer	트레일러	teu-re-il-leo

| comfortable (adj) | 편안한 | pyeon-an-han |
| used (adj) | 중고의 | jung-go-ui |

175. Cars. Bodywork

bonnet	보닛	bo-nit
wing	펜더	pen-deo
roof	지붕	ji-bung

windscreen	전면 유리	jeon-myeon nyu-ri
rear-view mirror	백미러	baeng-mi-reo
windscreen washer	워셔	wo-syeo
windscreen wipers	와이퍼	wa-i-peo

side window	옆 유리창	yeop pyu-ri-chang
electric window	파워윈도우	pa-wo-win-do-u
aerial	안테나	an-te-na
sunroof	선루프	seol-lu-peu

bumper	범퍼	beom-peo
boot	트렁크	teu-reong-keu
door	차문	cha-mun
door handle	도어핸들	do-eo-haen-deul
door lock	도어락	do-eo-rak

| number plate | 번호판 | beon-ho-pan |
| silencer | 머플러 | meo-peul-leo |

petrol tank	연료 탱크	yeol-lyo taeng-keu
exhaust pipe	배기관	bae-gi-gwan

accelerator	액셀	aek-sel
pedal	페달	pe-dal
accelerator pedal	액셀 페달	aek-sel pe-dal

brake	브레이크	beu-re-i-keu
brake pedal	브레이크 페달	beu-re-i-keu pe-dal
to brake (use the brake)	브레이크를 밟다	beu-re-i-keu-reul bap-da
handbrake	주차 브레이크	ju-cha beu-re-i-keu

clutch	클러치	keul-leo-chi
clutch pedal	클러치 페달	keul-leo-chi pe-dal
clutch disc	클러치 디스크	keul-leo-chi di-seu-keu
shock absorber	완충장치	wan-chung-jang-chi

wheel	바퀴	ba-kwi
spare tyre	스페어 타이어	seu-pe-eo ta-i-eo
tyre	타이어	ta-i-eo
wheel cover (hubcap)	휠캡	hwil-kaep

driving wheels	구동륜	gu-dong-nyun
front-wheel drive (as adj)	전륜 구동의	jeol-lyun gu-dong-ui
rear-wheel drive (as adj)	후륜 구동의	hu-ryun gu-dong-ui
all-wheel drive (as adj)	사륜 구동의	sa-ryun gu-dong-ui

gearbox	변속기	byeon-sok-gi
automatic (adj)	자동의	ja-dong-ui
mechanical (adj)	기계식의	gi-gye-si-gui
gear lever	기어	gi-eo

headlamp	헤드라이트	he-deu-ra-i-teu
headlights	헤드라이트	he-deu-ra-i-teu

dipped headlights	하향등	ha-hyang-deung
full headlights	상향등	sang-hyang-deung
brake light	브레이크 등	beu-re-i-keu deung

sidelights	미등	mi-deung
hazard lights	비상등	bi-sang-deung
fog lights	안개등	an-gae-deung
turn indicator	방향지시등	bang-hyang-ji-si-deung
reversing light	후미등	hu-mi-deung

176. Cars. Passenger compartment

car interior	내부	nae-bu
leather (as adj)	가죽의	ga-ju-gui
velour (as adj)	벨루어의	bel-lu-eo-ui
upholstery	커버	keo-beo

instrument (gage)	계기	gye-gi
dashboard	계기반	gye-gi-ban

| speedometer | 속도계 | sok-do-gye |
| needle (pointer) | 지침 | ji-chim |

mileometer	주행기록계	ju-haeng-gi-rok-gye
indicator (sensor)	센서	sen-seo
level	레벨	re-bel
warning light	경고등	gyeong-go-deung

steering wheel	핸들	haen-deul
horn	경적	gyeong-jeok
button	버튼	beo-teun
switch	스위치	seu-wi-chi

seat	좌석	jwa-seok
backrest	등받이	deung-ba-ji
headrest	머리 받침	meo-ri bat-chim
seat belt	안전 벨트	an-jeon bel-teu
to fasten the belt	안전 벨트를 매다	an-jeon bel-teu-reul mae-da
adjustment (of seats)	조절	jo-jeol

| airbag | 에어백 | e-eo-baek |
| air-conditioner | 에어컨 | e-eo-keon |

radio	라디오	ra-di-o
CD player	씨디 플레이어	ssi-di peul-le-i-eo
to turn on	켜다	kyeo-da
aerial	안테나	an-te-na
glove box	글러브 박스	geul-leo-beu bak-seu
ashtray	재떨이	jae-tteo-ri

177. Cars. Engine

engine	엔진	en-jin
motor	모터	mo-teo
diesel (as adj)	디젤의	di-je-rui
petrol (as adj)	가솔린	ga-sol-lin

engine volume	배기량	bae-gi-ryang
power	출력	chul-lyeok
horsepower	마력	ma-ryeok
piston	피스톤	pi-seu-ton
cylinder	실린더	sil-lin-deo
valve	밸브	bael-beu

injector	연료 분사기	yeol-lyo bun-sa-gi
generator (alternator)	발전기	bal-jeon-gi
carburettor	카뷰레터	ka-byu-re-teo
motor oil	엔진 오일	en-jin o-il

radiator	라디에이터	ra-di-e-i-teo
coolant	냉매	naeng-mae
cooling fan	냉각팬	paen
battery (accumulator)	배터리	bae-teo-ri
starter	시동기	si-dong-gi

| ignition | 점화 장치 | jeom-hwa jang-chi |
| sparking plug | 점화플러그 | jeom-hwa-peul-leo-geu |

terminal (battery ~)	전극	jeon-geuk
positive terminal	플러스	peul-leo-seu
negative terminal	마이너스	ma-i-neo-seu
fuse	퓨즈	pyu-jeu

air filter	공기 필터	gong-gi pil-teo
oil filter	오일 필터	o-il pil-teo
fuel filter	연료 필터	yeol-lyo pil-teo

178. Cars. Crash. Repair

car crash	사고	sa-go
traffic accident	교통 사고	gyo-tong sa-go
to crash (into the wall, etc.)	들이받다	deu-ri-bat-da
to get smashed up	부서지다	bu-seo-ji-da
damage	피해	pi-hae
intact (unscathed)	손상 없는	son-sang eom-neun

| to break down (vi) | 고장 나다 | go-jang na-da |
| towrope | 견인줄 | gyeon-in-jul |

puncture	펑크	peong-keu
to have a puncture	펑크 나다	peong-keu na-da
to pump up	타이어 부풀리다	ta-i-eo bu-pul-li-da
pressure	압력	am-nyeok
to check (to examine)	확인하다	hwa-gin-ha-da

repair	수리	su-ri
garage (auto service shop)	정비소	jeong-bi-so
spare part	예비 부품	ye-bi bu-pum
part	부품	bu-pum

bolt (with nut)	볼트	bol-teu
screw (fastener)	나사	na-sa
nut	너트	neo-teu
washer	와셔	wa-syeo
bearing (e.g. ball ~)	베어링	be-eo-ring

tube	파이프	pa-i-peu
gasket (head ~)	개스킷	gae-seu-kit
cable, wire	전선	jeon-seon

jack	잭	jaek
spanner	스패너	seu-pae-neo
hammer	망치	mang-chi
pump	펌프	peom-peu
screwdriver	나사돌리개	na-sa-dol-li-gae

fire extinguisher	소화기	so-hwa-gi
warning triangle	안전 삼각대	an-jeon sam-gak-dae
to stall (vi)	멎다	meot-da

| stall (n) | 정지 | jeong-ji |
| to be broken | 부서지다 | bu-seo-ji-da |

to overheat (vi)	과열되다	gwa-yeol-doe-da
to be clogged up	막히다	mak-i-da
to freeze up (pipes, etc.)	얼다	eol-da
to burst (vi, ab. tube)	터지다	teo-ji-da

pressure	압력	am-nyeok
level	레벨	re-bel
slack (~ belt)	느슨한	neu-seun-han

dent	덴트	den-teu
knocking noise (engine)	똑똑거리는 소음	ttok-ttok-geo-ri-neun so-eum
crack	균열	gyu-nyeol
scratch	긁힘	geuk-him

179. Cars. Road

road	도로	do-ro
motorway	고속도로	go-sok-do-ro
highway	고속도로	go-sok-do-ro
direction (way)	방향	bang-hyang
distance	거리	geo-ri

bridge	다리	da-ri
car park	주차장	ju-cha-jang
square	광장	gwang-jang
road junction	인터체인지	in-teo-che-in-ji
tunnel	터널	teo-neol

petrol station	주유소	ju-yu-so
car park	주차장	ju-cha-jang
petrol pump	가솔린 펌프	ga-sol-lin peom-peu
auto repair shop	정비소	jeong-bi-so
to fill up	기름을 넣다	gi-reu-meul leo-ta
fuel	연료	yeol-lyo
jerrycan	통	tong

asphalt, tarmac	아스팔트	a-seu-pal-teu
road markings	노면 표지	no-myeon pyo-ji
kerb	도로 경계석	do-ro gyeong-gye-seok
crash barrier	가드레일	ga-deu-re-il
ditch	도랑	do-rang
roadside (shoulder)	길가	gil-ga
lamppost	가로등	ga-ro-deung

to drive (a car)	운전하다	un-jeon-ha-da
to turn (e.g., ~ left)	돌다	dol-da
to make a U-turn	유턴하다	yu-teon-ha-da
reverse (~ gear)	후진 기어	hu-jin gi-eo

| to honk (vi) | 경적을 울리다 | gyeong-jeo-geul rul-li-da |
| honk (sound) | 경적 | gyeong-jeok |

to get stuck (in the mud, etc.)	빠지다	ppa-ji-da
to spin the wheels	미끄러지다	mi-kkeu-reo-ji-da
to cut, to turn off (vt)	멈추다	meom-chu-da

speed	속도	sok-do
to exceed the speed limit	과속으로 달리다	gwa-so-geu-ro dal-li-da
to give a ticket	딱지를 떼다	ttak-ji-reul tte-da
traffic lights	신호등	sin-ho-deung
driving licence	운전 면허증	un-jeon myeon-heo-jeung

level crossing	십자로	sip-ja-ro
crossroads	교차로	gyo-cha-ro
zebra crossing	횡단 보도	hoeng-dan bo-do
bend, curve	커브	keo-beu
pedestrian precinct	보행자 공간	bo-haeng-ja gong-gan

180. Signs

Highway Code	교통 규칙	gyo-tong gyu-chik
road sign (traffic sign)	도로 표지	do-ro pyo-ji
overtaking	추월	chu-wol
curve	커브	keo-beu
U-turn	유턴	yu-teon
roundabout	로터리	ro-teo-ri

No entry	진입 금지	ji-nip geum-ji
All vehicles prohibited	통행금지	tong-haeng-geum-ji
No overtaking	추월 금지	chu-wol geum-ji
No parking	주차금지	ju-cha-geum-ji
No stopping	정차 금지	jeong-cha geum-ji

dangerous curve	급커브	geup-keo-beu
steep descent	내리막경사	nae-ri-mak-gyeong-sa
one-way traffic	일방통행	il-bang-tong-haeng
zebra crossing	횡단 보도	hoeng-dan bo-do
slippery road	미끄러운 도로	mi-kkeu-reo-un do-ro
GIVE WAY	양보	yang-bo

PEOPLE. LIFE EVENTS

181. Holidays. Event

celebration, holiday	휴일	hyu-il
national day	국경일	guk-gyeong-il
public holiday	공휴일	gong-hyu-il
to commemorate (vt)	기념하다	gi-nyeom-ha-da
event (happening)	사건	sa-geon
event (organized activity)	이벤트	i-ben-teu
banquet (party)	연회	yeon-hoe
reception (formal party)	리셉션	ri-sep-syeon
feast	연회	yeon-hoe
anniversary	기념일	gi-nyeom-il
jubilee	기념일	gi-nyeom-il
to celebrate (vt)	경축하다	gyeong-chuk-a-da
New Year	새해	sae-hae
Happy New Year!	새해 복 많이 받으세요!	sae-hae bok ma-ni ba-deu-se-yo!
Father Christmas	산타클로스	san-ta-keul-lo-seu
Christmas	크리스마스	keu-ri-seu-ma-seu
Merry Christmas!	성탄을 축하합니다!	seong-ta-neul chuk-a-ham-ni-da!
Christmas tree	크리스마스트리	keu-ri-seu-ma-seu-teu-ri
fireworks (fireworks show)	불꽃놀이	bul-kkon-no-ri
wedding	결혼식	gyeol-hon-sik
groom	신랑	sil-lang
bride	신부	sin-bu
to invite (vt)	초대하다	cho-dae-ha-da
invitation card	초대장	cho-dae-jang
guest	손님	son-nim
to visit (~ your parents, etc.)	방문하다	bang-mun-ha-da
to meet the guests	손님을 맞이하다	son-ni-meul ma-ji-ha-da
gift, present	선물	seon-mul
to give (sth as present)	선물 하다	seon-mul ha-da
to receive gifts	선물 받다	seon-mul bat-da
bouquet (of flowers)	꽃다발	kkot-da-bal
congratulations	축하를	chuk-a-reul
to congratulate (vt)	축하하다	chuk-a-ha-da
greetings card	축하 카드	chuk-a ka-deu
to send a postcard	카드를 보내다	ka-deu-reul bo-nae-da

to get a postcard	카드 받다	ka-deu bat-da
toast	축배	chuk-bae
to offer (a drink, etc.)	대접하다	dae-jeo-pa-da
champagne	샴페인	syam-pe-in

to enjoy oneself	즐기다	jeul-gi-da
merriment (gaiety)	즐거움	jeul-geo-um
joy (emotion)	기쁨, 즐거움	gi-ppeun, jeul-geo-um

| dance | 춤 | chum |
| to dance (vi, vt) | 춤추다 | chum-chu-da |

| waltz | 왈츠 | wal-cheu |
| tango | 탱고 | taeng-go |

182. Funerals. Burial

cemetery	묘지	myo-ji
grave, tomb	무덤	mu-deom
cross	십자가	sip-ja-ga
gravestone	묘석	myo-seok
fence	울타리	ul-ta-ri
chapel	채플	chae-peul

death	죽음	ju-geum
to die (vi)	죽다	juk-da
the deceased	고인	go-in
mourning	상	sang

to bury (vt)	묻다	mut-da
undertakers	장례식장	jang-nye-sik-jang
funeral	장례식	jang-nye-sik

wreath	화환	hwa-hwan
coffin	관	gwan
hearse	영구차	yeong-gu-cha
shroud	수의	su-ui

| funerary urn | 유골 단지 | yu-gol dan-ji |
| crematorium | 화장장 | hwa-jang-jang |

obituary	부고	bu-go
to cry (weep)	울다	ul-da
to sob (vi)	흐느껴 울다	heu-neu-kkyeo ul-da

183. War. Soldiers

platoon	소대	so-dae
company	중대	jung-dae
regiment	연대	yeon-dae
army	군대	gun-dae
division	사단	sa-dan

| section, squad | 분대 | bun-dae |
| host (army) | 군대 | gun-dae |

| soldier | 군인 | gun-in |
| officer | 장교 | jang-gyo |

private	일병	il-byeong
sergeant	병장	byeong-jang
lieutenant	중위	jung-wi
captain	대위	dae-wi
major	소령	so-ryeong
colonel	대령	dae-ryeong
general	장군	jang-gun

sailor	선원	seon-won
captain	대위	dae-wi
boatswain	갑판장	gap-pan-jang

artilleryman	포병	po-byeong
paratrooper	낙하산 부대원	nak-a-san bu-dae-won
pilot	조종사	jo-jong-sa
navigator	항법사	hang-beop-sa
mechanic	정비공	jeong-bi-gong

pioneer (sapper)	공병대원	gong-byeong-dae-won
parachutist	낙하산병	nak-a-san-byeong
reconnaissance scout	정찰대	jeong-chal-dae
sniper	저격병	jeo-gyeok-byeong

patrol (group)	순찰	sun-chal
to patrol (vt)	순찰하다	sun-chal-ha-da
sentry, guard	경비병	gyeong-bi-byeong

warrior	전사	jeon-sa
patriot	애국자	ae-guk-ja
hero	영웅	yeong-ung
heroine	여걸	yeo-geol

traitor	매국노	mae-gung-no
deserter	탈영병	ta-ryeong-byeong
to desert (vi)	탈영하다	ta-ryeong-ha-da

mercenary	용병	yong-byeong
recruit	훈련병	hul-lyeon-byeong
volunteer	지원병	ji-won-byeong

dead (n)	사망자	sa-mang-ja
wounded (n)	부상자	bu-sang-ja
prisoner of war	포로	po-ro

184. War. Military actions. Part 1

| war | 전쟁 | jeon-jaeng |
| to be at war | 참전하다 | cham-jeon-ha-da |

civil war	내전	nae-jeon
treacherously (adv)	비겁하게	bi-geo-pa-ge
declaration of war	선전 포고	seon-jeon po-go
to declare (~ war)	선포하다	seon-po-ha-da
aggression	침략	chim-nyak
to attack (invade)	공격하다	gong-gyeo-ka-da

to invade (vt)	침략하다	chim-nyak-a-da
invader	침략자	chim-nyak-ja
conqueror	정복자	jeong-bok-ja

defence	방어	bang-eo
to defend (a country, etc.)	방어하다	bang-eo-ha-da
to defend (against …)	… 를 방어하다	… reul bang-eo-ha-da

enemy	적	jeok
foe, adversary	원수	won-su
enemy (as adj)	적의	jeo-gui

strategy	전략	jeol-lyak
tactics	전술	jeon-sul

order	명령	myeong-nyeong
command (order)	명령	myeong-nyeong
to order (vt)	명령하다	myeong-nyeong-ha-da
mission	임무	im-mu
secret (adj)	비밀의	bi-mi-rui

battle	전투	jeon-tu
battle	전투	jeon-tu
combat	전투	jeon-tu

attack	공격	gong-gyeok
charge (assault)	돌격	dol-gyeok
to storm (vt)	습격하다	seup-gyeok-a-da
siege (to be under ~)	포위 공격	po-wi gong-gyeok

offensive (n)	공세	gong-se
to go on the offensive	공격하다	gong-gyeo-ka-da

retreat	퇴각	toe-gak
to retreat (vi)	퇴각하다	toe-gak-a-da

encirclement	포위	po-wi
to encircle (vt)	둘러싸다	dul-leo-ssa-da

bombing (by aircraft)	폭격	pok-gyeok
to drop a bomb	폭탄을 투하하다	pok-ta-neul tu-ha-ha-da
to bomb (vt)	폭격하다	pok-gyeok-a-da
explosion	폭발	pok-bal

shot	발포	bal-po
to fire (~ a shot)	쏘다	sso-da
firing (burst of ~)	사격	sa-gyeok
to aim (to point a weapon)	겨냥대다	gyeo-nyang-dae-da
to point (a gun)	총을 겨누다	chong-eul gyeo-nu-da

to hit (the target)	맞히다	ma-chi-da
to sink (~ a ship)	가라앉히다	ga-ra-an-chi-da
hole (in a ship)	구멍	gu-meong
to founder, to sink (vi)	가라앉히다	ga-ra-an-chi-da

front (war ~)	전선	jeon-seon
evacuation	철수	cheol-su
to evacuate (vt)	대피시키다	dae-pi-si-ki-da

trench	참호	cham-ho
barbed wire	가시철사	ga-si-cheol-sa
barrier (anti tank ~)	장애물	jang-ae-mul
watchtower	감시탑	gam-si-tap

military hospital	군 병원	gun byeong-won
to wound (vt)	부상을 입히다	bu-sang-eul ri-pi-da
wound	부상	bu-sang
wounded (n)	부상자	bu-sang-ja
to be wounded	부상을 입다	bu-sang-eul rip-da
serious (wound)	심각한	sim-gak-an

185. War. Military actions. Part 2

captivity	사로잡힘	sa-ro-ja-pim
to take captive	포로로 하다	po-ro-ro ha-da
to be held captive	사로잡히어	sa-ro-ja-pi-eo
to be taken captive	포로가 되다	po-ro-ga doe-da

concentration camp	강제 수용소	gang-je su-yong-so
prisoner of war	포로	po-ro
to escape (vi)	탈출하다	tal-chul-ha-da

to betray (vt)	팔아먹다	pa-ra-meok-da
betrayer	배반자	bae-ban-ja
betrayal	배반	bae-ban

| to execute (by firing squad) | 총살하다 | chong-sal-ha-da |
| execution (by firing squad) | 총살형 | chong-sal-hyeong |

equipment (military gear)	군장	gun-jang
shoulder board	계급 견장	gye-geup gyeon-jang
gas mask	가스 마스크	ga-seu ma-seu-keu

field radio	군용무전기	gu-nyong-mu-jeon-gi
cipher, code	암호	am-ho
secrecy	비밀 유지	bi-mil ryu-ji
password	비밀번호	bi-mil-beon-ho

land mine	지뢰	ji-roe
to mine (road, etc.)	지뢰를 매설하다	ji-roe-reul mae-seol-ha-da
minefield	지뢰밭	ji-roe-bat

| air-raid warning | 공습 경보 | gong-seup gyeong-bo |
| alarm (alert signal) | 경보 | gyeong-bo |

| signal | 신호 | sin-ho |
| signal flare | 신호탄 | sin-ho-tan |

headquarters	본부	bon-bu
reconnaissance	정찰	jeong-chal
situation	정세	jeong-se
report	보고	bo-go
ambush	기습	gi-seup
reinforcement (army)	강화	gang-hwa

target	과녁	gwa-nyeok
training area	성능 시험장	seong-neung si-heom-jang
military exercise	군사 훈련	gun-sa hul-lyeon

panic	공황	gong-hwang
devastation	파멸	pa-myeol
destruction, ruins	파괴	pa-goe
to destroy (vt)	파괴하다	pa-goe-ha-da

to survive (vi, vt)	살아남다	sa-ra-nam-da
to disarm (vt)	무장해제하다	mu-jang-hae-je-ha-da
to handle (~ a gun)	다루다	da-ru-da

| Attention! | 차려! | cha-ryeo! |
| At ease! | 쉬어! | swi-eo! |

feat, act of courage	무훈	mu-hun
oath (vow)	맹세	maeng-se
to swear (an oath)	맹세하다	maeng-se-ha-da

decoration (medal, etc.)	훈장	hun-jang
to award (give a medal to)	훈장을 주다	hun-jang-eul ju-da
medal	메달	me-dal
order (e.g. ~ of Merit)	훈장	hun-jang

victory	승리	seung-ni
defeat	패배	pae-bae
armistice	휴전	hyu-jeon

standard (battle flag)	기	gi
glory (honour, fame)	영광	yeong-gwang
parade	퍼레이드	peo-re-i-deu
to march (on parade)	행진하다	haeng-jin-ha-da

186. Weapons

| weapons | 무기 | mu-gi |
| firearms | 화기 | hwa-gi |

chemical weapons	화학 병기	hwa-hak byeong-gi
nuclear (adj)	핵의	hae-gui
nuclear weapons	핵무기	haeng-mu-gi
bomb	폭탄	pok-tan
atomic bomb	원자폭탄	won-ja-pok-tan

pistol (gun)	권총	gwon-chong
rifle	장총	jang-chong
submachine gun	기관단총	gi-gwan-dan-chong
machine gun	기관총	gi-gwan-chong
muzzle	총구	chong-gu
barrel	총열	chong-yeol
calibre	구경	gu-gyeong
trigger	방아쇠	bang-a-soe
sight (aiming device)	가늠자	ga-neum-ja
butt (shoulder stock)	개머리	gae-meo-ri
hand grenade	수류탄	su-ryu-tan
explosive	폭약	po-gyak
bullet	총알	chong-al
cartridge	탄약통	ta-nyak-tong
charge	화약	hwa-yak
ammunition	탄약	ta-nyak
bomber (aircraft)	폭격기	pok-gyeok-gi
fighter	전투기	jeon-tu-gi
helicopter	헬리콥터	hel-li-kop-teo
anti-aircraft gun	대공포	dae-gong-po
tank	전차	jeon-cha
artillery	대포	dae-po
gun (cannon, howitzer)	대포	dae-po
to lay (a gun)	총을 겨누다	chong-eul gyeo-nu-da
shell (projectile)	탄피	tan-pi
mortar bomb	박격포탄	bak-gyeok-po-tan
mortar	박격포	bak-gyeok-po
splinter (shell fragment)	포탄파편	po-tan-pa-pyeon
submarine	잠수함	jam-su-ham
torpedo	어뢰	eo-roe
missile	미사일	mi-sa-il
to load (gun)	장탄하다	jang-tan-ha-da
to shoot (vi)	쏘다	sso-da
to point at (the cannon)	총을 겨누다	chong-eul gyeo-nu-da
bayonet	총검	chong-geom
rapier	레이피어	re-i-pi-eo
sabre (e.g. cavalry ~)	군도	gun-do
spear (weapon)	창	chang
bow	활	hwal
arrow	화살	hwa-sal
musket	머스킷	meo-seu-kit
crossbow	석궁	seok-gung

187. Ancient people

primitive (prehistoric)	원시적인	won-si-jeo-gin
prehistoric (adj)	선사시대의	seon-sa-si-dae-ui
ancient (~ civilization)	고대의	go-dae-ui
Stone Age	석기 시대	seok-gi si-dae
Bronze Age	청동기 시대	cheong-dong-gi si-dae
Ice Age	빙하 시대	bing-ha si-dae
tribe	부족	bu-jok
cannibal	식인종	si-gin-jong
hunter	사냥꾼	sa-nyang-kkun
to hunt (vi, vt)	사냥하다	sa-nyang-ha-da
mammoth	매머드	mae-meo-deu
cave	동굴	dong-gul
fire	불	bul
campfire	모닥불	mo-dak-bul
cave painting	동굴 벽화	dong-gul byeok-wa
tool (e.g. stone axe)	도구	do-gu
spear	창	chang
stone axe	돌도끼	dol-do-kki
to be at war	참전하다	cham-jeon-ha-da
to domesticate (vt)	길들이다	gil-deu-ri-da
idol	우상	u-sang
to worship (vt)	숭배하다	sung-bae-ha-da
superstition	미신	mi-sin
evolution	진화	jin-hwa
development	개발	gae-bal
disappearance (extinction)	멸종	myeol-jong
to adapt oneself	적응하다	jeo-geung-ha-da
archaeology	고고학	go-go-hak
archaeologist	고고학자	go-go-hak-ja
archaeological (adj)	고고학의	go-go-ha-gui
excavation site	발굴 현장	bal-gul hyeon-jang
excavations	발굴	bal-gul
find (object)	발견물	bal-gyeon-mul
fragment	파편	pa-pyeon

188. Middle Ages

people (ethnic group)	민족	min-jok
peoples	민족	min-jok
tribe	부족	bu-jok
tribes	부족들	bu-jok-deul
barbarians	오랑캐	o-rang-kae
Gauls	갈리아인	gal-li-a-in

Goths	고트족	go-teu-jok
Slavs	슬라브족	seul-la-beu-jok
Vikings	바이킹	ba-i-king

| Romans | 로마 사람 | ro-ma sa-ram |
| Roman (adj) | 로마의 | ro-ma-ui |

Byzantines	비잔티움 사람들	bi-jan-ti-um sa-ram-deul
Byzantium	비잔티움	bi-jan-ti-um
Byzantine (adj)	비잔틴의	bi-jan-tin-ui

emperor	황제	hwang-je
leader, chief (tribal ~)	추장	chu-jang
powerful (~ king)	강력한	gang-nyeo-kan
king	왕	wang
ruler (sovereign)	통치자	tong-chi-ja

knight	기사	gi-sa
feudal lord	봉건 영주	bong-geon nyeong-ju
feudal (adj)	봉건적인	bong-geon-jeo-gin
vassal	봉신	bong-sin

duke	공작	gong-jak
earl	백작	baek-jak
baron	남작	nam-jak
bishop	주교	ju-gyo

armour	갑옷	ga-bot
shield	방패	bang-pae
sword	검	geom
visor	얼굴 가리개	eol-gul ga-ri-gae
chainmail	미늘 갑옷	mi-neul ga-bot

| Crusade | 십자군 | sip-ja-gun |
| crusader | 십자군 전사 | sip-ja-gun jeon-sa |

territory	영토	yeong-to
to attack (invade)	공격하다	gong-gyeo-ka-da
to conquer (vt)	정복하다	jeong-bok-a-da
to occupy (invade)	점령하다	jeom-nyeong-ha-da

siege (to be under ~)	포위 공격	po-wi gong-gyeok
besieged (adj)	포위당한	po-wi-dang-han
to besiege (vt)	포위하다	po-wi-ha-da

inquisition	이단심문	i-dan-sim-mun
inquisitor	종교 재판관	jong-gyo jae-pan-gwan
torture	고문	go-mun
cruel (adj)	잔혹한	jan-hok-an
heretic	이단자	i-dan-ja
heresy	이단으로	i-da-neu-ro

seafaring	항해	hang-hae
pirate	해적	hae-jeok
piracy	해적 행위	hae-jeok aeng-wi
boarding (attack)	널판장	neol-pan-jang

loot, booty	노획물	no-hoeng-mul
treasure	보물	bo-mul
discovery	발견	bal-gyeon
to discover (new land, etc.)	발견하다	bal-gyeon-ha-da
expedition	탐험	tam-heom
musketeer	총병	chong-byeong
cardinal	추기경	chu-gi-gyeong
heraldry	문장학	mun-jang-hak
heraldic (adj)	문장학의	mun-jang-ha-gui

189. Leader. Chief. Authorities

king	왕	wang
queen	여왕	yeo-wang
royal (adj)	왕족의	wang-jo-gui
kingdom	왕국	wang-guk
prince	왕자	wang-ja
princess	공주	gong-ju
president	대통령	dae-tong-nyeong
vice-president	부통령	bu-tong-nyeong
senator	상원의원	sang-won-ui-won
monarch	군주	gun-ju
ruler (sovereign)	통치자	tong-chi-ja
dictator	독재자	dok-jae-ja
tyrant	폭군	pok-gun
magnate	거물	geo-mul
director	사장	sa-jang
chief	추장	chu-jang
manager (director)	지배인	ji-bae-in
boss	상사	sang-sa
owner	소유자	so-yu-ja
head (~ of delegation)	책임자	chae-gim-ja
authorities	당국	dang-guk
superiors	상사	sang-sa
governor	주지사	ju-ji-sa
consul	영사	yeong-sa
diplomat	외교관	oe-gyo-gwan
mayor	시장	si-jang
sheriff	보안관	bo-an-gwan
emperor	황제	hwang-je
tsar, czar	황제	hwang-je
pharaoh	파라오	pa-ra-o
khan	칸	kan

190. Road. Way. Directions

road	도로	do-ro
way (direction)	길	gil
highway	고속도로	go-sok-do-ro
motorway	고속도로	go-sok-do-ro
trunk road	광역	gwang-yeok
main road	대로	dae-ro
dirt road	비포장도로	bi-po-jang-do-ro
pathway	길	gil
footpath (troddenpath)	오솔길	o-sol-gil
Where?	어디?	eo-di?
Where (to)?	어디로?	eo-di-ro?
From where?	어디로부터?	eo-di-ro-bu-teo?
direction (way)	방향	bang-hyang
to point (~ the way)	가리키다	ga-ri-ki-da
to the left	왼쪽으로	oen-jjo-geu-ro
to the right	오른쪽으로	o-reun-jjo-geu-ro
straight ahead (adv)	똑바로	ttok-ba-ro
back (e.g. to turn ~)	뒤로	dwi-ro
bend, curve	커브	keo-beu
to turn (e.g., ~ left)	돌다	dol-da
to make a U-turn	유턴하다	yu-teon-ha-da
to be visible	보이다	bo-i-da
(mountains, castle, etc.)		
to appear (come into view)	나타나다	na-ta-na-da
stop, halt (e.g., during a trip)	정지	jeong-ji
to rest, to pause (vi)	쉬다	swi-da
rest (pause)	휴양	hyu-yang
to lose one's way	길을 잃다	gi-reul ril-ta
to lead to ... (ab. road)	··· 로 이어지다	... ro i-eo-ji-da
to came out	나가다	na-ga-da
(e.g., on the highway)		
stretch (of the road)	구간	gu-gan
asphalt	아스팔트	a-seu-pal-teu
kerb	도로 경계석	do-ro gyeong-gye-seok
ditch	도랑	do-rang
manhole	맨홀	maen-hol
roadside (shoulder)	길가	gil-ga
pit, pothole	패인 곳	pae-in got
to go (on foot)	가다	ga-da
to overtake (vt)	추월하다	chu-wol-ha-da
step (footstep)	걸음	geo-reum

on foot (adv)	도보로	do-bo-ro
to block (road)	길을 막다	gi-reul mak-da
boom gate	차단기	cha-dan-gi
dead end	막다른길	mak-da-reun-gil

191. Breaking the law. Criminals. Part 1

bandit	산적	san-jeok
crime	범죄	beom-joe
criminal (person)	범죄자	beom-joe-ja

thief	도둑	do-duk
to steal (vi, vt)	훔치다	hum-chi-da
stealing (larceny)	절도	jeol-do
theft	도둑질	do-duk-jil

to kidnap (vt)	납치하다	nap-chi-ha-da
kidnapping	유괴	yu-goe
kidnapper	유괴범	yu-goe-beom

| ransom | 몸값 | mom-gap |
| to demand ransom | 몸값을 요구하다 | mom-gap-seul ryo-gu-ha-da |

| to rob (vt) | 뺏다 | ppaet-da |
| robber | 강도 | gang-do |

to extort (vt)	갈취하다	gal-chwi-ha-da
extortionist	갈취자	gal-chwi-ja
extortion	갈취	gal-chwi

to murder, to kill	죽이다	ju-gi-da
murder	살인	sa-rin
murderer	살인자	sa-rin-ja

gunshot	발포	bal-po
to fire (~ a shot)	쏘다	sso-da
to shoot to death	쏘아 죽이다	sso-a ju-gi-da
to shoot (vi)	쏘다	sso-da
shooting	발사	bal-sa

incident (fight, etc.)	사건	sa-geon
fight, brawl	몸싸움	mom-ssa-um
victim	희생자	hui-saeng-ja

to damage (vt)	해치다	hae-chi-da
damage	피해	pi-hae
dead body, corpse	시신	si-sin
grave (~ crime)	중대한	jung-dae-han

to attack (vt)	공격하다	gong-gyeo-ka-da
to beat (to hit)	때리다	ttae-ri-da
to beat up	조지다	jo-ji-da
to take (rob of sth)	훔치다	hum-chi-da
to stab to death	찔러 죽이다	jjil-leo ju-gi-da

to maim (vt)	불구로 만들다	bul-gu-ro man-deul-da
to wound (vt)	부상을 입히다	bu-sang-eul ri-pi-da
blackmail	공갈	gong-gal
to blackmail (vt)	공갈하다	gong-gal-ha-da
blackmailer	공갈범	gong-gal-beom
protection racket	폭력단의 갈취 행위	pong-nyeok-dan-ui gal-chwi haeng-wi
racketeer	모리배	mo-ri-bae
gangster	갱	gaeng
mafia	마피아	ma-pi-a
pickpocket	소매치기	so-mae-chi-gi
burglar	빈집털이범	bin-jip-teo-ri-beom
smuggling	밀수입	mil-su-ip
smuggler	밀수입자	mil-su-ip-ja
forgery	위조	wi-jo
to forge (counterfeit)	위조하다	wi-jo-ha-da
fake (forged)	가짜의	ga-jja-ui

192. Breaking the law. Criminals. Part 2

rape	강간	gang-gan
to rape (vt)	강간하다	gang-gan-ha-da
rapist	강간범	gang-gan-beom
maniac	미치광이	mi-chi-gwang-i
prostitute (fem.)	매춘부	mae-chun-bu
prostitution	매춘	mae-chun
pimp	포주	po-ju
drug addict	마약 중독자	ma-yak jung-dok-ja
drug dealer	마약 밀매자	ma-yak mil-mae-ja
to blow up (bomb)	폭발하다	pok-bal-ha-da
explosion	폭발	pok-bal
to set fire	방화하다	bang-hwa-ha-da
arsonist	방화범	bang-hwa-beom
terrorism	테러리즘	te-reo-ri-jeum
terrorist	테러리스트	te-reo-ri-seu-teu
hostage	볼모	bol-mo
to swindle (deceive)	속이다	so-gi-da
swindle, deception	사기	sa-gi
swindler	사기꾼	sa-gi-kkun
to bribe (vt)	뇌물을 주다	noe-mu-reul ju-da
bribery	뇌물 수수	noe-mul su-su
bribe	뇌물	noe-mul
poison	독	dok
to poison (vt)	독살하다	dok-sal-ha-da

to poison oneself	음독하다	eum-dok-a-da
suicide (act)	자살	ja-sal
suicide (person)	자살자	ja-sal-ja

to threaten (vt)	협박하다	hyeop-bak-a-da
threat	협박	hyeop-bak
to make an attempt	살해를 꾀하다	sal-hae-reul kkoe-ha-da
attempt (attack)	미수	mi-su

| to steal (a car) | 훔치는 | hum-chi-da |
| to hijack (a plane) | 납치하다 | nap-chi-ha-da |

| revenge | 복수 | bok-su |
| to avenge (get revenge) | 복수하다 | bok-su-ha-da |

to torture (vt)	고문하다	go-mun-ha-da
torture	고문	go-mun
to torment (vt)	괴롭히다	goe-ro-pi-da

pirate	해적	hae-jeok
hooligan	난동꾼	nan-dong-kkun
armed (adj)	무장한	mu-jang-han
violence	폭력	pong-nyeok

| spying (espionage) | 간첩행위 | gan-cheo-paeng-wi |
| to spy (vi) | 간첩 행위를 하다 | gan-cheop paeng-wi-reul ha-da |

193. Police. Law. Part 1

| justice | 정의 | jeong-ui |
| court (see you in ~) | 법정 | beop-jeong |

judge	판사	pan-sa
jurors	배심원	bae-sim-won
jury trial	배심 재판	bae-sim jae-pan
to judge, to try (vt)	재판에 부치다	jae-pan-e bu-chi-da

lawyer, barrister	변호사	byeon-ho-sa
defendant	피고	pi-go
dock	피고인석	pi-go-in-seok

| charge | 혐의 | hyeom-ui |
| accused | 형사 피고인 | pi-go-in |

| sentence | 형량 | hyeong-nyang |
| to sentence (vt) | 선고하다 | seon-go-ha-da |

guilty (culprit)	유죄	yu-joe
to punish (vt)	처벌하다	cheo-beol-ha-da
punishment	벌	beol

| fine (penalty) | 벌금 | beol-geum |
| life imprisonment | 종신형 | jong-sin-hyeong |

death penalty	사형	sa-hyeong
electric chair	전기 의자	jeon-gi ui-ja
gallows	교수대	gyo-su-dae

| to execute (vt) | 집행하다 | ji-paeng-ha-da |
| execution | 처형 | cheo-hyeong |

| prison | 교도소 | gyo-do-so |
| cell | 감방 | gam-bang |

escort (convoy)	호송	ho-song
prison officer	간수	gan-su
prisoner	죄수	joe-su

| handcuffs | 수갑 | su-gap |
| to handcuff (vt) | 수갑을 채우다 | su-ga-beul chae-u-da |

prison break	탈옥	ta-rok
to break out (vi)	탈옥하다	ta-rok-a-da
to disappear (vi)	사라지다	sa-ra-ji-da
to release (from prison)	출옥하다	chu-rok-a-da
amnesty	사면	sa-myeon

police	경찰	gyeong-chal
police officer	경찰관	gyeong-chal-gwan
police station	경찰서	gyeong-chal-seo
truncheon	경찰봉	gyeong-chal-bong
megaphone (loudhailer)	메가폰	me-ga-pon

patrol car	순찰차	sun-chal-cha
siren	사이렌	sa-i-ren
to turn on the siren	사이렌을 켜다	sa-i-re-neul kyeo-da
siren call	사이렌 소리	sa-i-ren so-ri

crime scene	범죄현장	beom-joe-hyeon-jang
witness	목격자	mok-gyeok-ja
freedom	자유	ja-yu
accomplice	공범자	gong-beom-ja
to flee (vi)	달아나다	da-ra-na-da
trace (to leave a ~)	흔적	heun-jeok

194. Police. Law. Part 2

search (investigation)	조사	jo-sa
to look for ...	… 를 찾다	... reul chat-da
suspicion	혐의	hyeom-ui
suspicious (e.g., ~ vehicle)	의심스러운	ui-sim-seu-reo-un
to stop (cause to halt)	멈추다	meom-chu-da
to detain (keep in custody)	구류하다	gu-ryu-ha-da

case (lawsuit)	판례	pal-lye
investigation	조사	jo-sa
detective	형사	hyeong-sa
investigator	조사관	jo-sa-gwan

hypothesis	가설	ga-seol
motive	동기	dong-gi
interrogation	심문	sim-mun
to interrogate (vt)	신문하다	sin-mun-ha-da
to question	심문하다	sim-mun-ha-da
(~ neighbors, etc.)		
check (identity ~)	확인	hwa-gin

round-up (raid)	일제 검거	il-je geom-geo
search (~ warrant)	수색	su-saek
chase (pursuit)	추적	chu-jeok
to pursue, to chase	추적하다	chu-jeok-a-da
to track (a criminal)	추적하다	chu-jeok-a-da

arrest	체포	che-po
to arrest (sb)	체포하다	che-po-ha-da
to catch (thief, etc.)	붙잡다	but-jap-da
capture	체포	che-po

document	서류	seo-ryu
proof (evidence)	증거	jeung-geo
to prove (vt)	증명하다	jeung-myeong-ha-da
footprint	발자국	bal-ja-guk
fingerprints	지문	ji-mun
piece of evidence	증거물	jeung-geo-mul

alibi	알리바이	al-li-ba-i
innocent (not guilty)	무죄인	mu-joe-in
injustice	부정	bu-jeong
unjust, unfair (adj)	부당한	bu-dang-han

criminal (adj)	범죄의	beom-joe-ui
to confiscate (vt)	몰수하다	mol-su-ha-da
drug (illegal substance)	마약	ma-yak
weapon, gun	무기	mu-gi
to disarm (vt)	무장해제하다	mu-jang-hae-je-ha-da
to order (command)	명령하다	myeong-nyeong-ha-da
to disappear (vi)	사라지다	sa-ra-ji-da

law	법률	beom-nyul
legal, lawful (adj)	합법적인	hap-beop-jeo-gin
illegal, illicit (adj)	불법적인	bul-beop-jeo-gin

responsibility (blame)	책임	chae-gim
responsible (adj)	책임 있는	chae-gim in-neun

NATURE

The Earth. Part 1

space	우주	u-ju
space (as adj)	우주의	u-ju-ui
outer space	우주 공간	u-ju gong-gan
world	세계	se-gye
universe	우주	u-ju
galaxy	은하	eun-ha
star	별, 항성	byeol, hang-seong
constellation	별자리	byeol-ja-ri
planet	행성	haeng-seong
satellite	인공위성	in-gong-wi-seong
meteorite	운석	un-seok
comet	혜성	hye-seong
asteroid	소행성	so-haeng-seong
orbit	궤도	gwe-do
to revolve (~ around the Earth)	회전한다	hoe-jeon-han-da
atmosphere	대기	dae-gi
the Sun	태양	tae-yang
solar system	태양계	tae-yang-gye
solar eclipse	일식	il-sik
the Earth	지구	ji-gu
the Moon	달	dal
Mars	화성	hwa-seong
Venus	금성	geum-seong
Jupiter	목성	mok-seong
Saturn	토성	to-seong
Mercury	수성	su-seong
Uranus	천왕성	cheon-wang-seong
Neptune	해왕성	hae-wang-seong
Pluto	명왕성	myeong-wang-seong
Milky Way	은하수	eun-ha-su
Great Bear (Ursa Major)	큰곰자리	keun-gom-ja-ri
North Star	북극성	buk-geuk-seong
Martian	화성인	hwa-seong-in
extraterrestrial (n)	외계인	oe-gye-in

| alien | 외계인 | oe-gye-in |
| flying saucer | 비행 접시 | bi-haeng jeop-si |

| spaceship | 우주선 | u-ju-seon |
| space station | 우주 정거장 | u-ju jeong-nyu-jang |

engine	엔진	en-jin
nozzle	노즐	no-jeul
fuel	연료	yeol-lyo

| cockpit, flight deck | 조종석 | jo-jong-seok |
| aerial | 안테나 | an-te-na |

porthole	현창	hyeon-chang
solar panel	태양 전지	tae-yang jeon-ji
spacesuit	우주복	u-ju-bok

| weightlessness | 무중력 | mu-jung-nyeok |
| oxygen | 산소 | san-so |

| docking (in space) | 도킹 | do-king |
| to dock (vi, vt) | 도킹하다 | do-king-ha-da |

observatory	천문대	cheon-mun-dae
telescope	망원경	mang-won-gyeong
to observe (vt)	관찰하다	gwan-chal-ha-da
to explore (vt)	탐험하다	tam-heom-ha-da

196. The Earth

the Earth	지구	ji-gu
the globe (the Earth)	지구	ji-gu
planet	행성	haeng-seong

atmosphere	대기	dae-gi
geography	지리학	ji-ri-hak
nature	자연	ja-yeon

globe (table ~)	지구의	ji-gu-ui
map	지도	ji-do
atlas	지도첩	ji-do-cheop

| Europe | 유럽 | yu-reop |
| Asia | 아시아 | a-si-a |

| Africa | 아프리카 | a-peu-ri-ka |
| Australia | 호주 | ho-ju |

America	아메리카 대륙	a-me-ri-ka dae-ryuk
North America	북아메리카	bu-ga-me-ri-ka
South America	남아메리카	nam-a-me-ri-ka

| Antarctica | 남극 대륙 | nam-geuk dae-ryuk |
| the Arctic | 극지방 | geuk-ji-bang |

197. Cardinal directions

north	북쪽	buk-jjok
to the north	북쪽으로	buk-jjo-geu-ro
in the north	북쪽에	buk-jjo-ge
northern (adj)	북쪽의	buk-jjo-gui

south	남쪽	nam-jjok
to the south	남쪽으로	nam-jjo-geu-ro
in the south	남쪽에	nam-jjo-ge
southern (adj)	남쪽의	nam-jjo-gui

west	서쪽	seo-jjok
to the west	서쪽으로	seo-jjo-geu-ro
in the west	서쪽에	seo-jjo-ge
western (adj)	서쪽의	seo-jjo-gui

east	동쪽	dong-jjok
to the east	동쪽으로	dong-jjo-geu-ro
in the east	동쪽에	dong-jjo-ge
eastern (adj)	동쪽의	dong-jjo-gui

198. Sea. Ocean

sea	바다	ba-da
ocean	대양	dae-yang
gulf (bay)	만	man
straits	해협	hae-hyeop

continent (mainland)	대륙	dae-ryuk
island	섬	seom
peninsula	반도	ban-do
archipelago	군도	gun-do

bay, cove	만	man
harbour	항구	hang-gu
lagoon	석호	seok-o
cape	곶	got

atoll	환초	hwan-cho
reef	암초	am-cho
coral	산호	san-ho
coral reef	산호초	san-ho-cho

deep (adj)	깊은	gi-peun
depth (deep water)	깊이	gi-pi
trench (e.g. Mariana ~)	해구	hae-gu

current (Ocean ~)	해류	hae-ryu
to surround (bathe)	둘러싸다	dul-leo-ssa-da

shore	해변	hae-byeon
coast	바닷가	ba-dat-ga

flow (flood tide)	밀물	mil-mul
ebb (ebb tide)	썰물	sseol-mul
shoal	모래톱	mo-rae-top
bottom (~ of the sea)	해저	hae-jeo

wave	파도	pa-do
crest (~ of a wave)	물마루	mul-ma-ru
spume (sea foam)	거품	geo-pum

hurricane	허리케인	heo-ri-ke-in
tsunami	해일	hae-il
calm (dead ~)	고요함	go-yo-ham
quiet, calm (adj)	고요한	go-yo-han

| pole | 극 | geuk |
| polar (adj) | 극지의 | geuk-ji-ui |

latitude	위도	wi-do
longitude	경도	gyeong-do
parallel	위도선	wi-do-seon
equator	적도	jeok-do

sky	하늘	ha-neul
horizon	수평선	su-pyeong-seon
air	공기	gong-gi

lighthouse	등대	deung-dae
to dive (vi)	뛰어들다	ttwi-eo-deul-da
to sink (ab. boat)	가라앉다	ga-ra-an-da
treasure	보물	bo-mul

199. Seas & Oceans names

Atlantic Ocean	대서양	dae-seo-yang
Indian Ocean	인도양	in-do-yang
Pacific Ocean	태평양	tae-pyeong-yang
Arctic Ocean	북극해	buk-geuk-ae

Black Sea	흑해	heuk-ae
Red Sea	홍해	hong-hae
Yellow Sea	황해	hwang-hae
White Sea	백해	baek-ae

Caspian Sea	카스피 해	ka-seu-pi hae
Dead Sea	사해	sa-hae
Mediterranean Sea	지중해	ji-jung-hae

| Aegean Sea | 에게 해 | e-ge hae |
| Adriatic Sea | 아드리아 해 | a-deu-ri-a hae |

Arabian Sea	아라비아 해	a-ra-bi-a hae
Sea of Japan	동해	dong-hae
Bering Sea	베링 해	be-ring hae
South China Sea	남중국해	nam-jung-guk-ae

Coral Sea	산호해	san-ho-hae
Tasman Sea	태즈먼 해	tae-jeu-meon hae
Caribbean Sea	카리브 해	ka-ri-beu hae

| Barents Sea | 바렌츠 해 | ba-ren-cheu hae |
| Kara Sea | 카라 해 | ka-ra hae |

North Sea	북해	buk-ae
Baltic Sea	발트 해	bal-teu hae
Norwegian Sea	노르웨이 해	no-reu-we-i hae

200. Mountains

mountain	산	san
mountain range	산맥	san-maek
mountain ridge	능선	neung-seon

summit, top	정상	jeong-sang
peak	봉우리	bong-u-ri
foot (~ of the mountain)	기슭	gi-seuk
slope (mountainside)	경사면	gyeong-sa-myeon

volcano	화산	hwa-san
active volcano	활화산	hwal-hwa-san
dormant volcano	사화산	sa-hwa-san

eruption	폭발	pok-bal
crater	분화구	bun-hwa-gu
magma	마그마	ma-geu-ma
lava	용암	yong-am
molten (~ lava)	녹은	no-geun

canyon	협곡	hyeop-gok
gorge	협곡	hyeop-gok
crevice	갈라진	gal-la-jin

pass, col	산길	san-gil
plateau	고원	go-won
cliff	절벽	jeol-byeok
hill	언덕, 작은 산	eon-deok, ja-geun san

glacier	빙하	bing-ha
waterfall	폭포	pok-po
geyser	간헐천	gan-heol-cheon
lake	호수	ho-su

plain	평원	pyeong-won
landscape	경관	gyeong-gwan
echo	메아리	me-a-ri

alpinist	등산가	deung-san-ga
rock climber	암벽 등반가	am-byeok deung-ban-ga
to conquer (in climbing)	정복하다	jeong-bok-a-da
climb (an easy ~)	등반	deung-ban

201. Mountains names

The Alps	알프스 산맥	al-peu-seu san-maek
Mont Blanc	몽블랑 산	mong-beul-lang san
The Pyrenees	피레네 산맥	pi-re-ne san-maek
The Carpathians	카르파티아 산맥	ka-reu-pa-ti-a san-maek
The Ural Mountains	우랄 산맥	u-ral san-maek
The Caucasus Mountains	코카서스 산맥	ko-ka-seo-seu san-maek
Mount Elbrus	엘브루스 산	el-beu-ru-seu san
The Altai Mountains	알타이 산맥	al-ta-i san-maek
The Tian Shan	톈샨 산맥	ten-syan san-maek
The Pamirs	파미르 고원	pa-mi-reu go-won
The Himalayas	히말라야 산맥	hi-mal-la-ya san-maek
Mount Everest	에베레스트 산	e-be-re-seu-teu san
The Andes	안데스 산맥	an-de-seu san-maek
Mount Kilimanjaro	킬리만자로 산	kil-li-man-ja-ro san

202. Rivers

river	강	gang
spring (natural source)	샘	saem
riverbed (river channel)	강바닥	gang-ba-dak
basin (river valley)	유역	yu-yeok
to flow into ...	··· 로 흘러가다	... ro heul-leo-ga-da
tributary	지류	ji-ryu
bank (river ~)	둑	duk
current (stream)	흐름	heu-reum
downstream (adv)	하류로	gang ha-ryu-ro
upstream (adv)	상류로	sang-nyu-ro
inundation	홍수	hong-su
flooding	홍수	hong-su
to overflow (vi)	범람하다	beom-nam-ha-da
to flood (vt)	범람하다	beom-nam-ha-da
shallow (shoal)	얕은 곳	ya-teun got
rapids	여울	yeo-ul
dam	댐	daem
canal	운하	un-ha
reservoir (artificial lake)	저수지	jeo-su-ji
sluice, lock	수문	su-mun
water body (pond, etc.)	저장 수량	jeo-jang su-ryang
swamp (marshland)	늪, 소택지	neup, so-taek-ji
bog, marsh	수렁	su-reong
whirlpool	소용돌이	so-yong-do-ri
stream (brook)	개울, 시내	gae-ul, si-nae

| drinking (ab. water) | 마실 수 있는 | ma-sil su in-neun |
| fresh (~ water) | 민물의 | min-mu-rui |

| ice | 얼음 | eo-reum |
| to freeze over (ab. river, etc.) | 얼다 | eol-da |

203. Rivers names

| Seine | 센 강 | sen gang |
| Loire | 루아르 강 | ru-a-reu gang |

Thames	템스 강	tem-seu gang
Rhine	라인 강	ra-in gang
Danube	도나우 강	do-na-u gang

Volga	볼가 강	bol-ga gang
Don	돈 강	don gang
Lena	레나 강	re-na gang

Yellow River	황허강	hwang-heo-gang
Yangtze	양자강	yang-ja-gang
Mekong	메콩 강	me-kong gang
Ganges	갠지스 강	gaen-ji-seu gang

Nile River	나일 강	na-il gang
Congo River	콩고 강	kong-go gang
Okavango River	오카방고 강	o-ka-bang-go gang
Zambezi River	잠베지 강	jam-be-ji gang
Limpopo River	림포포 강	rim-po-po gang

204. Forest

| forest, wood | 숲 | sup |
| forest (as adj) | 산림의 | sal-li-mui |

thick forest	밀림	mil-lim
grove	작은 숲	ja-geun sup
forest clearing	빈터	bin-teo

| thicket | 덤불 | deom-bul |
| scrubland | 관목지 | gwan-mok-ji |

| footpath (troddenpath) | 오솔길 | o-sol-gil |
| gully | 도랑 | do-rang |

tree	나무	na-mu
leaf	잎	ip
leaves (foliage)	나뭇잎	na-mun-nip

fall of leaves	낙엽	na-gyeop
to fall (ab. leaves)	떨어지다	tteo-reo-ji-da
branch	가지	ga-ji

bough	큰 가지	keun ga-ji
bud (on shrub, tree)	잎눈	im-nun
needle (of the pine tree)	바늘	ba-neul
fir cone	솔방울	sol-bang-ul
tree hollow	구멍	gu-meong
nest	둥지	dung-ji
burrow (animal hole)	굴	gul
trunk	몸통	mom-tong
root	뿌리	ppu-ri
bark	껍질	kkeop-jil
moss	이끼	i-kki
to uproot (remove trees or tree stumps)	수목을 통째 뽑다	su-mo-geul tong-jjae ppop-da
to chop down	자르다	ja-reu-da
to deforest (vt)	삼림을 없애다	sam-ni-meul reop-sae-da
tree stump	그루터기	geu-ru-teo-gi
campfire	모닥불	mo-dak-bul
forest fire	산불	san-bul
to extinguish (vt)	끄다	kkeu-da
forest ranger	산림경비원	sal-lim-gyeong-bi-won
protection	보호	bo-ho
to protect (~ nature)	보호하다	bo-ho-ha-da
poacher	밀렵자	mil-lyeop-ja
steel trap	덫	deot
to gather, to pick (vt)	따다	tta-da
to lose one's way	길을 잃다	gi-reul ril-ta

205. Natural resources

natural resources	천연 자원	cheo-nyeon ja-won
deposits	매장량	mae-jang-nyang
field (e.g. oilfield)	지역	ji-yeok
to mine (extract)	채광하다	chae-gwang-ha-da
mining (extraction)	막장일	mak-jang-il
ore	광석	gwang-seok
mine (e.g. for coal)	광산	gwang-san
shaft (mine ~)	갱도	gaeng-do
miner	광부	gwang-bu
gas (natural ~)	가스	ga-seu
gas pipeline	가스관	ga-seu-gwan
oil (petroleum)	석유	seo-gyu
oil pipeline	석유 파이프라인	seo-gyu pa-i-peu-ra-in
oil well	유정	yu-jeong
derrick (tower)	유정탑	yu-jeong-tap
tanker	유조선	yu-jo-seon

sand	모래	mo-rae
limestone	석회석	seok-oe-seok
gravel	자갈	ja-gal
peat	토탄	to-tan
clay	점토	jeom-to
coal	석탄	seok-tan

iron (ore)	철	cheol
gold	금	geum
silver	은	eun
nickel	니켈	ni-kel
copper	구리	gu-ri

zinc	아연	a-yeon
manganese	망간	mang-gan
mercury	수은	su-eun
lead	납	nap

mineral	광물	gwang-mul
crystal	수정	su-jeong
marble	대리석	dae-ri-seok
uranium	우라늄	u-ra-nyum

The Earth. Part 2

weather	날씨	nal-ssi
weather forecast	일기 예보	il-gi ye-bo
temperature	온도	on-do
thermometer	온도계	on-do-gye
barometer	기압계	gi-ap-gye
humidity	습함, 습기	seu-pam, seup-gi
heat (extreme ~)	더위	deo-wi
hot (torrid)	더운	deo-un
it's hot	덥다	deop-da
it's warm	따뜻하다	tta-tteu-ta-da
warm (moderately hot)	따뜻한	tta-tteu-tan
it's cold	춥다	chup-da
cold (adj)	추운	chu-un
sun	해	hae
to shine (vi)	빛나다	bin-na-da
sunny (day)	화창한	hwa-chang-han
to come up (vi)	뜨다	tteu-da
to set (vi)	지다	ji-da
cloud	구름	gu-reum
cloudy (adj)	구름의	gu-reum-ui
somber (gloomy)	흐린	heu-rin
rain	비	bi
it's raining	비가 오다	bi-ga o-da
rainy (~ day, weather)	비가 오는	bi-ga o-neun
to drizzle (vi)	이슬비가 내리다	i-seul-bi-ga nae-ri-da
pouring rain	억수	eok-su
downpour	호우	ho-u
heavy (e.g. ~ rain)	심한	sim-han
puddle	웅덩이	ung-deong-i
to get wet (in rain)	젖다	jeot-da
fog (mist)	안개	an-gae
foggy	안개가 자욱한	an-gae-ga ja-uk-an
snow	눈	nun
it's snowing	눈이 오다	nun-i o-da

207. Severe weather. Natural disasters

thunderstorm	뇌우	noe-u
lightning (~ strike)	번개	beon-gae
to flash (vi)	번쩍이다	beon-jjeo-gi-da
thunder	천둥	cheon-dung
to thunder (vi)	천둥이 치다	cheon-dung-i chi-da
it's thundering	천둥이 치다	cheon-dung-i chi-da
hail	싸락눈	ssa-rang-nun
it's hailing	싸락눈이 내리다	ssa-rang-nun-i nae-ri-da
to flood (vt)	범람하다	beom-nam-ha-da
flood, inundation	홍수	hong-su
earthquake	지진	ji-jin
tremor, shoke	진동	jin-dong
epicentre	진앙	jin-ang
eruption	폭발	pok-bal
lava	용암	yong-am
twister	회오리바람	hoe-o-ri-ba-ram
tornado	토네이도	to-ne-i-do
typhoon	태풍	tae-pung
hurricane	허리케인	heo-ri-ke-in
storm	폭풍우	pok-pung-u
tsunami	해일	hae-il
fire (accident)	불	bul
disaster	재해	jae-hae
meteorite	운석	un-seok
avalanche	눈사태	nun-sa-tae
snowslide	눈사태	nun-sa-tae
blizzard	눈보라	nun-bo-ra
snowstorm	눈보라	nun-bo-ra

208. Noises. Sounds

silence (quiet)	고요함	go-yo-ham
sound	소리	so-ri
noise	소음	so-eum
to make noise	소리를 내다	so-ri-reul lae-da
noisy (adj)	시끄러운	si-kkeu-reo-un
loudly (to speak, etc.)	큰 소리로	keun so-ri-ro
loud (voice, etc.)	시끄러운	si-kkeu-reo-un
constant (e.g., ~ noise)	끊임없는	kkeu-nim-eom-neun
cry, shout (n)	고함을	go-ha-meul
to cry, to shout (vi)	소리를 치다	so-ri-reul chi-da

| whisper | 속삭임 | sok-sa-gim |
| to whisper (vi, vt) | 속삭이다 | sok-sa-gi-da |

| barking (dog's ~) | 짖는 소리 | jin-neun so-ri |
| to bark (vi) | 짖다 | jit-da |

groan (of pain, etc.)	신음 소리	si-neum so-ri
to groan (vi)	신음하다	si-neum-ha-da
cough	기침	gi-chim
to cough (vi)	기침을 하다	gi-chi-meul ha-da

whistle	휘파람	hwi-pa-ram
to whistle (vi)	휘파람을 불다	hwi-pa-ra-meul bul-da
knock (at the door)	노크	no-keu
to knock (on the door)	두드리다	du-deu-ri-da

| to crack (vi) | 날카로운 소리가 나다 | nal-ka-ro-un so-ri-ga na-da |
| crack (cracking sound) | 딱딱 튀는 소리 | ttak-ttak twi-neun so-ri |

siren	사이렌	sa-i-ren
whistle (factory ~, etc.)	경적	gyeong-jeok
to whistle (ab. train)	기적을 울리다	gi-jeo-geul rul-li-da
honk (car horn sound)	경적	gyeong-jeok
to honk (vi)	경적을 울리다	gyeong-jeo-geul rul-li-da

209. Winter

winter (n)	겨울	gyeo-ul
winter (as adj)	겨울의	gyeo-ul
in winter	겨울에	gyeo-u-re

snow	눈	nun
it's snowing	눈이 오다	nun-i o-da
snowfall	강설	gang-seol
snowdrift	눈더미	nun-deo-mi

snowflake	눈송이	nun-song-i
snowball	눈뭉치	nun-mung-chi
snowman	눈사람	nun-sa-ram
icicle	고드름	go-deu-reum

December	십이월	si-bi-wol
January	일월	i-rwol
February	이월	i-wol

| frost (severe ~, freezing cold) | 지독한 서리 | ji-dok-an seo-ri |
| frosty (weather, air) | 서리가 내리는 | seo-ri-ga nae-ri-neun |

| below zero (adv) | 영하 | yeong-ha |
| hoarfrost | 서리 | seo-ri |

cold (cold weather)	추위	chu-wi
it's cold	춥다	chup-da
fur coat	모피 외투	mo-pi oe-tu

mittens	벙어리장갑	beong-eo-ri-jang-gap
to fall ill	병에 걸리다	byeong-e geol-li-da
cold (illness)	감기	gam-gi
to catch a cold	감기에 걸리다	gam-gi-e geol-li-da
ice	얼음	eo-reum
black ice	빙판	bing-pan
to freeze over (ab. river, etc.)	얼다	eol-da
ice floe	부빙	bu-bing
skis	스키	seu-ki
skier	스키 타는 사람	seu-ki ta-neun sa-ram
to ski (vi)	스키를 타다	seu-ki-reul ta-da
to skate (vi)	스케이트를 타다	seu-ke-i-teu-reul ta-da

Fauna

predator	육식 동물	yuk-sik dong-mul
tiger	호랑이	ho-rang-i
lion	사자	sa-ja
wolf	이리	i-ri
fox	여우	yeo-u
jaguar	재규어	jae-gyu-eo
leopard	표범	pyo-beom
cheetah	치타	chi-ta
puma	퓨마	pyu-ma
snow leopard	눈표범	nun-pyo-beom
lynx	스라소니	seu-ra-so-ni
coyote	코요테	ko-yo-te
jackal	재칼	jae-kal
hyena	하이에나	ha-i-e-na

animal	동물	dong-mul
beast (animal)	짐승	jim-seung
squirrel	다람쥐	da-ram-jwi
hedgehog	고슴도치	go-seum-do-chi
hare	토끼	to-kki
rabbit	굴토끼	gul-to-kki
badger	오소리	o-so-ri
raccoon	너구리	neo-gu-ri
hamster	햄스터	haem-seu-teo
marmot	마멋	ma-meot
mole	두더지	du-deo-ji
mouse	생쥐	saeng-jwi
rat	시궁쥐	si-gung-jwi
bat	박쥐	bak-jwi
ermine	북방족제비	buk-bang-jok-je-bi
sable	검은담비	geo-meun-dam-bi
marten	담비	dam-bi
mink	밍크	ming-keu
beaver	비버	bi-beo
otter	수달	su-dal

horse	말	mal
moose	엘크, 무스	el-keu, mu-seu
deer	사슴	sa-seum
camel	낙타	nak-ta
bison	미국들소	mi-guk-deul-so
wisent	유럽들소	yu-reop-deul-so
buffalo	물소	mul-so
zebra	얼룩말	eol-lung-mal
antelope	영양	yeong-yang
roe deer	노루	no-ru
fallow deer	다마사슴	da-ma-sa-seum
chamois	샤모아	sya-mo-a
wild boar	멧돼지	met-dwae-ji
whale	고래	go-rae
seal	바다표범	ba-da-pyo-beom
walrus	바다코끼리	ba-da-ko-kki-ri
fur seal	물개	mul-gae
dolphin	돌고래	dol-go-rae
bear	곰	gom
polar bear	북극곰	buk-geuk-gom
panda	판다	pan-da
monkey	원숭이	won-sung-i
chimpanzee	침팬지	chim-paen-ji
orangutan	오랑우탄	o-rang-u-tan
gorilla	고릴라	go-ril-la
macaque	마카크	ma-ka-keu
gibbon	긴팔원숭이	gin-pa-rwon-sung-i
elephant	코끼리	ko-kki-ri
rhinoceros	코뿔소	ko-ppul-so
giraffe	기린	gi-rin
hippopotamus	하마	ha-ma
kangaroo	캥거루	kaeng-geo-ru
koala (bear)	코알라	ko-al-la
mongoose	몽구스	mong-gu-seu
chinchilla	친칠라	chin-chil-la
skunk	스컹크	seu-keong-keu
porcupine	호저	ho-jeo

212. Domestic animals

cat	고양이	go-yang-i
tomcat	수고양이	su-go-yang-i
horse	말	mal
stallion (male horse)	수말, 종마	su-mal, jong-ma
mare	암말	am-mal

cow	암소	am-so
bull	황소	hwang-so
ox	수소	su-so
sheep (ewe)	양, 암양	yang, a-myang
ram	수양	su-yang
goat	염소	yeom-so
billy goat, he-goat	숫염소	sun-nyeom-so
donkey	당나귀	dang-na-gwi
mule	노새	no-sae
pig	돼지	dwae-ji
piglet	돼지 새끼	dwae-ji sae-kki
rabbit	집토끼	jip-to-kki
hen (chicken)	암닭	am-tak
cock	수닭	su-tak
duck	집오리	ji-bo-ri
drake	수오리	su-o-ri
goose	집거위	jip-geo-wi
tom turkey, gobbler	수칠면조	su-chil-myeon-jo
turkey (hen)	칠면조	chil-myeon-jo
domestic animals	가축	ga-chuk
tame (e.g. ~ hamster)	길들여진	gil-deu-ryeo-jin
to tame (vt)	길들이다	gil-deu-ri-da
to breed (vt)	사육하다, 기르다	sa-yuk-a-da, gi-reu-da
farm	농장	nong-jang
poultry	가금	ga-geum
cattle	가축	ga-chuk
herd (cattle)	떼	tte
stable	마구간	ma-gu-gan
pigsty	돼지 우리	dwae-ji u-ri
cowshed	외양간	oe-yang-gan
rabbit hutch	토끼장	to-kki-jang
hen house	닭장	dak-jang

213. Dogs. Dog breeds

dog	개	gae
sheepdog	양치기 개	yang-chi-gi gae
poodle	푸들	pu-deul
dachshund	닥스훈트	dak-seu-hun-teu
bulldog	불독	bul-dok
boxer	복서	bok-seo
mastiff	매스티프	mae-seu-ti-peu
Rottweiler	로트와일러	ro-teu-wa-il-leo
Doberman	도베르만	do-be-reu-man

basset	바셋 하운드	ba-set ta-un-deu
bobtail	밥테일	bap-te-il
Dalmatian	달마시안	dal-ma-si-an
cocker spaniel	코커 스패니얼	ko-keo seu-pae-ni-eol
Newfoundland	뉴펀들랜드	nyu-peon-deul-laen-deu
Saint Bernard	세인트버나드	se-in-teu-beo-na-deu
husky	허스키	heo-seu-ki
spitz	스피츠	seu-pi-cheu
pug	퍼그	peo-geu

214. Sounds made by animals

barking (n)	짖는 소리	jin-neun so-ri
to bark (vi)	짖다	jit-da
to miaow (vi)	야옹 하고 울다	ya-ong ha-go ul-da
to purr (vi)	목을 가르랑거리다	mo-geul ga-reu-rang-geo-ri-da
to moo (vi)	음매 울다	eum-mae ul-da
to bellow (bull)	우렁찬 소리를 내다	u-reong-chan so-ri-reul lae-da
to growl (vi)	으르렁거리다	eu-reu-reong-geo-ri-da
howl (n)	울부짖음	ul-bu-ji-jeum
to howl (vi)	울다	ul-da
to whine (vi)	낑낑거리다	kking-kking-geo-ri-da
to bleat (sheep)	매애하고 울다	mae-ae-ha-go ul-da
to oink, to grunt (pig)	꿀꿀거리다	kkul-kkul-geo-ri-da
to squeal (vi)	하는 소리를 내다	ha-neun so-ri-reul lae-da
to croak (vi)	개골개골하다	gae-gol-gae-gol-ha-da
to buzz (insect)	윙윙거리다	wing-wing-geo-ri-da
to chirp (crickets, grasshopper)	찌르찌르 울다	jji-reu-jji-reu ul-da

215. Young animals

cub	새끼	sae-kki
kitten	새끼고양이	sae-kki-go-yang-i
baby mouse	아기 생쥐	a-gi saeng-jwi
puppy	강아지	gang-a-ji
leveret	토끼의 새끼	to-kki-ui sae-kki
baby rabbit	집토끼의 새끼	jip-to-kki-ui sae-kki
wolf cub	이리 새끼	i-ri sae-kki
fox cub	여우 새끼	yeo-u sae-kki
bear cub	곰 새끼	gom sae-kki
lion cub	사자의 새끼	sa-ja-ui sae-kki
tiger cub	호랑이 새끼	ho-rang-i sae-kki

elephant calf	코끼리의 새끼	ko-kki-ri-ui sae-kki
piglet	돼지 새끼	dwae-ji sae-kki
calf (young cow, bull)	송아지	song-a-ji
kid (young goat)	염소의 새끼	yeom-so-ui sae-kki
lamb	어린 양	eo-rin nyang
fawn (young deer)	새끼 사슴	sae-kki sa-seum
young camel	낙타새끼	nak-ta-sae-kki

snakelet (baby snake)	새끼 뱀	sae-kki baem
froglet (baby frog)	새끼 개구리	sae-kki gae-gu-ri

baby bird	새 새끼	sae sae-kki
chick (of chicken)	병아리	byeong-a-ri
duckling	오리새끼	o-ri-sae-kki

216. Birds

bird	새	sae
pigeon	비둘기	bi-dul-gi
sparrow	참새	cham-sae
tit (great tit)	박새	bak-sae
magpie	까치	kka-chi

raven	갈가마귀	gal-ga-ma-gwi
crow	까마귀	kka-ma-gwi
jackdaw	갈가마귀	gal-ga-ma-gwi
rook	떼까마귀	ttae-kka-ma-gwi

duck	오리	o-ri
goose	거위	geo-wi
pheasant	꿩	kkwong

eagle	독수리	dok-su-ri
hawk	매	mae
falcon	매	mae
vulture	독수리, 콘도르	dok-su-ri, kon-do-reu
condor (Andean ~)	콘도르	kon-do-reu

swan	백조	baek-jo
crane	두루미	du-ru-mi
stork	황새	hwang-sae

parrot	앵무새	aeng-mu-sae
hummingbird	벌새	beol-sae
peacock	공작	gong-jak

ostrich	타조	ta-jo
heron	왜가리	wae-ga-ri
flamingo	플라밍고	peul-la-ming-go
pelican	펠리컨	pel-li-keon

nightingale	나이팅게일	na-i-ting-ge-il
swallow	제비	je-bi
thrush	지빠귀	ji-ppa-gwi

song thrush	노래지빠귀	no-rae-ji-ppa-gwi
blackbird	대륙검은지빠귀	dae-ryuk-geo-meun-ji-ppa-gwi
swift	칼새	kal-sae
lark	종다리	jong-da-ri
quail	메추라기	me-chu-ra-gi
woodpecker	딱따구리	ttak-tta-gu-ri
cuckoo	뻐꾸기	ppeo-kku-gi
owl	올빼미	ol-ppae-mi
eagle owl	수리부엉이	su-ri-bu-eong-i
wood grouse	큰뇌조	keun-noe-jo
black grouse	멧닭	met-dak
partridge	자고	ja-go
starling	찌르레기	jji-reu-re-gi
canary	카나리아	ka-na-ri-a
chaffinch	되새	doe-sae
bullfinch	피리새	pi-ri-sae
seagull	갈매기	gal-mae-gi
albatross	신천옹	sin-cheon-ong
penguin	펭귄	peng-gwin

217. Birds. Singing and sounds

to sing (vi)	노래하다	no-rae-ha-da
to call (animal, bird)	울다	ul-da
to crow (cock)	꼬끼오 하고 울다	kko-kki-o ha-go ul-da
cock-a-doodle-doo	꼬끼오	kko-kki-o
to cluck (hen)	꼬꼬댁거리다	kko-kko-daek-geo-ri-da
to caw (crow call)	까악까악 울다	kka-ak-kka-ak gul-da
to quack (duck call)	꽥꽥 울다	kkwaek-kkwaek gul-da
to cheep (vi)	삐약삐약 울다	ppi-yak-ppi-yak gul-da
to chirp, to twitter	짹짹 울다	jjaek-jjaek gul-da

218. Fish. Marine animals

bream	도미류	do-mi-ryu
carp	잉어	ing-eo
perch	농어의 일종	nong-eo-ui il-jong
catfish	메기	me-gi
pike	북부민물꼬치고기	buk-bu-min-mul-kko-chi-go-gi
salmon	연어	yeon-eo
sturgeon	철갑상어	cheol-gap-sang-eo
herring	청어	cheong-eo
Atlantic salmon	대서양 연어	dae-seo-yang yeon-eo
mackerel	고등어	go-deung-eo

flatfish	넙치	neop-chi
cod	대구	dae-gu
tuna	참치	cham-chi
trout	송어	song-eo
eel	뱀장어	baem-jang-eo
electric ray	시끈가오리	si-kkeun-ga-o-ri
moray eel	곰치	gom-chi
piranha	피라니아	pi-ra-ni-a
shark	상어	sang-eo
dolphin	돌고래	dol-go-rae
whale	고래	go-rae
crab	게	ge
jellyfish	해파리	hae-pa-ri
octopus	낙지	nak-ji
starfish	불가사리	bul-ga-sa-ri
sea urchin	성게	seong-ge
seahorse	해마	hae-ma
oyster	굴	gul
prawn	새우	sae-u
lobster	바닷가재	ba-dat-ga-jae
spiny lobster	대하	dae-ha

219. Amphibians. Reptiles

snake	뱀	baem
venomous (snake)	독이 있는	do-gi in-neun
viper	살무사	sal-mu-sa
cobra	코브라	ko-beu-ra
python	비단뱀	bi-dan-baem
boa	보아	bo-a
grass snake	풀뱀	pul-baem
rattle snake	방울뱀	bang-ul-baem
anaconda	아나콘다	a-na-kon-da
lizard	도마뱀	do-ma-baem
iguana	이구아나	i-gu-a-na
salamander	도롱뇽	do-rong-nyong
chameleon	카멜레온	ka-mel-le-on
scorpion	전갈	jeon-gal
turtle	거북	geo-buk
frog	개구리	gae-gu-ri
toad	두꺼비	du-kkeo-bi
crocodile	악어	a-geo

220. Insects

insect	곤충	gon-chung
butterfly	나비	na-bi
ant	개미	gae-mi
fly	파리	pa-ri
mosquito	모기	mo-gi
beetle	딱정벌레	ttak-jeong-beol-le
wasp	말벌	mal-beol
bee	꿀벌	kkul-beol
bumblebee	호박벌	ho-bak-beol
gadfly (botfly)	쇠파리	soe-pa-ri
spider	거미	geo-mi
spider's web	거미줄	geo-mi-jul
dragonfly	잠자리	jam-ja-ri
grasshopper	메뚜기	me-ttu-gi
moth (night butterfly)	나방	na-bang
cockroach	바퀴벌레	ba-kwi-beol-le
tick	진드기	jin-deu-gi
flea	벼룩	byeo-ruk
midge	깔따구	kkal-tta-gu
locust	메뚜기	me-ttu-gi
snail	달팽이	dal-paeng-i
cricket	귀뚜라미	gwi-ttu-ra-mi
firefly	개똥벌레	gae-ttong-beol-le
ladybird	무당벌레	mu-dang-beol-le
cockchafer	왕풍뎅이	wang-pung-deng-i
leech	거머리	geo-meo-ri
caterpillar	애벌레	ae-beol-le
earthworm	지렁이	ji-reong-i
larva	애벌레	ae-beol-le

221. Animals. Body parts

beak	부리	bu-ri
wings	날개	nal-gae
foot (of the bird)	다리	da-ri
feathers (plumage)	깃털	git-teol
feather	깃털	git-teol
crest	볏	byeot
gills	아가미	a-ga-mi
spawn	알을 낳다	a-reul la-ta
larva	애벌레	ae-beol-le
fin	지느러미	ji-neu-reo-mi
scales (of fish, reptile)	비늘	bi-neul
fang (canine)	송곳니	song-gon-ni

paw (e.g. cat's ~)	발	bal
muzzle (snout)	주둥이	ju-dung-i
mouth (cat's ~)	입	ip
tail	꼬리	kko-ri
whiskers	수염	su-yeom

| hoof | 발굽 | bal-gup |
| horn | 뿔 | ppul |

carapace	등딱지	deung-ttak-ji
shell (mollusk ~)	조개 껍질	jo-gae kkeop-jil
eggshell	달걀 껍질	dal-gyal kkeop-jil

| animal's hair (pelage) | 털 | teol |
| pelt (hide) | 가죽 | ga-juk |

222. Actions of animals

to fly (vi)	날다	nal-da
to fly in circles	선회하다	seon-hoe-ha-da
to fly away	날아가버리다	na-ra-ga-beo-ri-da
to flap (~ the wings)	날개를 치다	nal-gae-reul chi-da

to peck (vi)	쪼다	jjo-da
to sit on eggs	알을 품다	a-reul pum-da
to hatch out (vi)	까다	kka-da
to build a nest	보금자리를 짓다	bo-geum-ja-ri-reul jit-da

to slither, to crawl	기다	gi-da
to sting, to bite (insect)	물다	mul-da
to bite (ab. animal)	물다	mul-da

to sniff (vt)	냄새맡다	naem-sae-mat-da
to bark (vi)	짖다	jit-da
to hiss (snake)	쉬익하는 소리를 내다	swi-ik-a-neun so-ri-reul lae-da

| to scare (vt) | 겁주다 | geop-ju-da |
| to attack (vt) | 공격하다 | gong-gyeo-ka-da |

to gnaw (bone, etc.)	쏠다	ssol-da
to scratch (with claws)	할퀴다	hal-kwi-da
to hide (vi)	숨기다	sum-gi-da

to play (kittens, etc.)	놀다	nol-da
to hunt (vi, vt)	사냥하다	sa-nyang-ha-da
to hibernate (vi)	동면하다	dong-myeon-ha-da
to go extinct	멸종하다	myeol-jong-ha-da

223. Animals. Habitats

| habitat | 서식지 | seo-sik-ji |
| migration | 이동 | i-dong |

mountain	산	san
reef	암초	am-cho
cliff	절벽	jeol-byeok
forest	숲	sup
jungle	정글	jeong-geul
savanna	대초원	dae-cho-won
tundra	툰드라	tun-deu-ra
steppe	스텝 지대	seu-tep ji-dae
desert	사막	sa-mak
oasis	오아시스	o-a-si-seu
sea	바다	ba-da
lake	호수	ho-su
ocean	대양	dae-yang
swamp (marshland)	늪, 소택지	neup, so-taek-ji
freshwater (adj)	민물의	min-mu-rui
pond	연못	yeon-mot
river	강	gang
den (bear's ~)	굴	gul
nest	둥지	dung-ji
tree hollow	구멍	gu-meong
burrow (animal hole)	굴	gul
anthill	개미탑	gae-mi-tap

224. Animal care

zoo	동물원	dong-mu-rwon
nature reserve	자연 보호구역	ja-yeon bo-ho-gu-yeok
breeder (cattery, kennel, etc.)	사육장	sa-yuk-jang
open-air cage	야외 사육장	ya-oe sa-yuk-jang
cage	우리	u-ri
kennel	개집	gae-jip
dovecot	비둘기장	bi-dul-gi-jang
aquarium (fish tank)	어항	eo-hang
to breed (animals)	사육하다, 기르다	sa-yuk-a-da, gi-reu-da
brood, litter	한 배 새끼	han bae sae-kki
to tame (vt)	길들이다	gil-deu-ri-da
to train (animals)	가르치다	ga-reu-chi-da
feed (fodder, etc.)	먹이	meo-gi
to feed (vt)	먹이다	meo-gi-da
pet shop	애완 동물 상점	ae-wan dong-mul sang-jeom
muzzle (for dog)	입마개	im-ma-gae
collar (e.g., dog ~)	개목걸이	gae-mok-geo-ri
name (of an animal)	이름	i-reum
pedigree (dog's ~)	족보	gye-tong yeon-gu

225. Animals. Miscellaneous

pack (wolves)	떼	tte
flock (birds)	새 떼	sae tte
shoal, school (fish)	떼	tte
herd (horses)	무리	mu-ri
male (n)	수컷	su-keot
female (n)	암컷	am-keot
hungry (adj)	배고픈	bae-go-peun
wild (adj)	야생의	ya-saeng-ui
dangerous (adj)	위험한	wi-heom-han

226. Horses

breed (race)	품종	pum-jong
foal	망아지	mang-a-ji
mare	암말	am-mal
mustang	무스탕	mu-seu-tang
pony	조랑말	jo-rang-mal
draught horse	짐수레말	jim-su-re-mal
mane	갈기	gal-gi
tail	꼬리	kko-ri
hoof	발굽	bal-gup
horseshoe	편자	pyeon-ja
to shoe (vt)	편자를 박다	pyeon-ja-reul bak-da
blacksmith	편자공	pyeon-ja-gong
saddle	안장	an-jang
stirrup	등자	deung-ja
bridle	굴레	gul-le
reins	고삐	go-ppi
whip (for riding)	채찍	chae-jjik
rider	기수는	gi-su-neun
to saddle up (vt)	안장을 얹다	an-jang-eul reon-da
to mount a horse	말에 타다	ma-re ta-da
gallop	갤럽	gael-leop
to gallop (vi)	전속력으로 달리다	jeon-song-nyeo-geu-ro dal-li-da
trot (n)	속보	sok-bo
at a trot (adv)	속보로	sok-bo-ro
racehorse	경마용 말	gyeong-ma-yong mal
horse racing	경마	gyeong-ma
stable	마구간	ma-gu-gan
to feed (vt)	먹이다	meo-gi-da

hay	건초	geon-cho
to water (animals)	물을 먹이다	mu-reul meo-gi-da
to wash (horse)	씻기다	ssit-gi-da

to graze (vi)	풀을 뜯다	pu-reul tteut-da
to neigh (vi)	울다	ul-da
to kick (to buck)	걷어차다	geo-deo-cha-da

Flora

tree	나무	na-mu
deciduous (adj)	낙엽수의	na-gyeop-su-ui
coniferous (adj)	침엽수의	chi-myeop-su-ui
evergreen (adj)	상록의	sang-no-gui
apple tree	사과나무	sa-gwa-na-mu
pear tree	배나무	bae-na-mu
cherry tree	벚나무	beon-na-mu
plum tree	자두나무	ja-du-na-mu
birch	자작나무	ja-jang-na-mu
oak	오크	o-keu
linden tree	보리수	bo-ri-su
aspen	사시나무	sa-si-na-mu
maple	단풍나무	dan-pung-na-mu
spruce	가문비나무	ga-mun-bi-na-mu
pine	소나무	so-na-mu
larch	낙엽송	na-gyeop-song
fir tree	전나무	jeon-na-mu
cedar	시다	si-da
poplar	포플러	po-peul-leo
rowan	마가목	ma-ga-mok
willow	버드나무	beo-deu-na-mu
alder	오리나무	o-ri-na-mu
beech	너도밤나무	neo-do-bam-na-mu
elm	느릅나무	neu-reum-na-mu
ash (tree)	물푸레나무	mul-pu-re-na-mu
chestnut	밤나무	bam-na-mu
magnolia	목련	mong-nyeon
palm tree	야자나무	ya-ja-na-mu
cypress	사이프러스	sa-i-peu-reo-seu
mangrove	맹그로브	maeng-geu-ro-beu
baobab	바오밥나무	ba-o-bam-na-mu
eucalyptus	유칼립투스	yu-kal-lip-tu-seu
sequoia	세쿼이아	se-kwo-i-a

bush	덤불	deom-bul
shrub	관목	gwan-mok

| grapevine | 포도 덩굴 | po-do deong-gul |
| vineyard | 포도밭 | po-do-bat |

raspberry bush	라즈베리	ra-jeu-be-ri
redcurrant bush	레드커런트 나무	re-deu-keo-reon-teu na-mu
gooseberry bush	구스베리 나무	gu-seu-be-ri na-mu

acacia	아카시아	a-ka-si-a
barberry	매자나무	mae-ja-na-mu
jasmine	재스민	jae-seu-min

juniper	두송	du-song
rosebush	장미 덤불	jang-mi deom-bul
dog rose	찔레나무	jjil-le-na-mu

229. Mushrooms

mushroom	버섯	beo-seot
edible mushroom	식용 버섯	si-gyong beo-seot
poisonous mushroom	독버섯	dok-beo-seot
cap	버섯의 갓	beo-seos-ui gat
stipe	줄기	jul-gi

| orange-cap boletus | 등색껄껄이그물버섯 | deung-saek-kkeol-kkeo-ri-geu-mul-beo-seot |
| birch bolete | 거친껄껄이그물버섯 | geo-chin-kkeol-kkeo-ri-geu-mul-beo-seot |

| chanterelle | 살구버섯 | sal-gu-beo-seot |
| russula | 무당버섯 | mu-dang-beo-seot |

morel	곰보버섯	gom-bo-beo-seot
fly agaric	광대버섯	gwang-dae-beo-seot
death cap	알광대버섯	al-gwang-dae-beo-seot

230. Fruits. Berries

apple	사과	sa-gwa
pear	배	bae
plum	자두	ja-du

strawberry (garden ~)	딸기	ttal-gi
sour cherry	신양	si-nyang
sweet cherry	양벚나무	yang-beon-na-mu
grape	포도	po-do

raspberry	라즈베리	ra-jeu-be-ri
blackcurrant	블랙커렌트	beul-laek-keo-ren-teu
redcurrant	레드커렌트	re-deu-keo-ren-teu
gooseberry	구스베리	gu-seu-be-ri
cranberry	크랜베리	keu-raen-be-ri
orange	오렌지	o-ren-ji
tangerine	귤	gyul

pineapple	파인애플	pa-in-ae-peul
banana	바나나	ba-na-na
date	대추야자	dae-chu-ya-ja
lemon	레몬	re-mon
apricot	살구	sal-gu
peach	복숭아	bok-sung-a
kiwi	키위	ki-wi
grapefruit	자몽	ja-mong
berry	장과	jang-gwa
berries	장과류	jang-gwa-ryu
cowberry	월귤나무	wol-gyul-la-mu
wild strawberry	야생딸기	ya-saeng-ttal-gi
bilberry	빌베리	bil-be-ri

231. Flowers. Plants

flower	꽃	kkot
bouquet (of flowers)	꽃다발	kkot-da-bal
rose (flower)	장미	jang-mi
tulip	튤립	tyul-lip
carnation	카네이션	ka-ne-i-syeon
gladiolus	글라디올러스	geul-la-di-ol-leo-seu
cornflower	수레국화	su-re-guk-wa
harebell	실잔대	sil-jan-dae
dandelion	민들레	min-deul-le
camomile	캐모마일	kae-mo-ma-il
aloe	알로에	al-lo-e
cactus	선인장	seon-in-jang
rubber plant, ficus	고무나무	go-mu-na-mu
lily	백합	baek-ap
geranium	제라늄	je-ra-nyum
hyacinth	히아신스	hi-a-sin-seu
mimosa	미모사	mi-mo-sa
narcissus	수선화	su-seon-hwa
nasturtium	한련	hal-lyeon
orchid	난초	nan-cho
peony	모란	mo-ran
violet	바이올렛	ba-i-ol-let
pansy	팬지	paen-ji
forget-me-not	물망초	mul-mang-cho
daisy	데이지	de-i-ji
poppy	양귀비	yang-gwi-bi
hemp	삼	sam
mint	박하	bak-a

lily of the valley	은방울꽃	eun-bang-ul-kkot
snowdrop	스노드롭	seu-no-deu-rop
nettle	쐐기풀	sswae-gi-pul
sorrel	수영	su-yeong
water lily	수련	su-ryeon
fern	고사리	go-sa-ri
lichen	이끼	i-kki
conservatory (greenhouse)	온실	on-sil
lawn	잔디	jan-di
flowerbed	꽃밭	kkot-bat
plant	식물	sing-mul
grass	풀	pul
blade of grass	풀잎	pu-rip
leaf	잎	ip
petal	꽃잎	kko-chip
stem	줄기	jul-gi
tuber	구근	gu-geun
young plant (shoot)	새싹	sae-ssak
thorn	가시	ga-si
to blossom (vi)	피우다	pi-u-da
to fade, to wither	시들다	si-deul-da
smell (odour)	향기	hyang-gi
to cut (flowers)	자르다	ja-reu-da
to pick (a flower)	따다	tta-da

232. Cereals, grains

grain	곡물	gong-mul
cereal crops	곡류	gong-nyu
ear (of barley, etc.)	이삭	i-sak
wheat	밀	mil
rye	호밀	ho-mil
oats	귀리	gwi-ri
millet	수수, 기장	su-su, gi-jang
barley	보리	bo-ri
maize	옥수수	ok-su-su
rice	쌀	ssal
buckwheat	메밀	me-mil
pea plant	완두	wan-du
kidney bean	강낭콩	gang-nang-kong
soya	콩	kong
lentil	렌즈콩	ren-jeu-kong
beans (pulse crops)	콩	kong

233. Vegetables. Greens

vegetables	채소	chae-so
greens	녹황색 채소	nok-wang-saek chae-so
tomato	토마토	to-ma-to
cucumber	오이	o-i
carrot	당근	dang-geun
potato	감자	gam-ja
onion	양파	yang-pa
garlic	마늘	ma-neul
cabbage	양배추	yang-bae-chu
cauliflower	컬리플라워	keol-li-peul-la-wo
Brussels sprouts	방울다다기 양배추	bang-ul-da-da-gi yang-bae-chu
beetroot	비트	bi-teu
aubergine	가지	ga-ji
marrow	애호박	ae-ho-bak
pumpkin	호박	ho-bak
turnip	순무	sun-mu
parsley	파슬리	pa-seul-li
dill	딜	dil
lettuce	양상추	yang-sang-chu
celery	셀러리	sel-leo-ri
asparagus	아스파라거스	a-seu-pa-ra-geo-seu
spinach	시금치	si-geum-chi
pea	완두	wan-du
beans	콩	kong
maize	옥수수	ok-su-su
kidney bean	강낭콩	gang-nang-kong
pepper	피망	pi-mang
radish	무	mu
artichoke	아티초크	a-ti-cho-keu

REGIONAL GEOGRAPHY

234. Western Europe

Europe	유럽	yu-reop
European Union	유럽 연합	yu-reop byeon-hap
European (n)	유럽 사람	yu-reop sa-ram
European (adj)	유럽의	yu-reo-bui
Austria	오스트리아	o-seu-teu-ri-a
Austrian (masc.)	오스트리아 사람	o-seu-teu-ri-a sa-ram
Austrian (fem.)	오스트리아 사람	o-seu-teu-ri-a sa-ram
Austrian (adj)	오스트리아의	o-seu-teu-ri-a-ui
Great Britain	영국	yeong-guk
England	잉글랜드	ing-geul-laen-deu
British (masc.)	영국 남자	yeong-guk nam-ja
British (fem.)	영국 여성	yeong-guk gyeo-ja
English, British (adj)	영국의	yeong-gu-gui
Belgium	벨기에	bel-gi-e
Belgian (masc.)	벨기에 사람	bel-gi-e sa-ram
Belgian (fem.)	벨기에 사람	bel-gi-e sa-ram
Belgian (adj)	벨기에의	bel-gi-e-ui
Germany	독일	do-gil
German (masc.)	독일 사람	do-gil sa-ram
German (fem.)	독일 사람	do-gil sa-ram
German (adj)	독일의	do-gi-rui
Netherlands	네덜란드	ne-deol-lan-deu
Holland	네덜란드	ne-deol-lan-deu
Dutch (masc.)	네덜란드 사람	ne-deol-lan-deu sa-ram
Dutch (fem.)	네덜란드 사람	ne-deol-lan-deu sa-ram
Dutch (adj)	네덜란드의	ne-deol-lan-deu-ui
Greece	그리스	geu-ri-seu
Greek (masc.)	그리스 사람	geu-ri-seu sa-ram
Greek (fem.)	그리스 사람	geu-ri-seu sa-ram
Greek (adj)	그리스의	geu-ri-seu-ui
Denmark	덴마크	den-ma-keu
Dane (masc.)	덴마크 사람	den-ma-keu sa-ram
Dane (fem.)	덴마크 사람	den-ma-keu sa-ram
Danish (adj)	덴마크의	den-ma-keu-ui
Ireland	아일랜드	a-il-laen-deu
Irish (masc.)	아일랜드 사람	a-il-laen-deu sa-ram
Irish (fem.)	아일랜드 사람	a-il-laen-deu sa-ram
Irish (adj)	아일랜드의	a-il-laen-deu-ui

Iceland	아이슬란드	a-i-seul-lan-deu
Icelander (masc.)	아이슬란드 사람	a-i-seul-lan-deu sa-ram
Icelander (fem.)	아이슬란드 사람	a-i-seul-lan-deu sa-ram
Icelandic (adj)	아이슬란드의	a-i-seul-lan-deu-ui

Spain	스페인	seu-pe-in
Spaniard (masc.)	스페인 사람	seu-pe-in sa-ram
Spaniard (fem.)	스페인 사람	seu-pe-in sa-ram
Spanish (adj)	스페인의	seu-pe-in-ui

Italy	이탈리아	i-tal-li-a
Italian (masc.)	이탈리아 사람	i-tal-li-a sa-ram
Italian (fem.)	이탈리아 사람	i-tal-li-a sa-ram
Italian (adj)	이탈리아의	i-tal-li-a-ui

Cyprus	키프로스	ki-peu-ro-seu
Cypriot (masc.)	키프로스 사람	ki-peu-ro-seu sa-ram
Cypriot (fem.)	키프로스 사람	ki-peu-ro-seu sa-ram
Cypriot (adj)	키프로스의	ki-peu-ro-seu-ui

Malta	몰타	mol-ta
Maltese (masc.)	몰타 사람	mol-ta sa-ram
Maltese (fem.)	몰타 사람	mol-ta sa-ram
Maltese (adj)	몰타의	mol-ta-ui

Norway	노르웨이	no-reu-we-i
Norwegian (masc.)	노르웨이 사람	no-reu-we-i sa-ram
Norwegian (fem.)	노르웨이사람	no-reu-we-i sa-ram
Norwegian (adj)	노르웨이의	no-reu-we-i-ui

Portugal	포르투갈	po-reu-tu-gal
Portuguese (masc.)	포르투갈 사람	po-reu-tu-gal sa-ram
Portuguese (fem.)	포르투갈 사람	po-reu-tu-gal sa-ram
Portuguese (adj)	포르투갈의	po-reu-tu-ga-rui

Finland	핀란드	pil-lan-deu
Finn (masc.)	핀란드 사람	pil-lan-deu sa-ram
Finn (fem.)	핀란드사람	pil-lan-deu-sa-ram
Finnish (adj)	핀란드의	pil-lan-deu-ui

France	프랑스	peu-rang-seu
French (masc.)	프랑스 사람	peu-rang-seu sa-ram
French (fem.)	프랑스 사람	peu-rang-seu sa-ram
French (adj)	프랑스의	peu-rang-seu-ui

Sweden	스웨덴	seu-we-den
Swede (masc.)	스웨덴 사람	seu-we-den sa-ram
Swede (fem.)	스웨덴 사람	seu-we-den sa-ram
Swedish (adj)	스웨덴의	seu-we-den-ui

Switzerland	스위스	seu-wi-seu
Swiss (masc.)	스위스 사람	seu-wi-seu sa-ram
Swiss (fem.)	스위스 사람	seu-wi-seu sa-ram
Swiss (adj)	스위스의	seu-wi-seu-ui
Scotland	스코틀랜드	seu-ko-teul-laen-deu
Scottish (masc.)	스코틀랜드 사람	seu-ko-teul-laen-deu sa-ram

| Scottish (fem.) | 스코틀랜드 사람 | seu-ko-teul-laen-deu sa-ram |
| Scottish (adj) | 스코틀랜드의 | seu-ko-teul-laen-deu-ui |

Vatican City	바티칸	ba-ti-kan
Liechtenstein	리히텐슈타인	ri-hi-ten-syu-ta-in
Luxembourg	룩셈부르크	ruk-sem-bu-reu-keu
Monaco	모나코	mo-na-ko

235. Central and Eastern Europe

Albania	알바니아	al-ba-ni-a
Albanian (masc.)	알바니아 사람	al-ba-ni-a sa-ram
Albanian (fem.)	알바니아 사람	al-ba-ni-a sa-ram
Albanian (adj)	알바니아의	al-ba-ni-a-ui

Bulgaria	불가리아	bul-ga-ri-a
Bulgarian (masc.)	불가리아 사람	bul-ga-ri-a sa-ram
Bulgarian (fem.)	불가리아 사람	bul-ga-ri-a sa-ram
Bulgarian (adj)	불가리아의	bul-ga-ri-a-ui

Hungary	헝가리	heong-ga-ri
Hungarian (masc.)	헝가리 사람	heong-ga-ri sa-ram
Hungarian (fem.)	헝가리 사람	heong-ga-ri sa-ram
Hungarian (adj)	헝가리의	heong-ga-ri-ui

Latvia	라트비아	ra-teu-bi-a
Latvian (masc.)	라트비아 사람	ra-teu-bi-a sa-ram
Latvian (fem.)	라트비아 사람	ra-teu-bi-a sa-ram
Latvian (adj)	라트비아의	ra-teu-bi-a-ui

Lithuania	리투아니아	ri-tu-a-ni-a
Lithuanian (masc.)	리투아니아 사람	ri-tu-a-ni-a sa-ram
Lithuanian (fem.)	리투아니아 사람	ri-tu-a-ni-a sa-ram
Lithuanian (adj)	리투아니아의	ri-tu-a-ni-a-ui

Poland	폴란드	pol-lan-deu
Pole (masc.)	폴란드 사람	pol-lan-deu sa-ram
Pole (fem.)	폴란드 사람	pol-lan-deu sa-ram
Polish (adj)	폴란드의	pol-lan-deu-ui

Romania	루마니아	ru-ma-ni-a
Romanian (masc.)	루마니아 사람	ru-ma-ni-a sa-ram
Romanian (fem.)	루마니아 사람	ru-ma-ni-a sa-ram
Romanian (adj)	루마니아의	ru-ma-ni-a-ui

Serbia	세르비아	se-reu-bi-a
Serbian (masc.)	세르비아 사람	se-reu-bi-a sa-ram
Serbian (fem.)	세르비아 사람	se-reu-bi-a sa-ram
Serbian (adj)	세르비아의	se-reu-bi-a-ui

Slovakia	슬로바키아	seul-lo-ba-ki-a
Slovak (masc.)	슬로바키아 사람	seul-lo-ba-ki-a sa-ram
Slovak (fem.)	슬로바키아 사람	seul-lo-ba-ki-a sa-ram
Slovak (adj)	슬로바키아의	seul-lo-ba-ki-a-ui

Croatia	크로아티아	keu-ro-a-ti-a
Croatian (masc.)	크로아티아 사람	keu-ro-a-ti-a sa-ram
Croatian (fem.)	크로아티아 사람	keu-ro-a-ti-a sa-ram
Croatian (adj)	크로아티아의	keu-ro-a-ti-a-ui

Czech Republic	체코	che-ko
Czech (masc.)	체코 사람	che-ko sa-ram
Czech (fem.)	체코 사람	che-ko sa-ram
Czech (adj)	체코의	che-ko-ui

Estonia	에스토니아	e-seu-to-ni-a
Estonian (masc.)	에스토니아 사람	e-seu-to-ni-a sa-ram
Estonian (fem.)	에스토니아 사람	e-seu-to-ni-a sa-ram
Estonian (adj)	에스토니아의	e-seu-to-ni-a-ui

| Bosnia and Herzegovina | 보스니아 헤르체코비나 | bo-seu-ni-a he-reu-che-ko-bi-na |

North Macedonia	마케도니아	ma-ke-do-ni-a
Slovenia	슬로베니아	seul-lo-be-ni-a
Montenegro	몬테네그로	mon-te-ne-geu-ro

236. Former USSR countries

Azerbaijan	아제르바이잔	a-je-reu-ba-i-jan
Azerbaijani (masc.)	아제르바이잔 사람	a-je-reu-ba-i-jan sa-ram
Azerbaijani (fem.)	아제르바이잔 사람	a-je-reu-ba-i-jan sa-ram
Azerbaijani, Azeri (adj)	아제르바이잔의	a-je-reu-ba-i-jan-ui

Armenia	아르메니아	a-reu-me-ni-a
Armenian (masc.)	아르메니아 사람	a-reu-me-ni-a sa-ram
Armenian (fem.)	아르메니아 사람	a-reu-me-ni-a sa-ram
Armenian (adj)	아르메니아의	a-reu-me-ni-a-ui

Belarus	벨로루시	bel-lo-ru-si
Belarusian (masc.)	벨로루시 사람	bel-lo-ru-si sa-ram
Belarusian (fem.)	벨로루시 사람	bel-lo-ru-si sa-ram
Belarusian (adj)	벨로루시의	bel-lo-ru-si-ui

Georgia	그루지야	geu-ru-ji-ya
Georgian (masc.)	그루지야 사람	geu-ru-ji-ya sa-ram
Georgian (fem.)	그루지야 사람	geu-ru-ji-ya sa-ram
Georgian (adj)	그루지야의	geu-ru-ji-ya-ui

Kazakhstan	카자흐스탄	ka-ja-heu-seu-tan
Kazakh (masc.)	카자흐스탄 사람	ka-ja-heu-seu-tan sa-ram
Kazakh (fem.)	카자흐스탄 사람	ka-ja-heu-seu-tan sa-ram
Kazakh (adj)	카자흐스탄의	ka-ja-heu-seu-tan-ui

Kirghizia	키르기스스탄	ki-reu-gi-seu-seu-tan
Kirghiz (masc.)	키르기스스탄 사람	ki-reu-gi-seu-seu-tan sa-ram
Kirghiz (fem.)	키르기스스탄 사람	ki-reu-gi-seu-seu-tan sa-ram
Kirghiz (adj)	키르기스스탄의	ki-reu-gi-seu-seu-tan-ui
Moldova, Moldavia	몰도바	mol-do-ba
Moldavian (masc.)	몰도바 사람	mol-do-ba sa-ram

| Moldavian (fem.) | 몰도바 사람 | mol-do-ba sa-ram |
| Moldavian (adj) | 몰도바의 | mol-do-ba-ui |

Russia	러시아	reo-si-a
Russian (masc.)	러시아 사람	reo-si-a sa-ram
Russian (fem.)	러시아 사람	reo-si-a sa-ram
Russian (adj)	러시아의	reo-si-a-ui

Tajikistan	타지키스탄	ta-ji-ki-seu-tan
Tajik (masc.)	타지키스탄 사람	ta-ji-ki-seu-tan sa-ram
Tajik (fem.)	타지키스탄 사람	ta-ji-ki-seu-tan sa-ram
Tajik (adj)	타지키스탄의	ta-ji-ki-seu-tan-ui

Turkmenistan	투르크메니스탄	tu-reu-keu-me-ni-seu-tan
Turkmen (masc.)	투르크메니스탄 사람	tu-reu-keu-me-ni-seu-tan sa-ram
Turkmen (fem.)	투르크메니스탄 사람	tu-reu-keu-me-ni-seu-tan sa-ram
Turkmenian (adj)	투르크메니스탄의	tu-reu-keu-me-ni-seu-tan-ui

Uzbekistan	우즈베키스탄	u-jeu-be-ki-seu-tan
Uzbek (masc.)	우즈베키스탄 사람	u-jeu-be-ki-seu-tan sa-ram
Uzbek (fem.)	우즈베키스탄 사람	u-jeu-be-ki-seu-tan sa-ram
Uzbek (adj)	우즈베키스탄의	u-jeu-be-ki-seu-tan-ui

Ukraine	우크라이나	u-keu-ra-i-na
Ukrainian (masc.)	우크라이나 사람	u-keu-ra-i-na sa-ram
Ukrainian (fem.)	우크라이나 사람	u-keu-ra-i-na sa-ram
Ukrainian (adj)	우크라이나의	u-keu-ra-i-na-ui

237. Asia

| Asia | 아시아 | a-si-a |
| Asian (adj) | 아시아의 | a-si-a-ui |

Vietnam	베트남	be-teu-nam
Vietnamese (masc.)	베트남 사람	be-teu-nam sa-ram
Vietnamese (fem.)	베트남 사람	be-teu-nam sa-ram
Vietnamese (adj)	베트남의	be-teu-nam-ui

India	인도	in-do
Indian (masc.)	인도 사람	in-do sa-ram
Indian (fem.)	인도 사람	in-do sa-ram
Indian (adj)	인도의	in-do-ui

Israel	이스라엘	i-seu-ra-el
Israeli (masc.)	이스라엘 사람	i-seu-ra-el sa-ram
Israeli (fem.)	이스라엘 사람	i-seu-ra-el sa-ram
Israeli (adj)	이스라엘의	i-seu-ra-e-rui

Jew (n)	유대인	yu-dae-in
Jewess (n)	유대인 여자	yu-dae-in nyeo-ja
Jewish (adj)	유대인의	yu-dae-in-ui
China	중국	jung-guk

Chinese (masc.)	중국 사람	jung-guk sa-ram
Chinese (fem.)	중국 사람	jung-guk sa-ram
Chinese (adj)	중국의	jung-gu-gui

Korean (masc.)	한국 사람	han-guk sa-ram
Korean (fem.)	한국 사람	han-guk sa-ram
Korean (adj)	한국의	han-gu-gui

Lebanon	레바논	re-ba-non
Lebanese (masc.)	레바논 사람	re-ba-non sa-ram
Lebanese (fem.)	레바논 사람	re-ba-non sa-ram
Lebanese (adj)	레바논의	re-ba-non-ui

Mongolia	몽골	mong-gol
Mongolian (masc.)	몽골 사람	mong-gol sa-ram
Mongolian (fem.)	몽골 사람	mong-gol sa-ram
Mongolian (adj)	몽골의	mong-go-rui

Malaysia	말레이시아	mal-le-i-si-a
Malaysian (masc.)	말레이시아 사람	mal-le-i-si-a sa-ram
Malaysian (fem.)	말레이시아 사람	mal-le-i-si-a sa-ram
Malaysian (adj)	말레이시아의	mal-le-i-si-a-ui

Pakistan	파키스탄	pa-ki-seu-tan
Pakistani (masc.)	파키스탄 사람	pa-ki-seu-tan sa-ram
Pakistani (fem.)	파키스탄 사람	pa-ki-seu-tan sa-ram
Pakistani (adj)	파키스탄의	pa-ki-seu-tan-ui

Saudi Arabia	사우디아라비아	sa-u-di-a-ra-bi-a
Arab (masc.)	아랍 사람	a-rap sa-ram
Arab (fem.)	아랍 사람	a-rap sa-ram
Arabic, Arabian (adj)	아랍인의	sa-u-di-a-ra-bi-a-ui

Thailand	태국	tae-guk
Thai (masc.)	태국 사람	tae-guk sa-ram
Thai (fem.)	태국 사람	tae-guk sa-ram
Thai (adj)	태국의	tae-gu-gui

Taiwan	대만	dae-man
Taiwanese (masc.)	대만 사람	dae-man sa-ram
Taiwanese (fem.)	대만 사람	dae-man sa-ram
Taiwanese (adj)	대만의	dae-man-ui

Turkey	터키	teo-ki
Turk (masc.)	터키 사람	teo-ki sa-ram
Turk (fem.)	터키 사람	teo-ki sa-ram
Turkish (adj)	터키의	teo-ki-ui

Japan	일본	il-bon
Japanese (masc.)	일본 사람	il-bon sa-ram
Japanese (fem.)	일본 사람	il-bon sa-ram
Japanese (adj)	일본의	il-bon-ui

Afghanistan	아프가니스탄	a-peu-ga-ni-seu-tan
Bangladesh	방글라데시	bang-geul-la-de-si
Indonesia	인도네시아	in-do-ne-si-a

Jordan	요르단	yo-reu-dan
Iraq	이라크	i-ra-keu
Iran	이란	i-ran
Cambodia	캄보디아	kam-bo-di-a
Kuwait	쿠웨이트	ku-we-i-teu
Laos	라오스	ra-o-seu
Myanmar	미얀마	mi-yan-ma
Nepal	네팔	ne-pal
United Arab Emirates	아랍에미리트	a-ra-be-mi-ri-teu
Syria	시리아	si-ri-a
Palestine	팔레스타인	pal-le-seu-ta-in
South Korea	한국	han-guk
North Korea	북한	buk-an

238. North America

United States of America	미국	mi-guk
American (masc.)	미국 사람	mi-guk sa-ram
American (fem.)	미국 사람	mi-guk sa-ram
American (adj)	미국의	mi-gu-gui
Canada	캐나다	kae-na-da
Canadian (masc.)	캐나다 사람	kae-na-da sa-ram
Canadian (fem.)	캐나다 사람	kae-na-da sa-ram
Canadian (adj)	캐나다의	kae-na-da-ui
Mexico	멕시코	mek-si-ko
Mexican (masc.)	멕시코 사람	mek-si-ko sa-ram
Mexican (fem.)	멕시코 사람	mek-si-ko sa-ram
Mexican (adj)	멕시코의	mek-si-ko-ui

239. Central and South America

Argentina	아르헨티나	a-reu-hen-ti-na
Argentinian (masc.)	아르헨티나 사람	a-reu-hen-ti-na sa-ram
Argentinian (fem.)	아르헨티나 사람	a-reu-hen-ti-na sa-ram
Argentinian (adj)	아르헨티나의	a-reu-hen-ti-na-ui
Brazil	브라질	beu-ra-jil
Brazilian (masc.)	브라질 사람	beu-ra-jil sa-ram
Brazilian (fem.)	브라질 사람	beu-ra-jil sa-ram
Brazilian (adj)	브라질의	beu-ra-ji-rui
Colombia	콜롬비아	kol-lom-bi-a
Colombian (masc.)	콜롬비아 사람	kol-lom-bi-a sa-ram
Colombian (fem.)	콜롬비아 사람	kol-lom-bi-a sa-ram
Colombian (adj)	콜롬비아의	kol-lom-bi-a-ui
Cuba	쿠바	ku-ba
Cuban (masc.)	쿠바 사람	ku-ba sa-ram

| Cuban (fem.) | 쿠바 사람 | ku-ba sa-ram |
| Cuban (adj) | 쿠바의 | ku-ba-ui |

Chile	칠레	chil-le
Chilean (masc.)	칠레 사람	chil-le sa-ram
Chilean (fem.)	칠레 사람	chil-le sa-ram
Chilean (adj)	칠레의	chil-le-ui

Bolivia	볼리비아	bol-li-bi-a
Venezuela	베네수엘라	be-ne-su-el-la
Paraguay	파라과이	pa-ra-gwa-i
Peru	페루	pe-ru
Suriname	수리남	su-ri-nam
Uruguay	우루과이	u-ru-gwa-i
Ecuador	에콰도르	e-kwa-do-reu

The Bahamas	바하마	ba-ha-ma
Haiti	아이티	a-i-ti
Dominican Republic	도미니카 공화국	do-mi-ni-ka gong-hwa-guk
Panama	파나마	pa-na-ma
Jamaica	자메이카	ja-me-i-ka

240. Africa

Egypt	이집트	i-jip-teu
Egyptian (masc.)	이집트 사람	i-jip-teu sa-ram
Egyptian (fem.)	이집트 사람	i-jip-teu sa-ram
Egyptian (adj)	이집트의	i-jip-teu-ui

Morocco	모로코	mo-ro-ko
Moroccan (masc.)	모로코 사람	mo-ro-ko sa-ram
Moroccan (fem.)	모로코 사람	mo-ro-ko sa-ram
Moroccan (adj)	모로코의	mo-ro-ko-ui

Tunisia	튀니지	twi-ni-ji
Tunisian (masc.)	튀니지 사람	twi-ni-ji sa-ram
Tunisian (fem.)	튀니지 사람	twi-ni-ji sa-ram
Tunisian (adj)	튀니지의	twi-ni-ji-ui

Ghana	가나	ga-na
Zanzibar	잔지바르	jan-ji-ba-reu
Kenya	케냐	ke-nya
Libya	리비아	ri-bi-a
Madagascar	마다가스카르	ma-da-ga-seu-ka-reu

Namibia	나미비아	na-mi-bi-a
Senegal	세네갈	se-ne-gal
Tanzania	탄자니아	tan-ja-ni-a
South Africa	남아프리카 공화국	nam-a-peu-ri-ka gong-hwa-guk

African (masc.)	아프리카 사람	a-peu-ri-ka sa-ram
African (fem.)	아프리카 사람	a-peu-ri-ka sa-ram
African (adj)	아프리카의	a-peu-ri-ka-ui

241. Australia. Oceania

Australia	호주	ho-ju
Australian (masc.)	호주 사람	ho-ju sa-ram
Australian (fem.)	호주 사람	ho-ju sa-ram
Australian (adj)	호주의	ho-ju-ui
New Zealand	뉴질랜드	nyu-jil-laen-deu
New Zealander (masc.)	뉴질랜드 사람	nyu-jil-laen-deu sa-ram
New Zealander (fem.)	뉴질랜드 사람	nyu-jil-laen-deu sa-ram
New Zealand (as adj)	뉴질랜드의	nyu-jil-laen-deu-ui
Tasmania	태즈메이니아	tae-jeu-me-i-ni-a
French Polynesia	폴리네시아	pol-li-ne-si-a

242. Cities

Amsterdam	암스테르담	am-seu-te-reu-dam
Ankara	앙카라	ang-ka-ra
Athens	아테네	a-te-ne
Baghdad	바그다드	ba-geu-da-deu
Bangkok	방콕	bang-kok
Barcelona	바르셀로나	ba-reu-sel-lo-na
Beijing	베이징	be-i-jing
Beirut	베이루트	be-i-ru-teu
Berlin	베를린	be-reul-lin
Mumbai (Bombay)	봄베이, 뭄바이	bom-be-i, mum-ba-i
Bonn	본	bon
Bordeaux	보르도	bo-reu-do
Bratislava	브라티슬라바	beu-ra-ti-seul-la-ba
Brussels	브뤼셀	beu-rwi-sel
Bucharest	부쿠레슈티	bu-ku-re-syu-ti
Budapest	부다페스트	bu-da-pe-seu-teu
Cairo	카이로	ka-i-ro
Kolkata (Calcutta)	캘커타	kael-keo-ta
Chicago	시카고	si-ka-go
Copenhagen	코펜하겐	ko-pen-ha-gen
Dar-es-Salaam	다르에스살람	da-reu-e-seu-sal-lam
Delhi	델리	del-li
Dubai	두바이	du-ba-i
Dublin	더블린	deo-beul-lin
Düsseldorf	뒤셀도르프	dwi-sel-do-reu-peu
Florence	플로렌스	peul-lo-ren-seu
Frankfurt	프랑크푸르트	peu-rang-keu-pu-reu-teu
Geneva	제네바	je-ne-ba
The Hague	헤이그	he-i-geu
Hamburg	함부르크	ham-bu-reu-keu
Hanoi	하노이	ha-no-i

Havana	아바나	a-ba-na
Helsinki	헬싱키	hel-sing-ki
Hiroshima	히로시마	hi-ro-si-ma
Hong Kong	홍콩	hong-kong

Istanbul	이스탄불	i-seu-tan-bul
Jerusalem	예루살렘	ye-ru-sal-lem
Kyiv	키예프	ki-ye-peu
Kuala Lumpur	콸라룸푸르	kwal-la-rum-pu-reu
Lisbon	리스본	ri-seu-bon
London	런던	reon-deon
Los Angeles	로스앤젤레스	ro-seu-aen-jel-le-seu
Lyons	리옹	ri-ong

Madrid	마드리드	ma-deu-ri-deu
Marseille	마르세유	ma-reu-se-yu
Mexico City	멕시코시티	mek-si-ko-si-ti
Miami	마이애미	ma-i-ae-mi
Montreal	몬트리올	mon-teu-ri-ol
Moscow	모스크바	mo-seu-keu-ba
Munich	뮌헨	mwin-hen
Nairobi	나이로비	na-i-ro-bi
Naples	나폴리	na-pol-li
New York	뉴욕	nyu-yok
Nice	니스	ni-seu
Oslo	오슬로	o-seul-lo
Ottawa	오타와	o-ta-wa

Paris	파리	pa-ri
Prague	프라하	peu-ra-ha
Rio de Janeiro	리우데자네이루	ri-u-de-ja-ne-i-ru
Rome	로마	ro-ma

| Saint Petersburg | 상트페테르부르크 | sang-teu-pe-te-reu-bu-reu-keu |

Seoul	서울	seo-ul
Shanghai	상하이	sang-ha-i
Singapore	싱가포르	sing-ga-po-reu
Stockholm	스톡홀름	seu-tok-ol-leum
Sydney	시드니	si-deu-ni

Taipei	타이베이	ta-i-be-i
Tokyo	도쿄	do-kyo
Toronto	토론토	to-ron-to

Venice	베니스	be-ni-seu
Vienna	빈	bin
Warsaw	바르샤바	ba-reu-sya-ba
Washington	워싱턴	wo-sing-teon

243. Politics. Government. Part 1

| politics | 정치 | jeong-chi |
| political (adj) | 정치의 | jeong-chi-ui |

politician	정치가	jeong-chi-ga
state (country)	국가	guk-ga
citizen	시민	si-min
citizenship	시민권	si-min-gwon

| national emblem | 국장 | guk-jang |
| national anthem | 국가 | guk-ga |

government	정부	jeong-bu
head of state	국가 수장	guk-ga su-jang
parliament	의회	ui-hoe
party	정당	jeong-dang

| capitalism | 자본주의 | ja-bon-ju-ui |
| capitalist (adj) | 자본주의의 | ja-bon-ju-ui-ui |

| socialism | 사회주의 | sa-hoe-ju-ui |
| socialist (adj) | 사회주의의 | sa-hoe-ju-ui-ui |

communism	공산주의	gong-san-ju-ui
communist (adj)	공산주의의	gong-san-ju-ui-ui
communist (n)	공산주의자	gong-san-ju-ui-ja

democracy	민주주의	min-ju-ju-ui
democrat	민주주의자	min-ju-ju-ui-ja
democratic (adj)	민주주의의	min-ju-ju-ui-ui
Democratic party	민주당	min-ju-dang

liberal (n)	자유주의자	ja-yu-ju-ui-ja
Liberal (adj)	자유주의의	ja-yu-ju-ui-ui
conservative (n)	보수주의자	bo-su-ju-ui-ja
conservative (adj)	보수적인	bo-su-jeo-gin

republic (n)	공화국	gong-hwa-guk
republican (n)	공화당원	gong-hwa-dang-won
Republican party	공화당	gong-hwa-dang

elections	선거	seon-geo
to elect (vt)	선거하다	seon-geo-ha-da
elector, voter	유권자	yu-gwon-ja
election campaign	선거 운동	seon-geo un-dong

voting (n)	선거	seon-geo
to vote (vi)	투표하다	tu-pyo-ha-da
suffrage, right to vote	투표권	tu-pyo-gwon

candidate	후보자	hu-bo-ja
to run for (~ President)	입후보하다	i-pu-bo-ha-da
campaign	캠페인	kaem-pe-in

| opposition (as adj) | 반대의 | ban-dae-ui |
| opposition (n) | 반대 | ban-dae |

visit	방문	bang-mun
official visit	공식 방문	gong-sik bang-mun
international (adj)	국제적인	guk-je-jeo-gin

| negotiations | 협상 | hyeop-sang |
| to negotiate (vi) | 협상하다 | hyeop-sang-ha-da |

244. Politics. Government. Part 2

society	사회	sa-hoe
constitution	헌법	heon-beop
power (political control)	권력	gwol-lyeok
corruption	부패	bu-pae

| law (justice) | 법률 | beom-nyul |
| legal (legitimate) | 합법적인 | hap-beop-jeo-gin |

| justice (fairness) | 정의 | jeong-ui |
| just (fair) | 공정한 | gong-jeong-han |

committee	위원회	wi-won-hoe
bill (draft law)	법안	beo-ban
budget	예산	ye-san
policy	정책	jeong-chaek
reform	개혁	gae-hyeok
radical (adj)	급진적인	geup-jin-jeo-gin

power (strength, force)	힘	him
powerful (adj)	강력한	gang-nyeo-kan
supporter	지지자	ji-ji-ja
influence	영향	yeong-hyang

regime (e.g. military ~)	정권	jeong-gwon
conflict	갈등	gal-deung
conspiracy (plot)	음모	eum-mo
provocation	도발	do-bal

to overthrow (regime, etc.)	타도하다	ta-do-ha-da
overthrow (of a government)	전복	jeon-bok
revolution	혁명	hyeong-myeong

| coup d'état | 쿠데타 | ku-de-ta |
| military coup | 군사 쿠데타 | gun-sa ku-de-ta |

crisis	위기	wi-gi
economic recession	경기침체	gyeong-gi-chim-che
demonstrator (protester)	시위자	si-wi-ja
demonstration	데모	de-mo
martial law	계엄령	gye-eom-nyeong
military base	군사 거점	gun-sa geo-jeom

| stability | 안정 | an-jeong |
| stable (adj) | 안정된 | an-jeong-doen |

exploitation	착취	chak-chwi
to exploit (workers)	착취하다	chak-chwi-ha-da
racism	인종차별주의	in-jong-cha-byeol-ju-ui
racist	인종차별주의자	in-jong-cha-byeol-ju-ui-ja

fascism	파시즘	pa-si-jeum
fascist	파시스트	pa-si-seu-teu

245. Countries. Miscellaneous

foreigner	외국인	oe-gu-gin
foreign (adj)	외국의	oe-gu-gui
abroad (in a foreign country)	해외로	hae-oe-ro
emigrant	이민자	i-min-ja
emigration	이민	i-min
to emigrate (vi)	이주하다	i-ju-ha-da
the West	서양	seo-yang
the East	동양	dong-yang
the Far East	극동	geuk-dong
civilization	문명	mun-myeong
humanity (mankind)	인류	il-lyu
the world (earth)	세계	se-gye
peace	평화	pyeong-hwa
worldwide (adj)	세계의	se-gye-ui
homeland	고향	go-hyang
people (population)	국민	gung-min
population	인구	in-gu
people (a lot of ~)	사람들	sa-ram-deul
nation (people)	국가	guk-ga
generation	세대	se-dae
territory (area)	영토	yeong-to
region	지방, 지역	ji-bang, ji-yeok
state (part of a country)	주	ju
tradition	전통	jeon-tong
custom (tradition)	풍습	pung-seup
ecology	생태학	saeng-tae-hak
Indian (Native American)	인디언	in-di-eon
Gypsy (masc.)	집시	jip-si
Gypsy (fem.)	집시	jip-si
Gypsy (adj)	집시의	jip-si-ui
empire	제국	je-guk
colony	식민지	sing-min-ji
slavery	노예제도	no-ye-je-do
invasion	침략	chim-nyak
famine	기근	gi-geun

246. Major religious groups. Confessions

religion	종교	jong-gyo
religious (adj)	종교의	jong-gyo-ui

faith, belief	믿음	mi-deum
to believe (in God)	믿다	mit-da
believer	신자	sin-ja

| atheism | 무신론 | mu-sin-non |
| atheist | 무신론자 | mu-sin-non-ja |

Christianity	기독교	gi-dok-gyo
Christian (n)	기독교도	gi-dok-gyo-do
Christian (adj)	기독교의	gi-dok-gyo-ui

Catholicism	가톨릭	ga-tol-lik
Catholic (n)	가톨릭 신자	ga-tol-lik sin-ja
Catholic (adj)	가톨릭의	ga-tol-li-gui

Protestantism	개신교	gae-sin-gyo
Protestant Church	개신교 교회	gae-sin-gyo gyo-hoe
Protestant (n)	개신교도	gae-sin-gyo-do

Orthodoxy	동방정교	dong-bang-jeong-gyo
Orthodox Church	동방정교회	dong-bang-jeong-gyo-hoe
Orthodox (n)	동방정교 신자	dong-bang-jeong-gyo sin-ja

Presbyterianism	장로교	jang-no-gyo
Presbyterian Church	장로교회	jang-no-gyo-hoe
Presbyterian (n)	장로교 교인	jang-no-gyo gyo-in

| Lutheranism | 루터교회 | ru-teo-gyo-hoe |
| Lutheran (n) | 루터 교회 신자 | ru-teo gyo-hoe sin-ja |

| Baptist Church | 침례교 | chim-nye-gyo |
| Baptist (n) | 침례교도 | chim-nye-gyo-do |

| Anglican Church | 성공회 | seong-gong-hoe |
| Anglican (n) | 성공회 신자 | seong-gong-hoe sin-ja |

| Mormonism | 모르몬교 | mo-reu-mon-gyo |
| Mormon (n) | 모르몬 교도 | mo-reu-mon gyo-do |

| Judaism | 유대교 | yu-dae-gyo |
| Jew (n) | 유대인 | yu-dae-in |

| Buddhism | 불교 | bul-gyo |
| Buddhist (n) | 불교도 | bul-gyo-do |

| Hinduism | 힌두교 | hin-du-gyo |
| Hindu (n) | 힌두교도 | hin-du-gyo-do |

Islam	이슬람교	i-seul-lam-gyo
Muslim (n)	이슬람교도	i-seul-lam-gyo-ui
Muslim (adj)	이슬람의	i-seul-la-mui

Shiah Islam	시아파 이슬람	si-a-pa i-seul-lam
Shiite (n)	시아파 신도	si-a-pa sin-do
Sunni Islam	수니파 이슬람	su-ni-pa i-seul-lam
Sunnite (n)	수니파 신도	su-ni-pa sin-do

247. Religions. Priests

priest	사제	sa-je
the Pope	교황	gyo-hwang
monk, friar	수도사	su-do-sa
nun	수녀	su-nyeo
abbot	수도원장	su-do-won-jang
vicar (parish priest)	교구 목사	gyo-gu mok-sa
bishop	주교	ju-gyo
cardinal	추기경	chu-gi-gyeong
preacher	전도사	jeon-do-sa
preaching	설교	seol-gyo
parishioners	교구민	gyo-gu-min
believer	신자	sin-ja
atheist	무신론자	mu-sin-non-ja

248. Faith. Christianity. Islam

Adam	아담	a-dam
Eve	이브	i-beu
God	신	sin
the Lord	하나님	ha-na-nim
the Almighty	전능의 신	jeon-neung-ui sin
sin	죄	joe
to sin (vi)	죄를 범하다	joe-reul beom-ha-da
sinner (masc.)	죄인	joe-in
sinner (fem.)	죄인	joe-in
hell	지옥	ji-ok
paradise	천국	cheon-guk
Jesus	예수	ye-su
Jesus Christ	예수 그리스도	ye-su geu-ri-seu-do
the Holy Spirit	성령	seong-nyeong
the Saviour	구세주	gu-se-ju
the Virgin Mary	성모 마리아	seong-mo ma-ri-a
the Devil	악마	ang-ma
devil's (adj)	악마의	ang-ma-ui
Satan	사탄	sa-tan
satanic (adj)	사탄의	sa-tan-ui
angel	천사	cheon-sa
guardian angel	수호천사	su-ho-cheon-sa
angelic (adj)	천사의	cheon-sa-ui
apostle	사도	sa-do

| archangel | 대천사 | dae-cheon-sa |
| the Antichrist | 적그리스도 | jeok-geu-ri-seu-do |

Church	교회	gyo-hoe
Bible	성경	seong-gyeong
biblical (adj)	성경의	seong-gyeong-ui

Old Testament	구약성서	gu-yak-seong-seo
New Testament	신약성서	si-nyak-seong-seo
Gospel	복음	bo-geum
Holy Scripture	성서	seong-seo
Heaven	하늘나라	ha-neul-la-ra

Commandment	율법	yul-beop
prophet	예언자	ye-eon-ja
prophecy	예언	ye-eon

Allah	알라	al-la
Mohammed	마호메트	ma-ho-me-teu
the Koran	코란	ko-ran

mosque	모스크	mo-seu-keu
mullah	물라	mul-la
prayer	기도	gi-do
to pray (vi, vt)	기도하다	gi-do-ha-da

pilgrimage	순례 여행	sul-lye yeo-haeng
pilgrim	순례자	sul-lye-ja
Mecca	메카	me-ka

church	교회	gyo-hoe
temple	사원, 신전	sa-won, sin-jeon
cathedral	대성당	dae-seong-dang
Gothic (adj)	고딕 양식의	go-dik gyang-si-gui
synagogue	유대교 회당	yu-dae-gyo hoe-dang
mosque	모스크	mo-seu-keu

chapel	채플	chae-peul
abbey	수도원	su-do-won
convent	수녀원	su-nyeo-won
monastery	수도원	su-do-won

bell (church ~s)	종	jong
bell tower	종루	jong-nu
to ring (ab. bells)	울리다	ul-li-da

cross	십자가	sip-ja-ga
cupola (roof)	둥근 지붕	dung-geun ji-bung
icon	성상	seong-sang

soul	영혼	yeong-hon
fate (destiny)	운명	un-myeong
evil (n)	악	ak
good (n)	선	seon
vampire	흡혈귀	heu-pyeol-gwi
witch (evil ~)	마녀	ma-nyeo

demon	악령	ang-nyeong
spirit	정신, 영혼	jeong-sin, yeong-hon
redemption (giving us ~)	구원	gu-won
to redeem (vt)	상환하다	sang-hwan-ha-da
church service	예배, 미사	ye-bae, mi-sa
to say mass	미사를 올리다	mi-sa-reul rol-li-da
confession	고해	go-hae
to confess (vi)	고해하다	go-hae-ha-da
saint (n)	성인	seong-in
sacred (holy)	신성한	sin-seong-han
holy water	성수	seong-su
ritual (n)	의식	ui-sik
ritual (adj)	의식의	ui-si-gui
sacrifice	제물	je-mul
superstition	미신	mi-sin
superstitious (adj)	미신의	mi-sin-ui
afterlife	내세	nae-se
eternal life	영생	yeong-saeng

MISCELLANEOUS

249. Various useful words

background (green ~)	배경	bae-gyeong
balance (of the situation)	균형	gyun-hyeong
barrier (obstacle)	장벽	jang-byeok
base (basis)	근거	geun-geo
beginning	시작	si-jak
category	범주	beom-ju
cause (reason)	이유	i-yu
choice	선택	seon-taek
coincidence	우연	u-yeon
comfortable (~ chair)	편안한	pyeon-an-han
comparison	비교	bi-gyo
compensation	배상	bae-sang
degree (extent, amount)	정도	jeong-do
development	개발	gae-bal
difference	다름	da-reum
effect (e.g. of drugs)	효과	hyo-gwa
effort (exertion)	노력	no-ryeok
element	요소	yo-so
end (finish)	끝	kkeut
example (illustration)	예	ye
fact	사실	sa-sil
frequent (adj)	빈번한	bin-beon-han
growth (development)	성장	seong-jang
help	도움	do-um
ideal	이상	i-sang
kind (sort, type)	종류	jong-nyu
labyrinth	미궁	mi-gung
mistake, error	실수	sil-su
moment	순간	sun-gan
object (thing)	대상	dae-sang
obstacle	장애	jang-ae
original (original copy)	원본	won-bon
part (~ of sth)	부분	bu-bun
particle, small part	입자	ip-ja
pause (break)	휴식	hyu-sik
position	위치	wi-chi
principle	원칙	won-chik
problem	문제	mun-je
process	과정	gwa-jeong

progress	진척	jin-cheok
property (quality)	특질	teuk-jil
reaction	반응	ba-neung
risk	위험	wi-heom

secret	비밀	bi-mil
series	일련	il-lyeon
shape (outer form)	모양	mo-yang
situation	상황	sang-hwang
solution	해결	hae-gyeol

standard (adj)	기준의	gi-jun-ui
standard (level of quality)	기준	gi-jun
stop (pause)	정지	jeong-ji
style	스타일	seu-ta-il

system	체계	che-gye
table (chart)	표	pyo
tempo, rate	완급	wan-geup
term (word, expression)	용어	yong-eo
thing (object, item)	물건	mul-geon

truth (e.g. moment of ~)	진리	jil-li
turn (please wait your ~)	차례	cha-rye
type (sort, kind)	형태, 종류	hyeong-tae, jong-nyu
urgent (adj)	긴급한	gin-geu-pan
urgently	급히	geu-pi

utility (usefulness)	유용성	yu-yong-seong
variant (alternative)	변종	byeon-jong
way (means, method)	방법	bang-beop
zone	지대	ji-dae

250. Modifiers. Adjectives. Part 1

additional (adj)	추가의	chu-ga-ui
ancient (~ civilization)	고대의	go-dae-ui
artificial (adj)	인공의	in-gong-ui
back, rear (adj)	뒤의	dwi-ui
bad (adj)	나쁜	na-ppeun

beautiful (~ palace)	아름다운	a-reum-da-un
beautiful (person)	아름다운	a-reum-da-un
big (in size)	큰	keun
bitter (taste)	쓴	sseun
blind (sightless)	눈먼	nun-meon

calm, quiet (adj)	고요한	go-yo-han
careless (negligent)	부주의한	bu-ju-ui-han
caring (~ father)	배려하는	bae-ryeo-ha-neun
central (adj)	중앙의	jung-ang-ui

cheap (low-priced)	싼	ssan
cheerful (adj)	명랑한	myeong-nang-han

children's (adj)	어린이의	eo-ri-ni-ui
civil (~ law)	시민의	si-min-ui
clandestine (secret)	은밀한	eun-mil-han

clean (free from dirt)	깨끗한	kkae-kkeu-tan
clear (explanation, etc.)	명쾌한	myeong-kwae-han
clever (intelligent)	영리한	yeong-ni-han
close (near in space)	가까운	ga-kka-un
closed (adj)	닫힌	da-chin

cloudless (sky)	구름 없는	gu-reum eom-neun
cold (drink, weather)	차가운	cha-ga-un
compatible (adj)	호환이 되는	ho-hwan-i doe-neun
contented (satisfied)	만족한	man-jok-an
continuous (uninterrupted)	연속적인	yeon-sok-jeo-gin

cool (weather)	서늘한	seo-neul-han
dangerous (adj)	위험한	wi-heom-han
dark (room)	어두운	eo-du-un
dead (not alive)	죽은	ju-geun
dense (fog, smoke)	밀집한	mil-ji-pan

destitute (extremely poor)	극빈한	geuk-bin-han
different (not the same)	다른	da-reun
difficult (decision)	어려운	eo-ryeo-un
difficult (problem, task)	어려운	eo-ryeo-un
dim, faint (light)	희미한	hui-mi-han

dirty (not clean)	더러운	deo-reo-un
distant (in space)	먼	meon
dry (clothes, etc.)	마른	ma-reun
easy (not difficult)	쉬운	swi-un

empty (glass, room)	빈	bin
even (e.g. ~ surface)	고른	go-reun
exact (amount)	정확한	jeong-hwak-an
excellent (adj)	우수한	u-su-han
excessive (adj)	과도한	gwa-do-han

expensive (adj)	비싼	bi-ssan
exterior (adj)	외부의	oe-bu-ui
far (the ~ East)	먼	meon
fast (quick)	빠른	ppa-reun
fatty (food)	지방이 많은	ji-bang-i ma-neun

fertile (land, soil)	비옥한	bi-ok-an
flat (~ panel display)	평평한	pyeong-pyeong-han
foreign (adj)	외국의	oe-gu-gui
fragile (china, glass)	깨지기 쉬운	kkae-ji-gi swi-un

free (at no cost)	무료의	mu-ryo-ui
free (unrestricted)	한가한	han-ga-han
fresh (~ water)	민물의	min-mu-rui
fresh (e.g. ~ bread)	신선한	sin-seon-han
frozen (food)	언	naeng-dong-doen
full (completely filled)	가득 찬	ga-deuk chan

gloomy (house, forecast)	어둑어둑한	eo-du-geo-duk-an
good (book, etc.)	좋은	jo-eun
good, kind (kindhearted)	착한	cha-kan
grateful (adj)	감사하는	gam-sa-ha-neun
happy (adj)	행복한	haeng-bok-an
hard (not soft)	단단한	dan-dan-han
heavy (in weight)	무거운	mu-geo-un
hostile (adj)	적대적인	jeok-dae-jeo-gin
hot (adj)	뜨거운	tteu-geo-un
huge (adj)	거대한	geo-dae-han
humid (adj)	습한	seu-pan
hungry (adj)	배고픈	bae-go-peun
ill (sick, unwell)	병든	byeong-deun
immobile (adj)	동요되지 않는	dong-yo-doe-ji an-neun
important (adj)	중요한	jung-yo-han
impossible (adj)	불가능한	bul-ga-neung-han
incomprehensible	이해할 수 없는	i-hae-hal su eom-neun
indispensable (adj)	필수적인	pil-su-jeo-gin
inexperienced (adj)	경험 없는	gyeong-heom eom-neun
insignificant (adj)	중요하지 않은	jung-yo-ha-ji a-neun
interior (adj)	내부의	nae-bu-ui
joint (~ decision)	공동의	gong-dong-ui
last (e.g. ~ week)	지난	ji-nan
last (final)	마지막의	ma-ji-ma-gui
left (e.g. ~ side)	왼쪽의	oen-jjo-gui
legal (legitimate)	합법적인	hap-beop-jeo-gin
light (in weight)	가벼운	ga-byeo-un
light (pale color)	밝은	bal-geun
limited (adj)	한정된	han-jeong-doen
liquid (fluid)	액체의	aek-che-ui
long (e.g. ~ hair)	긴	gin
loud (voice, etc.)	시끄러운	si-kkeu-reo-un
low (voice)	낮은	na-jeun

251. Modifiers. Adjectives. Part 2

main (principal)	주요한	ju-yo-han
matt, matte	무광의	mu-gwang-ui
meticulous (job)	꼼꼼한	kkom-kkom-han
mysterious (adj)	신비한	sin-bi-han
narrow (street, etc.)	좁은	jo-beun
native (~ country)	태어난 곳의	tae-eo-nan gos-ui
nearby (adj)	인근의	in-geu-nui
needed (necessary)	필요한	pi-ryo-han
negative (~ response)	부정적인	bu-jeong-jeo-gin
neighbouring (adj)	이웃의	i-us-ui
nervous (adj)	신경질의	sin-gyeong-ji-rui

new (adj)	새로운	sae-ro-un
next (e.g. ~ week)	다음의	da-eum-ui
nice (agreeable)	친절한	chin-jeol-han
pleasant (voice)	좋은	jo-eun
normal (adj)	평범한	pyeong-beom-han
not big (adj)	크지 않은	keu-ji a-neun
not difficult (adj)	힘들지 않은	him-deul-ji a-neun
obligatory (adj)	의무적인	ui-mu-jeo-gin
old (house)	오래된	o-rae-doen
open (adj)	열린	yeol-lin
opposite (adj)	반대의	ban-dae-ui
ordinary (usual)	보통의	bo-tong-ui
original (unusual)	독창적인	dok-chang-jeo-gin
past (recent)	지나간	ji-na-gan
permanent (adj)	영구적인	yeong-gu-jeo-gin
personal (adj)	개인의	gae-in-ui
polite (adj)	공손한	gong-son-han
poor (not rich)	가난한	ga-nan-han
possible (adj)	가능한	ga-neung-han
present (current)	현재의	hyeon-jae-ui
principal (main)	주요한	ju-yo-han
private (~ jet)	사적인	sa-jeo-gin
probable (adj)	개연성 있는	gae-yeon-seong in-neun
prolonged (e.g. ~ applause)	장기적인	jang-gi-jeo-gin
public (open to all)	공공의	gong-gong-ui
punctual (person)	시간을 지키는	si-ga-neul ji-ki-neun
quiet (tranquil)	조용한	jo-yong-han
rare (adj)	드문	deu-mun
raw (uncooked)	날것의	nal-geos-ui
right (not left)	오른쪽의	o-reun-jjo-gui
right, correct (adj)	맞는	man-neun
ripe (fruit)	익은	i-geun
risky (adj)	위험한	wi-heom-han
sad (~ look)	슬픈	seul-peun
sad (depressing)	슬픈	seul-peun
safe (not dangerous)	안전한	an-jeon-han
salty (food)	짠	jjan
satisfied (customer)	만족한	man-jok-an
second hand (adj)	중고의	jung-go-ui
shallow (water)	얕은	ya-teun
sharp (blade, etc.)	날카로운	nal-ka-ro-un
short (in length)	짧은	jjal-beun
short, short-lived (adj)	단기의	dan-gi-ui
short-sighted (adj)	근시의	geun-si-ui
significant (notable)	중요한	jung-yo-han
similar (adj)	비슷한	bi-seu-tan

simple (easy)	단순한	dan-sun-han
skinny	깡마른	kkang-ma-reun
small (in size)	작은	ja-geun
smooth (surface)	매끈한	mae-kkeun-han
soft (~ toys)	부드러운	bu-deu-reo-un
solid (~ wall)	튼튼한	teun-teun-han
sour (flavour, taste)	시큼한	si-keum-han
spacious (house, etc.)	넓은	neol-beun
special (adj)	특별한	teuk-byeol-han
straight (line, road)	곧은	go-deun
strong (person)	강한	gang-han
stupid (foolish)	미련한	mi-ryeon-han
suitable (e.g. ~ for drinking)	적합한	jeo-ka-pan
sunny (day)	화창한	hwa-chang-han
superb, perfect (adj)	우수한, 완벽한	u-su-han, wan-byeok-an
swarthy (dark-skinned)	거무스레한	geo-mu-seu-re-han
sweet (sugary)	단	dan
tanned (adj)	햇볕에 탄	haet-byeo-te tan
tasty (delicious)	맛있는	man-nin-neun
tender (affectionate)	자상한	ja-sang-han
the highest (adj)	가장 높은	ga-jang no-peun
the most important	가장 중요한	ga-jang jung-yo-han
the nearest	가장 가까운	ga-jang ga-kka-un
the same, equal (adj)	같은	ga-teun
thick (e.g. ~ fog)	짙은	ji-teun
thick (wall, slice)	두툼한	du-tum-han
thin (person)	야윈	ya-win
tired (exhausted)	피곤한	pi-gon-han
tiring (adj)	지치는	ji-chi-neun
transparent (adj)	투명한	tu-myeong-han
unclear (adj)	불분명한	bul-bun-myeong-han
unique (exceptional)	독특한	dok-teuk-an
various (adj)	다양한	da-yang-han
warm (moderately hot)	따뜻한	tta-tteu-tan
wet (e.g. ~ clothes)	젖은	jeo-jeun
whole (entire, complete)	전체의	jeon-che-ui
wide (e.g. ~ road)	넓은	neol-beun
young (adj)	젊은	jeol-meun

MAIN 500 VERBS

to accompany (vt)	동반하다	dong-ban-ha-da
to accuse (vt)	비난하다	bi-nan-ha-da
to act (take action)	행동하다	haeng-dong-ha-da
to add (supplement)	추가하다	chu-ga-ha-da
to address (speak to)	말을 걸다	ma-reul geol-da
to admire (vi)	존경하다	jon-gyeong-ha-da
to advertise (vt)	광고하다	gwang-go-ha-da
to advise (vt)	조언하다	jo-eon-ha-da
to affirm (assert)	확언하다	hwa-geon-ha-da
to agree (say yes)	동의하다	dong-ui-ha-da
to aim (to point a weapon)	겨냥대다	gyeo-nyang-dae-da
to allow (sb to do sth)	허락하다	heo-rak-a-da
to amputate (vt)	절단하다	jeol-dan-ha-da
to answer (vi, vt)	대답하다	dae-da-pa-da
to apologize (vi)	사과하다	sa-gwa-ha-da
to appear (come into view)	나타나다	na-ta-na-da
to applaud (vi, vt)	박수를 치다	bak-su-reul chi-da
to appoint (assign)	지명하다	ji-myeong-ha-da
to approach (come closer)	가까이 가다	ga-kka-i ga-da
to arrive (ab. train)	도착하다	do-chak-a-da
to ask (~ sb to do sth)	부탁하다	bu-tak-a-da
to aspire to ...	... 를 열망하다	... reul ryeol-mang-ha-da
to assist (help)	원조하다	won-jo-ha-da
to attack (mil.)	공격하다	gong-gyeo-ka-da
to attain (objectives)	달성하다	dal-seong-ha-da
to avenge (get revenge)	복수하다	bok-su-ha-da
to avoid (danger, task)	피하다	pi-ha-da
to award (give a medal to)	훈장을 주다	hun-jang-eul ju-da
to battle (vi)	전투하다	jeon-tu-ha-da
to be (vi)	있다	it-da
to be a cause of ...	... 의 이유가 되다	... ui i-yu-ga doe-da
to be afraid	무서워하다	mu-seo-wo-ha-da
to be angry (with ...)	... 에게 화내다	... e-ge hwa-nae-da
to be at war	참전하다	cham-jeon-ha-da
to be based (on ...)	... 에 근거하다	... e geun-geo-ha-da
to be bored	심심하다	sim-sim-ha-da
to be convinced	확신하다	hwak-sin-ha-da

to be enough	충분하다	chung-bun-ha-da
to be envious	부러워하다	bu-reo-wo-ha-da
to be indignant	분개하다	bun-gae-ha-da
to be interested in ...	··· 에 관심을 가지다	... e gwan-si-meul ga-ji-da

to be lost in thought	생각에 잠기다	saeng-ga-ge jam-gi-da
to be lying (~ on the table)	놓여 있다	no-yeo it-da
to be needed	필요하다	pi-ryo-ha-da
to be perplexed (puzzled)	뻥뻥하다	ppeong-ppeong-ha-da

to be preserved	보존되다	bo-jon-doe-da
to be required	필요하다	pi-ryo-ha-da
to be surprised	놀라다	nol-la-da
to be worried	걱정하다	geok-jeong-ha-da

to beat (to hit)	때리다	ttae-ri-da
to become (e.g. ~ old)	되다	doe-da
to behave (vi)	행동하다	haeng-dong-ha-da
to believe (think)	믿다	mit-da

to belong to ...	··· 에 속하다	... e sok-a-da
to berth (moor)	정박시키다	jeong-bak-si-ki-da
to blind (other drivers)	앞이 안 보이게 만들다	a-pi an bo-i-ge man-deul-da
to blow (wind)	불다	bul-da

to blush (vi)	붉히다	buk-hi-da
to boast (vi)	자랑하다	ja-rang-ha-da
to borrow (money)	빌리다	bil-li-da
to break (branch, toy, etc.)	깨뜨리다	kkae-tteu-ri-da

to breathe (vi)	호흡하다	ho-heu-pa-da
to bring (sth)	가져오다	ga-jyeo-o-da
to burn (paper, logs)	태우다	tae-u-da
to buy (purchase)	사다	sa-da

to call (~ for help)	부르다, 요청하다	bu-reu-da, yo-cheong-ha-da
to call (yell for sb)	부르다	bu-reu-da
to calm down (vt)	진정시키다	jin-jeong-si-ki-da
can (v aux)	할 수 있다	hal su it-da

to cancel (call off)	취소하다	chwi-so-ha-da
to cast off (of a boat or ship)	출항하다	chul-hang-ha-da
to catch (e.g. ~ a ball)	잡다	jap-da
to change (~ one's opinion)	바꾸다	ba-kku-da
to change (exchange)	교환하다	gyo-hwan-ha-da

to charm (vt)	매료하다	mae-ryo-ha-da
to choose (select)	선택하다	seon-taek-a-da
to chop off (with an axe)	잘라내다	jal-la-nae-da
to clean (e.g. kettle from scale)	닦다	dak-da

to clean (shoes, etc.)	닦다	dak-da
to clean up (tidy)	청소하다	cheong-so-ha-da
to close (vt)	닫다	dat-da
to comb one's hair	빗질하다	bit-jil-ha-da

to come down (the stairs)	내려오다	nae-ryeo-o-da
to come out (book)	출간되다	chul-gan-doe-da
to compare (vt)	비교하다	bi-gyo-ha-da
to compensate (vt)	보상하다	bo-sang-ha-da
to compete (vi)	경쟁하다	gyeong-jaeng-ha-da
to compile (~ a list)	작성하다	jak-seong-ha-da
to complain (vi, vt)	불평하다	bul-pyeong-ha-da
to complicate (vt)	복잡하게 하다	bok-ja-pa-ge ha-da
to compose (music, etc.)	작곡하다	jak-gok-a-da
to compromise (reputation)	위태롭게 하다	wi-tae-rop-ge ha-da
to concentrate (vi)	집중하다	jip-jung-ha-da
to confess (criminal)	고백하다	go-baek-a-da
to confuse (mix up)	혼동하다	hon-dong-ha-da
to congratulate (vt)	축하하다	chuk-a-ha-da
to consult (doctor, expert)	상담하다	sang-dam-ha-da
to continue (~ to do sth)	계속하다	gye-sok-a-da
to control (vt)	제어하다	je-eo-ha-da
to convince (vt)	납득시키다	nap-deuk-si-ki-da
to cooperate (vi)	협동하다	hyeop-dong-ha-da
to coordinate (vt)	조정하다	jo-jeong-ha-da
to correct (an error)	고치다	go-chi-da
to cost (vt)	값이 … 이다	gap-si … i-da
to count (money, etc.)	세다	se-da
to count on …	… 에 의지하다	… e ui-ji-ha-da
to crack (ceiling, wall)	갈라지다	gal-la-ji-da
to create (vt)	창조하다	chang-jo-ha-da
to crush, to squash (~ a bug)	눌러서 뭉개다	nul-leo-seo mung-gae-da
to cry (weep)	울다	ul-da
to cut off (with a knife)	자르다	ja-reu-da

253. Verbs D-G

to dare (~ to do sth)	감히 … 하다	gam-hi … ha-da
to date from …	… 부터 시작되다	… bu-teo si-jak-doe-da
to deceive (vi, vt)	속이다	so-gi-da
to decide (~ to do sth)	결심하다	gyeol-sim-ha-da
to decorate (tree, street)	장식하다	jang-sik-a-da
to dedicate (book, etc.)	헌정하다	heon-jeong-ha-da
to defend (a country, etc.)	방어하다	bang-eo-ha-da
to defend oneself	자기 보호하다	ja-gi bo-ho-ha-da
to demand (request firmly)	요구하다	yo-gu-ha-da
to denounce (vt)	고발하다	go-bal-ha-da
to deny (vt)	거부하다	geo-bu-ha-da
to depend on …	… 을 신뢰하다	… seul sil-loe-ha-da
to deprive (vt)	박탈하다	bak-tal-ha-da
to deserve (vt)	받을 만하다	ba-deul man-ha-da

to design (machine, etc.)	설계하다	seol-gye-ha-da
to desire (want, wish)	원하다	won-ha-da
to despise (vt)	경멸하다	gyeong-myeol-ha-da
to destroy (documents, etc.)	파괴하다	pa-goe-ha-da
to differ (from sth)	다르다	da-reu-da
to dig (tunnel, etc.)	파다	pa-da
to direct (point the way)	안내하다	an-nae-ha-da
to disappear (vi)	사라지다	sa-ra-ji-da
to discover (new land, etc.)	발견하다	bal-gyeon-ha-da
to discuss (vt)	의논하다	ui-non-ha-da
to distribute (leaflets, etc.)	배포하다	bae-po-ha-da
to disturb (vt)	방해하다	bang-hae-ha-da
to dive (vi)	뛰어들다	ttwi-eo-deul-da
to divide (math)	나누다	na-nu-da
to do (vt)	하다	ha-da
to do the laundry	빨래하다	ppal-lae-ha-da
to double (increase)	두 배로 하다	du bae-ro ha-da
to doubt (have doubts)	의심하다	ui-sim-ha-da
to draw a conclusion	결론을 내다	gyeol-lo-neul lae-da
to dream (daydream)	꿈꾸다	kkum-kku-da
to dream (in sleep)	꿈을 꾸다	kku-meul kku-da
to drink (vi, vt)	마시다	ma-si-da
to drive a car	자동차를 운전하다	ja-dong-cha-reul run-jeon-ha-da
to drive away (scare away)	몰아내다	mo-ra-nae-da
to drop (let fall)	떨어뜨리다	tteo-reo-tteu-ri-da
to drown (ab. person)	익사하다	ik-sa-ha-da
to dry (clothes, hair)	말리다	mal-li-da
to eat (vi, vt)	먹다	meok-da
to eavesdrop (vi)	엿듣다	yeot-deut-da
to emit (diffuse - odor, etc.)	발산하다	bal-san-ha-da
to enjoy oneself	즐기다	jeul-gi-da
to enter (on the list)	적어 넣다	jeo-geo neo-ta
to enter (room, house, etc.)	들어가다	deu-reo-ga-da
to entertain (amuse)	즐겁게 하다	jeul-geop-ge ha-da
to equip (fit out)	설비하다	seol-bi-ha-da
to examine (proposal)	조사하다	jo-sa-ha-da
to exchange (sth)	교환하다	gyo-hwan-ha-da
to excuse (forgive)	용서하다	yong-seo-ha-da
to exist (vi)	존재하다	jon-jae-ha-da
to expect (anticipate)	예상하다	ye-sang-ha-da
to expect (foresee)	예상하다	ye-sang-ha-da
to expel (from school, etc.)	제명하다	je-myeong-ha-da
to explain (vt)	설명하다	seol-myeong-ha-da
to express (vt)	표현하다	pyo-hyeon-ha-da
to extinguish (a fire)	끄다	kkeu-da

to fall in love (with …)	… 와 사랑에 빠지다	… wa sa-rang-e ppa-ji-da
to fancy (vt)	좋아하다	jo-a-ha-da
to feed (provide food)	먹이다	meo-gi-da

to fight (against the enemy)	싸우다	ssa-u-da
to fight (vi)	싸우다	ssa-u-da
to fill (glass, bottle)	채우다	chae-u-da
to find (~ lost items)	찾다	chat-da

to finish (vt)	끝내다	kkeun-nae-da
to fish (angle)	낚시질하다	nak-si-jil-ha-da
to fit (ab. dress, etc.)	어울리다	eo-ul-li-da
to flatter (vt)	아첨하다	a-cheom-ha-da

to fly (bird, plane)	날다	nal-da
to follow … (come after)	… 를 따라가다	… reul tta-ra-ga-da
to forbid (vt)	금지하다	geum-ji-ha-da
to force (compel)	강요하다	gang-yo-ha-da

to forget (vi, vt)	잊다	it-da
to forgive (pardon)	용서하다	yong-seo-ha-da
to form (constitute)	이루다	i-ru-da
to get dirty (vi)	더러워지다	deo-reo-wo-ji-da

to get infected (with …)	옮다	om-da
to get irritated	짜증을 부리다	jja-jeung-eul bu-ri-da
to get married	결혼하다	gyeol-hon-ha-da
to get rid of …	… 를 제거하다	… reul je-geo-ha-da

to get tired	피곤하다	pi-gon-ha-da
to get up (arise from bed)	일어나다	i-reo-na-da
to give a bath (to bath)	목욕시키다	mo-gyok-si-ki-da

to give a hug, to hug (vt)	껴안다	kkyeo-an-da
to give in (yield to)	굴복하다	gul-bok-a-da
to glimpse (vt)	잠깐 보다	jam-kkan bo-da
to go (by car, etc.)	가다	ga-da

to go (on foot)	가다	ga-da
to go for a swim	수영하다	su-yeong-ha-da
to go out (for dinner, etc.)	나가다	na-ga-da
to go to bed (go to sleep)	잠자리에 들다	jam-ja-ri-e deul-da

to greet (vt)	인사하다	in-sa-ha-da
to grow (plants)	기르다	gi-reu-da
to guarantee (vt)	보증하다	bo-jeung-ha-da
to guess (the answer)	추측하다	chu-cheuk-a-da

254. Verbs H-M

to hand out (distribute)	나누어 주다	na-nu-eo ju-da
to hang (curtains, etc.)	걸다	geol-da
to have (vt)	가지다	ga-ji-da
to have a bath	목욕하다	mo-gyok-a-da

to have a try	시도하다	si-do-ha-da
to have breakfast	아침을 먹다	a-chi-meul meok-da
to have dinner	저녁을 먹다	jeo-nyeo-geul meok-da
to have lunch	점심을 먹다	jeom-si-meul meok-da
to head (group, etc.)	이끌다	i-kkeul-da
to hear (vt)	듣다	deut-da
to heat (vt)	데우다	de-u-da
to help (vt)	도와주다	do-wa-ju-da
to hide (vt)	숨기다	sum-gi-da
to hire (e.g. ~ a boat)	임대하다	im-dae-ha-da
to hire (staff)	고용하다	go-yong-ha-da
to hope (vi, vt)	희망하다	hui-mang-ha-da
to hunt (for food, sport)	사냥하다	sa-nyang-ha-da
to hurry (vi)	서두르다	seo-du-reu-da
to imagine (to picture)	상상하다	sang-sang-ha-da
to imitate (vt)	모방하다	mo-bang-ha-da
to implore (vt)	애걸하다	ae-geol-ha-da
to import (vt)	수입하다	su-i-pa-da
to increase (vi)	늘다	neul-da
to increase (vt)	늘리다	neul-li-da
to infect (vt)	감염시키다	gam-nyeom-si-ki-da
to influence (vt)	영향을 미치다	yeong-hyang-eul mi-chi-da
to inform (e.g. ~ the police about ...)	알리다	al-li-da
to inform (vt)	알리다	al-li-da
to inherit (vt)	상속하다	sang-sok-a-da
to inquire (about ...)	··· 에 관하여 묻다	... e gwan-ha-yeo mut-da
to insert (put in)	넣다	neo-ta
to insinuate (imply)	암시하다	am-si-ha-da
to insist (vi, vt)	주장하다	ju-jang-ha-da
to inspire (vt)	영감을 주다	yeong-ga-meul ju-da
to instruct (teach)	교육하다	gyo-yuk-a-da
to insult (offend)	모욕하다	mo-yok-a-da
to interest (vt)	관심을 끌다	gwan-si-meul kkeul-da
to intervene (vi)	간섭하다	gan-seo-pa-da
to introduce (sb to sb)	소개하다	so-gae-ha-da
to invent (machine, etc.)	발명하다	bal-myeong-ha-da
to invite (vt)	초대하다	cho-dae-ha-da
to iron (clothes)	다림질하다	da-rim-jil-ha-da
to irritate (annoy)	짜증나게 하다	jja-jeung-na-ge ha-da
to isolate (vt)	고립시키다	go-rip-si-ki-da
to join (political party, etc.)	가입하다	ga-i-pa-da
to joke (be kidding)	농담하다	nong-dam-ha-da
to keep (old letters, etc.)	보관하다	bo-gwan-ha-da
to keep silent, to hush	침묵을 지키다	chim-mu-geul ji-ki-da
to kill (vt)	죽이다	ju-gi-da
to knock (on the door)	두드리다	du-deu-ri-da
to know (sb)	알다	al-da

to know (sth)	알다	al-da
to laugh (vi)	웃다	ut-da
to launch (start up)	착수하다	chak-su-ha-da

to leave (~ for Mexico)	떠나다	tteo-na-da
to leave (forget sth)	두고 오다	du-go o-da
to leave (spouse)	떠나다	tteo-na-da
to liberate (city, etc.)	해방하다	hae-bang-ha-da
to lie (~ on the floor)	눕다	nup-da

to lie (tell untruth)	거짓말하다	geo-jin-mal-ha-da
to light (campfire, etc.)	불을 붙이다	bu-reul bu-chi-da
to light up (illuminate)	비추다	bi-chu-da
to limit (vt)	제한하다	je-han-ha-da
to listen (vi)	듣다	deut-da
to live (~ in France)	살다	sal-da
to live (exist)	살다	sal-da
to load (gun)	장탄하다	jang-tan-ha-da
to load (vehicle, etc.)	싣다	sit-da

to look (I'm just ~ing)	보다	bo-da
to look for ... (search)	… 를 찾다	... reul chat-da
to look like (resemble)	닮다	dam-da
to lose (umbrella, etc.)	잃어버리다	i-reo-beo-ri-da
to love (e.g. ~ dancing)	좋아하다	jo-a-ha-da

to love (sb)	사랑하다	sa-rang-ha-da
to lower (blind, head)	내리다	nae-ri-da
to make (~ dinner)	요리하다	yo-ri-ha-da
to make a mistake	실수하다	sil-su-ha-da
to make angry	화나게 하다	hwa-na-ge ha-da

to make easier	쉽게 하다	swip-ge ha-da
to make multiple copies	복사하다	bok-sa-ha-da
to make the acquaintance	… 와 아는 사이가 되다	... wa a-neun sa-i-ga doe-da
to make use (of ...)	… 를 사용하다	... reul sa-yong-ha-da
to manage, to run	운영하다	u-nyeong-ha-da

to mark (make a mark)	표시하다	pyo-si-ha-da
to mean (signify)	의미하다	ui-mi-ha-da
to memorize (vt)	외우다	oe-u-da
to mention (talk about)	언급하다	eon-geu-pa-da
to miss (school, etc.)	결석하다	gyeol-seok-a-da

to mix (combine, blend)	섞다	seok-da
to mock (make fun of)	조롱하다	jo-rong-ha-da
to move (to shift)	옮기다	om-gi-da
to multiply (math)	곱하다	go-pa-da
must (v aux)	… 해야 하다	... hae-ya ha-da

255. Verbs N-R

| to name, to call (vt) | 부르다 | bu-reu-da |
| to negotiate (vi) | 협상하다 | hyeop-sang-ha-da |

| to note (write down) | 적다 | jeok-da |
| to notice (see) | 알아차리다 | a-ra-cha-ri-da |

to obey (vi, vt)	복종하다	bok-jong-ha-da
to object (vi, vt)	반대하다	ban-dae-ha-da
to observe (see)	지켜보다	ji-kyeo-bo-da
to offend (vt)	모욕하다	mo-yok-a-da

to omit (word, phrase)	생략하다	saeng-nyak-a-da
to open (vt)	열다	yeol-da
to order (in restaurant)	주문하다	ju-mun-ha-da
to order (mil.)	명령하다	myeong-nyeong-ha-da
to organize (concert, party)	조직하다	jo-jik-a-da

to overestimate (vt)	과대평가하다	gwa-dae-pyeong-ga-ha-da
to own (possess)	소유하다	so-yu-ha-da
to participate (vi)	참가하다	cham-ga-ha-da
to pass through (by car, etc.)	지나다	ji-na-da
to pay (vi, vt)	지불하다	ji-bul-ha-da

to peep, to spy on	엿보다	yeot-bo-da
to penetrate (vt)	꿰뚫다	kkwe-ttul-ta
to permit (vt)	허락하다	heo-rak-a-da
to pick (flowers)	따다	tta-da
to place (put, set)	배치하다	bae-chi-ha-da

to plan (~ to do sth)	계획하다	gye-hoek-a-da
to play (actor)	연기하다	yeon-gi-ha-da
to play (children)	놀다	nol-da
to point (~ the way)	가리키다	ga-ri-ki-da

to pour (liquid)	따르다	tta-reu-da
to pray (vi, vt)	기도하다	gi-do-ha-da
to prefer (vt)	선호하다	seon-ho-ha-da
to prepare (~ a plan)	준비하다	jun-bi-ha-da

to present (sb to sb)	소개하다	so-gae-ha-da
to preserve (peace, life)	보호하다	bo-ho-ha-da
to prevail (vt)	발호하다	bal-ho-ha-da
to progress (move forward)	나아가다	na-a-ga-da

to promise (vt)	약속하다	yak-sok-a-da
to pronounce (vt)	발음하다	ba-reum-ha-da
to propose (vt)	제안하다	je-an-ha-da
to protect (e.g. ~ nature)	보호하다	bo-ho-ha-da

to protest (vi)	항의하다	hang-ui-ha-da
to prove (vt)	증명하다	jeung-myeong-ha-da
to provoke (vt)	도발하다	do-bal-ha-da
to pull (~ the rope)	잡아당기다	ja-ba-dang-gi-da

to punish (vt)	벌주다, 처벌하다	beol-ju-da, cheo-beol-ha-da
to push (~ the door)	밀다	mil-da
to put away (vt)	치우다	chi-u-da
to put in order	정리하다	jeong-ni-ha-da
to put, to place	놓다	no-ta

to quote (cite)	인용하다	i-nyong-ha-da
to reach (arrive at)	이르다	i-reu-da
to read (vi, vt)	읽다	ik-da
to realize (a dream)	현실로 만들다	hyeon-sil-lo man-deul-da
to recognize (identify sb)	알아보다	a-ra-bo-da
to recommend (vt)	추천하다	chu-cheon-ha-da
to recover (~ from flu)	회복하다	hoe-bok-a-da
to redo (do again)	다시 하다	da-si ha-da
to reduce (speed, etc.)	줄이다	ju-ri-da
to refuse (~ sb)	거부하다	geo-bu-ha-da
to regret (be sorry)	후회하다	hu-hoe-ha-da
to reinforce (vt)	강화하다	gang-hwa-ha-da
to remember (Do you ~ me?)	기억하다	gi-eok-a-da
to remember (I can't ~ her name)	기억하다	gi-eok-a-da
to remind of ...	··· 을 생각나게 하다	... eul saeng-gang-na-ge ha-da
to remove (~ a stain)	없애다	eop-sae-da
to remove (~ an obstacle)	제거하다	je-geo-ha-da
to rent (sth from sb)	임대하다	im-dae-ha-da
to repair (mend)	보수하다	bo-su-ha-da
to repeat (say again)	반복하다	ban-bok-a-da
to report (make a report)	보고하다	bo-go-ha-da
to reproach (vt)	책망하다	chaeng-mang-ha-da
to reserve, to book	예약하다	ye-yak-a-da
to restrain (hold back)	억누르다	eong-nu-reu-da
to return (come back)	되돌아가다	doe-do-ra-ga-da
to risk, to take a risk	위험을 무릅쓰다	wi-heo-meul mu-reup-sseu-da
to rub out (erase)	지우다	ji-u-da
to run (move fast)	달리다	dal-li-da
to rush (hurry sb)	재촉하다	jae-chok-a-da

256. Verbs S-W

to satisfy (please)	만족시키다	man-jok-si-ki-da
to save (rescue)	구조하다	gu-jo-ha-da
to say (~ thank you)	말하다	mal-ha-da
to scold (vt)	꾸짖다	kku-jit-da
to scratch (with claws)	할퀴다	hal-kwi-da
to select (to pick)	고르다	go-reu-da
to sell (goods)	팔다	pal-da
to send (a letter)	보내다	bo-nae-da
to send back (vt)	돌려보내다	dol-lyeo-bo-nae-da
to sense (~ danger)	감지하다	gam-ji-ha-da
to sentence (vt)	선고하다	seon-go-ha-da

to serve (in restaurant)	서빙을 하다	seo-bing-eul ha-da
to settle (a conflict)	해결하다	hae-gyeol-ha-da
to shake (vt)	흔들다	heun-deul-da
to shave (vi)	깎다	kkak-da
to shine (gleam)	빛나다	bin-na-da
to shiver (with cold)	추워서 떨다	chu-wo-seo tteol-da
to shoot (vi)	쏘다	sso-da
to shout (vi)	소리치다	so-ri-chi-da
to show (to display)	보여주다	bo-yeo-ju-da
to shudder (vi)	몸을 떨다	mo-meul tteol-da
to sigh (vi)	한숨을 쉬다	han-su-meul swi-da
to sign (document)	서명하다	seo-myeong-ha-da
to signify (mean)	의미하다	ui-mi-ha-da
to simplify (vt)	단순화하다	dan-sun-hwa-ha-da
to sin (vi)	죄를 범하다	joe-reul beom-ha-da
to sit (be sitting)	앉다	an-da
to sit down (vi)	앉다	an-da
to smell (emit an odor)	냄새가 나다	naem-sae-ga na-da
to smell (inhale the odor)	냄새를 맡다	naem-sae-reul mat-da
to smile (vi)	미소를 짓다	mi-so-reul jit-da
to snap (vi, ab. rope)	부러뜨리다	bu-reo-tteu-ri-da
to solve (problem)	해결하다	hae-gyeol-ha-da
to sow (seed, crop)	뿌리다	ppu-ri-da
to spill (liquid)	엎지르다	eop-ji-reu-da
to spit (vi)	뱉다	baet-da
to stand (toothache, cold)	참다	cham-da
to start (begin)	시작하다	si-jak-a-da
to steal (money, etc.)	훔치다	hum-chi-da
to stop (for pause, etc.)	정지하다	jeong-ji-ha-da
to stop (please ~ calling me)	그만두다	geu-man-du-da
to stop talking	말하기를 멈추다	mal-ha-gi-reul meom-chu-da
to stroke (caress)	쓰다듬다	sseu-da-deum-da
to study (vt)	공부하다	gong-bu-ha-da
to suffer (feel pain)	고통을 겪다	go-tong-eul gyeok-da
to support (cause, idea)	지지하다	ji-ji-ha-da
to suppose (assume)	추측하다	chu-cheuk-a-da
to surface (ab. submarine)	떠오르다	tteo-o-reu-da
to surprise (amaze)	놀라게 하다	nol-la-ge ha-da
to suspect (vt)	수상히 여기다	su-sang-hi yeo-gi-da
to swim (vi)	수영하다	su-yeong-ha-da
to take (get hold of)	잡다	jap-da
to take a rest	쉬다	swi-da
to take away (e.g. about waiter)	가져가다	ga-jyeo-ga-da
to take off (aeroplane)	이륙하다	i-ryuk-a-da
to take off (painting, curtains, etc.)	떼다	tte-da

to take pictures	사진을 찍다	sa-ji-neul jjik-da
to talk to ...	… 와 말하다	… wa mal-ha-da
to teach (give lessons)	가르치다	ga-reu-chi-da

to tear off, to rip off (vt)	찢다	jjit-da
to tell (story, joke)	이야기하다	i-ya-gi-ha-da
to thank (vt)	감사하다	gam-sa-ha-da
to think (believe)	믿다	mit-da

to think (vi, vt)	생각하다	saeng-gak-a-da
to threaten (vt)	협박하다	hyeop-bak-a-da
to throw (stone, etc.)	던지다	deon-ji-da
to tie to ...	… 에 묶다	… e muk-da

to tie up (prisoner)	묶다	muk-da
to tire (make tired)	피곤하게 하다	pi-gon-ha-ge ha-da
to touch (one's arm, etc.)	만지다	man-ji-da
to tower (over ...)	우뚝 솟다	u-ttuk sot-da
to train (animals)	가르치다	ga-reu-chi-da

to train (sb)	훈련하다	hul-lyeon-ha-da
to train (vi)	훈련하다	hul-lyeon-ha-da
to transform (vt)	변형시키다	byeon-hyeong-si-ki-da
to translate (vt)	번역하다	beo-nyeok-a-da

to treat (illness)	치료하다	chi-ryo-ha-da
to trust (vt)	신뢰하다	sil-loe-ha-da
to try (attempt)	해보다	hae-bo-da
to turn (e.g., ~ left)	돌다	dol-da

to turn away (vi)	돌아서다	do-ra-seo-da
to turn off (the light)	끄다	kkeu-da
to turn on (computer, etc.)	켜다	kyeo-da
to turn over (stone, etc.)	뒤집다	dwi-jip-da

to underestimate (vt)	과소평가하다	gwa-so-pyeong-ga-ha-da
to underline (vt)	밑줄을 긋다	mit-ju-reul geut-da
to understand (vt)	이해하다	i-hae-ha-da
to undertake (vt)	착수하다	chak-su-ha-da

to unite (vt)	연합하다	yeon-ha-pa-da
to untie (vt)	풀다	pul-da
to use (phrase, word)	사용하다	sa-yong-ha-da
to vaccinate (vt)	접종하다	jeop-jong-ha-da

to vote (vi)	투표하다	tu-pyo-ha-da
to wait (vt)	기다리다	gi-da-ri-da
to wake (sb)	깨우다	kkae-u-da
to want (wish, desire)	원하다	won-ha-da

to warn (of a danger)	경고하다	gyeong-go-ha-da
to wash (clean)	씻다	ssit-da
to water (plants)	물을 주다	mu-reul ju-da
to wave (the hand)	손을 흔들다	so-neul heun-deul-da
to weigh (have weight)	무게를 달다	mu-ge-reul dal-da
to work (vi)	일하다	il-ha-da

to worry (make anxious)	걱정하게 만들다	geok-jeong-ha-ge man-deul-da
to worry (vi)	걱정하다	geok-jeong-ha-da
to wrap (parcel, etc.)	포장하다	po-jang-ha-da
to wrestle (sport)	레슬링하다	re-seul-ling-ha-da
to write (vt)	쓰다	sseu-da
to write down	적다	jeok-da